Your Kin-dom Come

Your Kin-dom Come

The Lord's Prayer in a Global Age

William Thompson-Uberuaga

CASCADE Books • Eugene, Oregon

YOUR KIN-DOM COME
The Lord's Prayer in a Global Age

Copyright © 2018 William Thompson-Uberuaga. All rights reserved. Except for brief quotations in critical publications or reviews, no part of this book may be reproduced in any manner without prior written permission from the publisher. Write: Permissions, Wipf and Stock Publishers, 199 W. 8th Ave., Suite 3, Eugene, OR 97401.

Cascade Books
An Imprint of Wipf and Stock Publishers
199 W. 8th Ave., Suite 3
Eugene, OR 97401

www.wipfandstock.com

PAPERBACK ISBN: 978-1-5326-1032-5
HARDCOVER ISBN: 978-1-5326-1034-9
EBOOK ISBN: 978-1-5326-1033-2

Cataloguing-in-Publication data:

Names: Thompson-Uberuaga.

Title: Your kin-dom come : the Lord's Prayer in a global age / William Thompson-Uberuaga.

Description: Eugene, OR: Cascade Books, 2018. Includes bibliographical references and index.

Identifiers: ISBN 978-1-5326-1032-5 (paperback) | ISBN 978-1-5326-1034-9 (hardcover) | ISBN 978-1-5326-1033-2 (ebook)

Subjects: LCSH: Lord's prayer. | Prayer History. | Title.

Classification: BV230 .T456 2018 (print) | BV230 (ebook)

Manufactured in the U.S.A.   MARCH 18, 2022

Scripture quotations are from New Revised Standard Version Bible, copyright @ 1989 National Council of the Churches of Christ in the United States of America. Used by permission. All rights reserved worldwide.

Excerpt from "A Clean, Well-Lighted Place," by Ernest Hemingway, reprinted with permission of Scribner, a division of Simon & Schuster, Inc., from *The Short Stories of Ernest Hemingway* by Ernest Hemingway. Copyright @ 1933 by Charles Scribner's Sons. Copyright renewed 1961 by Mary Hemingway.

Excerpt from *The Collected Works of St. John of the Cross*, translated by Kieran Kavanaugh and Otilio Rodriguez Copyright © 1964, 1979, 1991 by Washington Province of Discalced Carmelites ICS Publications 2131 Lincoln Road, NE, Washington, DC 20002-1199 U.S.A. www.icspublications.org.

Excerpt from *The Handmaid's Tale* by Margaret Atwood @ 1985 O. W. Todd Ltd., used by permission of the Author. Published in the United States by Doubleday (Trade) and Houghton Mifflin (Ebook). All rights reserved.

The Lord's Prayer version for Night Prayer, "Eternal Spirit, Earth-maker, Pain-bearer," as adapted from Prayer at Night by Jim Cotter, Cairns Publications, is being used by permission of *A New Zealand Prayer Book —He Karakia Mihinare o Aotearoa*, copyright @ 1989 The General Secretary, The Anglican Church in Aotearoa, New Zealand and Polynesia.

"A Prayer before Reading the Bible," reprinted with permission of Catholic Online www.catholic.org.

For Patricia
beloved wife and best of friends,
a truly wonderful and loving mother,
fellow searcher, teacher, and theologian,
together members of the kin-dom!

Table of Contents

      Illustrations ix

      Preface xi

one   An Introduction: An Ecumenical Approach? 1

two   Texts and Versions 10

three   The Medium and the Message 35

four   Addressing the Holy Mystery 50

five   The "You" Petitions 77

six   The "We" Petitions 101

seven   The Lord's Prayer and Spirituality:
      Liturgical and Personal, Cathedral and Monastic 134

      Conclusion: A Prayer of Immense Hospitality 153

      Bibliography 165

      Index 175

      Scripture and Sacred Documents Index 185

Illustrations

Figure 1: The Primary Field and Secondary Field 122

Figure 2: The Lord's Prayer in the Form of a Triptych and as a Form of Crescendo Biblical Parallelisms 132

Preface

St. Michael's Episcopal Cathedral, Boise, Idaho, through the invitation of Dean Richard Demarest, and St. Stephen's Episcopal Church, also of Boise, through the invitation of its rector, Father David Wettstein, provided the "primary" field on which this book took root. A devoted group of fellow searchers, at both parishes, shared with me a fascination for a prayer we have been praying for untold and likely unknown years. I hope they know how much I appreciated their interest, their questions, their insights, and their support. And I hope they know how thankful I am to them. It was one of those experiences of the kin-dom.

None of us really had any idea that this study of perhaps Christianity's greatest prayer would end up in this form of a book. That was one of those great surprises. But as time passed, and as we discussed, and as the author researched, and simply did a fair amount of "sitting in his cell," well, in one of those mysterious forms of gestation, this work emerged. It is still perhaps the most surprising of all this author's writings.

What was and is the Spirit up to? I only have some inklings. The Lord's Prayer is traditionally thought of as a summary of the gospel. Was the Spirit leading this author to a new "summary" or overall evaluation of his endeavors as a spiritual seeker, teacher, and scholar? If so, it came in a most unexpected form. If it is a "summary," it is not one of the usual sort. It is more like a lens, a constellation of rich, primary images and symbols, which always gesture, always allure, always open up. But it does seem to have a unity to it, a connectivity, like the opening address and petitions of the Lord's Prayer. Each seems to lead to the other somehow, if each is pondered and explored, and if the seeker allows oneself to be carried along by the energy of the prayer.

Being carried along by the energy of the prayer: Hopefully that is part of the promise awaiting the reader of this book. It led the author to a new appreciation of the catholic and universal movement of the Our Father.

Who is the "our"? It is the family of *Abba*, we believe. And is any one person or creature excluded from *Abba*? The prayer seems to take us on a journey into the catholic and universal. Into the many mansions spoken of by the Jesus of John's Gospel (14:2).

A crucially important part of the movement into the catholicity of the Our Father is also the author's always growing and certainly unending recognition of and gratitude to the many people, and even animal friends and many, many creatures and our cosmic home (!), all enriching him over the years. The Lord's name is truly hallowed by all of these, those known and the many more who remain unknown: family, friends, colleagues, students, Cascade Books and its wonderful staff, and so many more.

The kin-dom comes in so many ways!

one

An Introduction: An Ecumenical Approach?

In late November, 2015, Pope Francis, during his visit to Africa, went to the Ugandan shrines in memory of twenty-three Anglican and twenty-two Roman Catholic Christians who were martyred for their faith. In his sermon at the Roman shrine he spoke of how their collective "witness of love for Christ and his Church has truly gone 'to the end of the earth.'" He powerfully added: "We remember also the Anglican martyrs whose deaths for Christ testify to the ecumenism of blood." This witness was a "gift of the Holy Spirit . . . . It unites us to one another as believers and living members of Christ's mystical body." Earlier at the Anglican shrine, the Pope and Archbishop Stanley Ntagali, Primate of the Anglican Church of Uganda, together blessed the assembled people. Pope Francis, when he emerged from the museum at the Anglican shrine, upon being greeted by an enthusiastic crowd, invited everyone to pray the Lord's Prayer together.

Why the Lord's Prayer? The Holy Spirit works in and with us in very practical ways, and we might surmise that the Pope knew that the Lord's Prayer is one which would be widely known by Christians, whether Roman Catholic, Anglican, and more. But there is something particularly inspired and appropriate about praying this prayer in an ecumenical setting. It is the prayer of the family of Christians, united under their one Father. It is a prayer giving expression to the truth of the African proverb alluded to by Archbishop Stanley: "If we want to go fast, let us go alone. As the wider Christian community in Uganda, however, if we want to go far, let us go together. This is why we were very happy to welcome the Pope of the Roman Catholic Church to the [Anglican] Church of Uganda."[1]

[1]. Francis, "Uganda Martyrs." Please note that unless otherwise specified, we will be using the New Revised Standard Version for our biblical citations.

Your Kin-dom Come

The Lord's Prayer is "our" prayer addressed to "our" Father. Somehow as we pray it—expressing the truth of that African proverb—we do so as one family, becoming even more one family, and that family has a long history, stretching back at least to the first generation of Christians, and moving forward to an ever-growing and changing extensive family of descendants. Like all families, this family is a rich treasury of memories and stories, a kind of song with lyrics that remain largely the same throughout history, but whose melody has taken many forms. Melodies are like renderings or interpretations. We could say that the Bible is the "lyric," and its various melodies are the way that Bible has been received in the family's history. Or perhaps those with a pronounced liturgical sensitivity might want to say that the Eucharist—word and altar together—is the lyric, and the various ways in which that has been and is celebrated in gesture, word, and song, make up the various melodies.

Following an old tradition, we might think of the Lord's Prayer as a summary of the Bible, a little Bible, or a concentrated expression of the Bible, as Christians have come to understand it.[2] If this be so in some meaningful way, then the Lord's Prayer becomes a wonderful key to the Bible as a whole, a sort of map into its depths. And it would be surprising if its varying forms of reception and interpretation—its melodies, so to speak—were not of great value for us as we seek to "receive" the revealed word of Scripture. Or again, to follow up on the liturgical approach, can we say that the Lord's Prayer is in some way a summary of the Eucharist, a concentrated resumé of what the eucharistic word and table are? As we have seen, it has been thought to be a succinct condensation of the good news ("gospel"), but it also occurs typically in the eucharistic celebrations of the Christian churches, and in some way it gives expression to our need for the eucharistic manna or bread necessary for our Christian journey. As one colleague suggested to me, it may well be the oldest form of consecration of the elements.[3] The various melodies of the Lord's Prayer, its rich and varied history of reception and interpretation, may well offer us a rich entry into the meaning of our sacramental and liturgical practice from this point of view.

Who is this family that is praying, or at least trying to pray? We may think of the two famous "lungs" of the church, that is, the Eastern Christian

---

2. See, for example, the second/third-century Tertullian's *On Prayer* 1, 42: "[A] summary of the whole Gospel is to be found in the prayer."

3. Email from Robert Davis Hughes, 12/30/2014.

An Introduction: An Ecumenical Approach?

churches and the Western Christian churches. That is largely how this book will think of it. This book is and desires to be ecumenical. The two lungs of East and West, if they are to breathe in a healthy way, need to be united in and through one heart, and it is this book's wager that the Lord's Prayer is a royal road to that heart. As we pray it and sing it in its rich melodies of East and West, we are experiencing that heart at work. The ecumenical movement in its deepest sense is a struggle of recovery of that one heart. When that one heart is stressed in varying ways, as it has been between East and West, and within East and West by their various divisions, then the lungs cannot breathe healthily. The Lord's Prayer has a rich and powerful role to play in the preservation of the health of our one great heart. The various melodies, so to speak, to which its lyrics have been put, in East and West, among, that is, the Oriental Orthodox, the Orthodox, and the Eastern Catholic churches, and among the Roman, the Anglican, and the Protestant and evangelical churches of the West, will be our guide to that one heart. Doing this exhaustively is beyond the competence of any one person. We can only hope to do this in a representative way.[4]

Like all families, this our Christian family is not an island unto itself. It dwells in a richly diversified world reaching out beyond the Christian orbit. To some extent I think we will see that this "world" has had and will continue to have its contribution to make to our reception of the Lord's Prayer. Jesus, for example, was nurtured by his Jewish heritage, and much of that is transparent in his great prayer. The Latin and Greek cultures have contributed much to the church's growing theological reception of its heritage and its prayer. And so too each culture has enriched and challenged the churches as the latter enter into them. This enrichment and challenge must be recognized in our living and praying the Lord's Prayer. The ecumenical is truly global today, embracing increasingly all thought-forms and cultures beyond the Christian. This, too, should be reflected somehow in our appropriation of this prayer. It might be that the one family spoken of in this great prayer is one much larger than the Christian, and always has

---

4. "[T]he Church must breathe with her two lungs," said Pope John Paul II of the churches of West and East, *Ut Unum Sint*, no. 54. Although the Pope does not seem to speak of the heart as the unifying and basic organ of this breathing, he implies it; he writes of the "conversion of hearts guided by love" (no. 21) as a crucial foundation of unity. For an overview of the various churches of the East, see Robertson, *The Eastern Churches*. See Louth, *Modern Orthodox Thinkers*, 321, for Vyacheslav Ivanov as the possible source behind John Paul II.

been, and perhaps our new experience of the global offers us a chance to discover this in a more forceful way.

"Our Father in heaven . . . Your will be done on earth, as it is in heaven." There is an implied universality in those words: a reign that embraces past, present, and future; every religion, many of whose prayers might well be similar or at least richly if variously equivalent; all creatures then, now, and to come, including, it would seem and maybe we are seeing it a bit more clearly now, our fellow animates, animal and sentient, and even all the galaxies, the cosmos in the fullest sense. Does the Lord's Prayer stretch us globally? Is it a peculiarly apt prayer in a global and interstellar age? Would praying it somehow help us in becoming "universal" ourselves? Would this be a new way of experiencing the old medieval axiom that the "soul is potentially everything"?

Keeping this movement into universality, and the Lord's Prayer as a guide into and toward this, in mind, several thoughts come to mind at this point. First, our "ecumenical" approach is a movement toward this universality, at best. It is part of our evolving movement, even if it is all too often accompanied by forms of regression and sin, or "devolution," if you will. So there is an important distinction between the "ecumenical" and the "universal." The truly universal would seem to be an eschatological reality, something toward which we move and in which we participate, but never fully accomplish, at least this side of the full eschaton (or end). How can we accomplish this, if it is to embrace all, past, present, and to come? We need to remain modest, or "real," if you will![5]

At the same time, we might think of prayer, and especially the Lord's Prayer, as a way in which Jesus teaches us how "to process" this movement toward and into universality. This will necessitate our thinking about and reading this prayer in a more ecumenical-toward-universal way, seeing it as our Christian way of processing our evolution toward wholeness.[6] Following Franciscan Richard Rohr's suggestion, we might want to consider this processing-through-prayer as one which requires a shift from the

---

5. See Voegelin, *The Ecumenic Age*, 192–93, for helpful observations about the distinction between "ecumenicity" and "universality." See 177 for Voegelin's tracing of the technical use of the word *oikoumene* as "the whole inhabited world" back to Polybius' *Histories*. See Delio, *Making All Things New*, 12, for a similar distinction between "catholic" and "universal." Delio's work is a superb introduction to a more cosmological understanding of reality, and it has prodded me toward a more cosmological reading of the Lord's Prayer.

6. Delio's influence is patent here.

An Introduction: An Ecumenical Approach?

"calculating mind" of the narcissistic ego to the "contemplative mind" of the one seeking to pray in and with the "mind of Christ," a mind oriented outward toward the all and the whole. Approaching the Lord's Prayer in this way may help us experience it as a process of widening our lenses to see from Christ's perspective.[7]

As we widen our lenses, then we begin to see what has remained hidden from us. On a personal level, perhaps this refers to dimensions of ourselves we do not know well enough, nor befriend well enough. When we pray for our needed bread, or ask forgiveness, some of these dimensions may come to mind. On the social and political levels we may also begin to see and befriend what has remained hidden from us. In a way, we begin to be decolonized by the Prayer, moved out beyond our limited and comfortable colonies, whether of gender, of culture, of nation, of sexual orientation, of religion, of ethnicity, of social class, and all the other colonies in which we dwell.

This prayer is also a prayer for the imperfect. Suggestively Dante offers his retelling of this prayer in canto 11 of his *Purgatorio*. That is the place of the sinful and the imperfect. One might almost say, as has been suggested, that our way is really not a "way of perfection" but a "way of imperfection."[8] We doubt, we sin, we hurt ourselves and others, we see so little in comparison with what we do not see. Some of us are in fact so "imperfect" that barely a crack remains through which the light might enter. And maybe most of us have had our moments like that. And in some way the various churches, and indeed entire societies, have had those moments, too, and continue to do so.

There are also agnostics, atheists, and anti-theists, these latter sometimes converting their atheism into a rebellion against theism, and at times a violence toward it. But perhaps somehow this prayer, this humble prayer, can emerge, even in these hearts, if sometimes only in a questioning, partial, not quite despairing way. We need the bread: "Give us this day our daily bread." We stumble, sometimes terribly, and others do the same vis-à-vis us: "Forgive us our sins as we forgive those who sin against us." We, too, in moments of ruthless honesty fear that we can lose it all; and we hope, sometimes only questioningly, that we "will not be led into temptation," that we will not meet "the evil one" who can overcome us.

---

7. See Rohr, Daily Meditation for December 3, 2015.
8. See Murray, *Praying with Confidence*, for thoughts along these lines.

Perhaps the reader has stumbled across Ernest Hemingway's fascinating and somewhat painful retelling of the Lord's Prayer in his short story, "A Clean, Well-Lighted Place":

> Our nada who art in nada, nada be thy name thy kingdom nada thy will be nada in nada as it is in nada. Give us this nada our daily nada and nada us not into nada but deliver us from nada; pues nada. Hail nothing full of nothing, nothing is with thee.[9]

Is this an atheist's parody of the Lord's Prayer, or an anti-theist's more violent mocking of the Lord's Prayer, along with a similar parody or mocking of Mary's "Ave Maria"? Or is it simply everyone's prayer of our imperfection, for the imperfect? A shadow side expression of the Lord's Prayer? The "Lord's Prayer of the Shadow." The *nada*/nothing of the café waiter in Hemingway's story is in the light, after all. This is even better than the light that peeks through the cracks. And the nothing? It may well be sheer negativity, but if it is, how can the nada deliver us from the nada? Is this perhaps the nada kingdom of John of the Cross and other mystics, the emptiness, like Christ's emptiness in Paul's Philippians 2:7, which is the "space" of openness for the illuminating and transfiguring grace of God? Or somewhat equivalently, like the *śūnyatā* emptiness of the Buddhist mystic? Jesus' mother, Mary, was full of this kind of emptiness. *Ave Maria*, you who said let it be done to me according to your will (Luke 1:28, 38). But sometimes we do seem simply "empty," at least for us imperfect wayfarers. And we *are* empty. Were there not a true carving out of our narcissism, how could the light of the kingdom shine through? This may well be the "place" in which we all meet, believers, non-believers, all creatures of all places and times.

A truly ecumenical approach to the Lord's Prayer must be one which includes the praying of us all: those praying in the silence of being overlooked, ignored, excluded, and abused; the imperfect; the almost praying of the agnostic; the atheist's and anti-theist's protest against it; the mystic's kenotic living of it in all the radicality possible for one; and the similar or equivalent praying of all the world's religions, past, present, and to come; and the gestures, expressions, and groaning in "other" languages of our interstellar, our sentient and our animal sisters and brothers.

Can this book account for all of that? Not very well, probably. At best, only suggestively, representatively, and very partially. And certainly not by itself. What gives this writer hope, however, is that the Lord's Prayer is Jesus'

---

9. Hemingway, "A Clean, Well-Lighted Place," 347.

An Introduction: An Ecumenical Approach?

prayer, and hopefully then our praying of it is a participation in Jesus' own praying of it. "When we cry, 'Abba! Father!' it is that very Spirit [of God] bearing witness with our spirit that we are children of God, and if children, then heirs, heirs of God and joint heirs with Christ . . ." (Rom 8:15–17).

The Chapters Ahead

In our second chapter we will offer a basic look at the texts of this prayer as we have them in the New Testament, and at their Jewish foundations. Matthew 6 and Luke 11 contain the two major texts of the prayer as we have received them, but there are likely partial parallels in other New Testament passages, and we will look at these too. We will also offer a look at the major translations of this prayer which are in use in the English language, how those came to be, and which of these are used by the various English-speaking Christian churches. Contemporary inclusive language translations in English will also be considered. Why do some pray "forgive us our debts," while others pray "forgive us our trespasses"? Why do some add a concluding doxology, "For thine is the kingdom, and the power, and the glory, forever and ever," and others do not, or do it a bit differently in liturgical prayer but not in personal prayer? When we come to contemporary inclusive language translations, how are these justified? Do these flow from the inner spirit of the Lord's Prayer itself, or are they "against its grain"?

Our third chapter will offer an overview of the prayer's structure as a whole. How many different parts or verses are there? Do all agree on this? Why are the first few addressed to God the Father, and the last few, to considerations of our needs as creatures? Is this structure purely accidental, or are there some significant reasons for the shape the prayer takes? Good musicians and other artists know that the way something is expressed often has a good deal to do with what is being expressed and how that can be experienced. This gets us into the form/content discussion, or the medium/message question. Some very significant work is being done along these lines. But it may not be only a matter of literary structures, important as they may be. Significant theological and spiritual issues may be at stake too.

The fourth chapter will offer a meditative consideration of what we might call the prayer's introduction, or better, the invocatory address. "Our Father, who art in heaven," in one common translation. Is this address an overture or preface, which decisively shapes our entire ability to enter into this prayer? Is the entire rest of the prayer a kind of bracket to this address?

As we study each part of the prayer, beginning with the address, we will attempt a consideration of the historical and literary meaning of the parts, in the original context as best we can do that, and then, in the texts that we have in the New Testament, and in what we are calling the "surplus of meaning," how the later tradition has come to wrestle with these texts and what kinds of further significance that tradition may offer. We are using the word "tradition" widely, embracing the ongoing "handing on" (*tradere*) of this prayer, into our present time.[10]

Context, text, and surplus of meaning are loaded words, carrying all kinds of implications. How can we really come to know the context of the Lord's Prayer? How does that context shape the text of the prayer itself? There are some historical agnostics, so to speak, who do not put much stock in retrieving contexts; others more optimistically do. We will have to think about this as we go along, and stake out our position for better or worse. The contested nature of an historical context also carries over into a consideration of possible surpluses of meaning. When do these surpluses simply import meanings back into the text, for whatever reasons, or when they do not, what are we saying? Do these texts have a depth, so to speak, which can be varyingly sounded under different circumstances? How do we know that, or how might we explain that?

The fifth and sixth chapters, respectively, will consider what are known as the "You petitions" (hallowed be *your* name; *your* kingdom come; *your* will be done) and the "We petitions" (give *us* . . . *our* daily bread; forgive *us* *our* sins; lead *us* not into temptation, but deliver *us*). God and the rest of us, Creator and creation, love of God and love of neighbor, like a Christian equivalent of the two parts of the decalogue/ten commandments—those are all so many ways of characterizing these petitionary parts of the prayer. Again we will survey context, text, and surplus of meaning. If it be true that the Lord's Prayer is both the Bible and the Eucharist "in miniature," or in "condensed, abbreviated form," then we are moving into the heart and substance of the Christian Mystery as we study this prayer. Perhaps this prayer is Jesus' suggestion for how we should live out our spirituality and do theology.

---

10. "Surplus of meaning" means different things in different authors, but Ricoeur, *Interpretation Theory*, is the place to start. Congar, *Tradition and Traditions*, proposed the helpful distinction between "Tradition," on the one hand, as the ongoing process of handing on or receiving while interpreting originating revelation, and "traditions," on the other, as the "fixed" expressions resulting from that ongoing process, such as Bible, doctrines, spiritual devotions, etc.

An Introduction: An Ecumenical Approach?

Since Jesus' time the Lord's Prayer has been used for both personal prayer, and likely for liturgical prayer as well. In our seventh chapter we will see that it has a rich historical role in the liturgical prayers of the Christian churches, East and West, as well as in the more personal spiritualities of those churches. What can we learn from this? Does this prayer play a special role in liturgy, especially the Eucharist? Does this liturgical use of the Lord's Prayer in church worship help us in our own personal appropriation of this prayer? What might be some ways of thinking fruitfully about the relationship between the personal and liturgical uses of this prayer? This might also be an appropriate time to think about whether and how the Lord's Prayer might be a paradigm for all prayer, Christian prayer, certainly, but perhaps all prayer in some way, if the Spirit who breathes universally and cosmically be the Lord's Prayer's source. St. Teresa of Avila had recommended, toward the end of her great commentary on the Lord's Prayer, that if "[we] understand how to recite the Lord's Prayer well," then we "will know how to recite all [of our] vocal prayers."[11] Would it be plausible to extend this recommendation to all praying, vocal or not? These will be some of the topics approached in chapter seven.

Our final chapter will offer a concluding meditation on the prayer as a whole, returning to some of the questions and themes we have noted in this introduction. How have we done? How ecumenical have we been? Is this prayer able to be seen by us now more plausibly as a port of entry to the one great heart, not only of the Christian churches of East and West, and of the world's religions, but of creation and cosmos as a whole?

---

11. Teresa of Avila, *The Way of Perfection* 42.4, 203. See similarly John of the Cross, *The Ascent of Mount Carmel* 3.44.4, 346–47.

two

Texts and Versions

Did Jesus himself actually teach us the Lord's Prayer? It is a simple question, but it requires a somewhat complicated response.

The Title

Commonly we see or hear this prayer referred to as "The Lord's Prayer," or the "Our Father," or sometimes even as the *Paternoster*, an older name based on the Latin words for "our Father" (*pater*, for "father," and *noster*, for "our"). Our possibly earliest known reference for the actual title "The Lord's Prayer" comes from the third-century church father Cyprian of Carthage, who wrote a treatise titled *On the Lord's Prayer*.[1] But did Jesus use this title? Perhaps his disciples did at times, or later followers of his original disciples, as Jesus' importance and significance became more evident. Paul typically refers to Jesus as "Lord," for example. As we will see, there are echoes of perhaps the entire prayer found in Paul's letters. The prayer may have circulated in his circles and others, and it may have been referred to by various titles, among which may have been "The Lord's Prayer." It seems an almost natural title to take hold among Jesus' disciples, who were very early on coming to regard Jesus as "Lord" in a very special way.

However, to this writer it seems a stretch too many to think that Jesus himself referred to himself as "Lord" or to his prayer as "The Lord's Prayer."

---

1. See Cyprian, *On the Lord's Prayer* 9, 70.

Texts and Versions

The Synoptic Gospels of Matthew, Mark, and Luke rather present Jesus as someone who is oriented toward his Father and his Father's reign. The "Lord" or *Adonai* in Jesus' estimation would likely have been the Father.[2] But that Jesus very early on is regarded as the "Lord" indicates a growing realization of how closely Jesus is united with the Father, and that his special prayer is a special pathway into the Father's heart.

The title "Our Father" likely derives from the version of this prayer that we find in Matthew's Gospel. The version in Luke simply begins with "Father."[3] The longer form of the prayer which we find in Matthew, including the longer address of "Our Father in heaven," is typical of Jewish public prayer in general. As we will see, the Jewish features of Matthew's Gospel, along with the echoes of the great Jewish prayers of early times in the Lord's Prayer, alert us to the rich Jewish background of the Lord's Prayer and to Jesus' own profoundly Jewish formation and orientation. It is not unlikely that he would have prayed "Our Father in heaven" as he was teaching his disciples this prayer, or as he was simply praying this prayer along with them. It is a very Jewish way to pray. I do not think we need to argue that he always prayed it this way. Luke's more simple and direct version also seems to have its solid foundation in Jesus' experience and ministry. Jewish praying is a praying of a certain amount of imaginative creativity and adaptability, after all. So, yes, the title "Our Father" may quite possibly and even probably derive from Jesus' own usage itself. But more on this later. But before moving on from this question of the title of the Lord's Prayer, we assume that the reader will likely know that the traditional Latin title of *Paternoster* is a later title, derived from the Latin-speaking zones of the Christian tradition. We have no solid evidence that it derives from Jesus!

---

2. We know, for example, that the Greek translation of the Hebrew Bible, the Septuagint, translated the Hebrew word for God, *Adonai*, by the Greek term for "Lord," namely, *Kyrios*. Thus, as the disciples, like Paul, come to regard Jesus as the "Lord," they are using a title loaded with echoes of *Adonai*.

3. Some Lukan manuscripts do have the longer address of Matthew; see Johnson, *The Gospel of Luke*, 177.

The Two Versions of Matthew and Luke

MATTHEW'S	LUKE'S
6:9 Our Father in heaven,	11:2 Father,
hallowed be your name.	hallowed be your name.
6:10 Your kingdom come.	Your kingdom come.
Your will be done	
on earth as it is in heaven.	
6:11 Give us this day our daily bread.	11:3 Give us each day our daily bread.
6:12 And forgive us our debts,	11:4 And forgive us our sins,
as we also have forgiven our debtors.	for we ourselves forgive everyone indebted to us.
6:13 And do not bring us to the time of trial,	And do not bring us to the time of trial.
but rescue us from the evil one.	

Some basic comparisons:

As noted earlier, Matthew has the longer address typical of Jewish prayer, "Our Father in heaven," while Luke, with the exception of some manuscripts, has the more "direct" and simple address, "Father," which seems typical of how the Gospels and Paul remember Jesus praying. "He said, 'Abba, Father, for you all things are possible . . .'" (Mark 14:36); ". . . God has sent the Spirit of his son into our hearts, crying, 'Abba, Father!'" (Gal 4:6).

Notice also that Matthew's version has three "You" petitions, while Luke's has only two. Matthew's "Your will be done on earth as it is in heaven" is missing in Luke. This kind of addition in Matthew is also typical of Jewish prayer, and we might surmise that it would be typical of the Jewish Jesus as well. It is a form of parallelism found very commonly in Jewish prayer; for example, in the psalms. In this case, it is a form of repetition of hallowing the name and praying for the kingdom's coming, but with a new twist. If God's name is really hallowed and the kingdom truly comes, then God's will shall in fact be done.

There are also a few other differences. You will notice that Matthew asks the Father to give us *this day* our daily bread, while Luke requests it for *each day*. Perhaps the reader can sense a certain but subtle nuance between *this* day and *each* day. For now it will be good to have just noted this and let the question of a possible nuance gestate for a while. When we come to a more ample discussion of these petitions in later chapters, we can return to this possible shift in nuance. Similarly, the reader will note the use of the word "debts" in Matthew, and that of "sins" in Luke. And, finally, Matthew ends with a request to be rescued from the evil one, something missing in Luke. Again, our more ample discussion of these petitions in later chapters will be the place to come back to a consideration of these somewhat subtle nuances. But let us "ponder" them before we "wander" into them.

How many "We" petitions does each version have? Perhaps each has three, but the answer seems to hinge on whether being rescued from the evil one in Matthew is a separate petition, or rather another way of praying not to be brought to the trial. If it is the latter, each version would then offer three "We" petitions. Being delivered from the evil one would be a further parallelism within the larger parallelism of all the petitions. We will return to this later.

Contexts and language:

Matthew's version occurs within the context of the third part (6:1–18) of the five parts of the Sermon on the Mount. Notice that it falls within the approximate center of the Sermon, and that may suggest that it is the "center" or core meaning of the Sermon as a whole. Here I will follow Daniel Harrington's outline; he offers a commonsense approach within the thicket of two thousand years of interpretation of this famous text: (1) Introduction (5:1–20); (2) The Antitheses (5:21–48); (3) Three Acts of Piety: Almsgiving, Prayer, and Fasting (6:1–18); (4) Other Teachings (6:19—7:12); and (5) Warnings about Judgment (7:13–29). If the key theme of the entire Sermon is that Jesus came to fulfill the law and prophets (5:17), and if the Lord's Prayer is the central core meaning of the entire Sermon, then it offers us a pathway to the meaning of both law and prophets. Thinking about the prayer in this way may then offer us a key to walking through the thicket of diverse interpretations of the Sermon itself. For example, is the Sermon a utopian blueprint? Well, we might ask: Is it unrealizable now, like all utopias, or is it in progress, at least in part, as the Prayer suggests? And does it hold out hope for its further and perhaps fullest realization, as the Prayer also suggests? And is the Sermon only for the elite, those called to "perfection," or is it addressed to the imperfect, as the Prayer suggests?[4]

Another feature of Matthew's text is the use of the aorist Greek tense. This may seem arcane, but it is worth our attention. Matthew and Luke use the aorist imperative, although Luke uses the present for "give" and our own "forgive." The aorist imperative, Greek scholars tell us, can be difficult to interpret, but in the imperative, as here in Matthew, it tends to refer to some action to be done now, for a limited period of time. It can be repeated, but within this limited time. This would suggest that Matthew is reflecting a more "eschatological" perspective: *now* is the special, limited time of the "end," that is, of the establishment of the reign of God.

That may partially reflect Jesus' own sense that the reign of God is in some way already being inaugurated within his earthly ministry: "But if it is by the Spirit of God that I cast out demons, then the kingdom of God has come to you" (Matt 12:28). But simultaneously that may also reflect something of the later view, after Jesus' death and resurrection, the time in which Matthew's Gospel originated, that the fullness of the reign of God is occurring. It would take some time to work out the already and not yet dimensions of the reign of God, and we are not finished with the task yet. On the other hand, Luke may be suggesting less of a sense of the fullness of God's reign having been established. In our present times each of us must keep on asking that the reign will come. This would then enable us to see the subtle shade in meaning in Luke's use of the words "*each* day": "Give us each day our daily bread"; that is, each present day in which we are living. Matthew's "Give us *this* day" might then reflect the "last day/time," the time of the end in which he felt his community was living.[5]

Like Matthew, Luke has placed his version of the Lord's Prayer within his own narrative of Jesus' prophetic ministry on behalf of the reign of God. The Prayer comes within the context of Jesus' journey to Jerusalem (9:51—19:27). Like John the Baptist, Jesus teaches his followers how to

---

4. See Harrington, *The Gospel of Matthew*, 96–98.

5. See Stevenson, *The Lord's Prayer*, 21–22. This is perhaps the best and most thorough study of the history of the Lord's Prayer in post-biblical tradition. For the Greek tenses, see, for example, Baugh, *A New Testament Greek Primer*, 121.

Texts and Versions

pray. Jesus is like John: a prophet who prays, and like many prophets, one who must bring his prophetic word to Jerusalem. Luke has shown Jesus in prayer twice within this section of his Gospel (10:21, 11:1), the Lord's Prayer coming immediately after one of his disciples, seeing him in prayer, says: "Lord, teach us to pray, as John taught his disciples" (11:1). Luke is well known for emphasizing how prayer occurs at critical moments within Jesus' and his followers' ministry in the early church (Luke 3:21; 5:16; 6:12; 22:44; Acts 1:24; 6:6; 9:11; 11:5; 13:3; 14:23; 16:25; 20:36; 21:5; 22:17; 28:8). Luke's version of the Lord's Prayer offers us perhaps the central or core message of Jesus. Notice how it falls approximately within the Gospel's center, just as Matthew's version occurs within the center of the Sermon on the Mount.[6] It is rather remarkable in some ways that both Matthew and Luke give us this central role of the Prayer, as if it were the key to understanding and participating in the reign of God.

Luke's version is simpler and shorter than Matthew's, as we have seen. Also, the Lukan version is considered "Q" material, a hypothetical source posited by scholars, which may reflect many or most of the original sayings of Jesus during his historical ministry. This "Q" material ("Q" for the German for "source," *Quelle*) seems to be the source behind the sayings of Jesus which are more or less both found in Matthew and Luke. Here may then be another appropriate moment to ask if or whether these versions or parts of them can be said to be based on Jesus' own preaching and teaching itself.

Of arguments about whether the Gospels reflect Jesus' own words and message, or rather that of the later growing movement of disciples after his death and resurrection, there is no end, especially since the entry of modern historical science into biblical studies. That seems natural, in fact, and leads many of us to that kind of "second naivete" of which philosopher Paul Ricoeur wrote upon revisiting these biblical texts.[7] Like Ricoeur, many of us, "beyond the desert of criticism, wish to be called again" by the biblical texts, but how can we do so without sliding into a simple naivete?[8] For this author, it is helpful to follow some useful criteria, which can help us avoid sliding into simple wishful thinking. What follows is one modest suggestion. Most importantly, the message of the Lord's Prayer coheres with the central message of Jesus offered us by the earliest Gospels (Matthew, Mark, and Luke), as well as by Paul, namely both the proclamation of the

---

6. See Johnson, *The Gospel of Luke*, 179; Balch, "Luke," 1127–28.
7. Ricoeur, *The Symbolism of Evil*, 351.
8. Ibid., 349.

dawning reign of God, and the rootedness of that reign in *Abba*, Father. So on grounds of coherence we can accept a continuity of message between the Lord's Prayer and Jesus' own historical message.

This does not necessarily mean that we have the precise words of Jesus. He spoke Aramaic, and we have only a few instances of that in the Gospels, *Abba* ("Father") being perhaps the most notable. What we have is mostly translations into Greek. Did Jesus know Greek? I agree with those who find it hard not to believe that he was not only exposed to Greek speakers, but may have learned some Greek, a "street Greek," as well, even if only a little. After all, Sepphoris, where Greek would have been spoken, a growing city rebuilt by Herod Antipas, was only five miles from Nazareth. It is possible, although we have no proof, that Jesus worked there on various building projects, perhaps learning a carpenter's trade and some of the Greek language involved in that.[9]

Jesus, like all good Jewish preachers, creatively adapted his message to different audiences. Especially in the oral situation of his ministry, and that of his followers, there likely was a fair amount of fluidity.[10] The two versions of Matthew and Luke are a reflection of this fluidity. But formal, collective prayer is one of those kinds of "discourse" that lends itself to memorization and repetition, while the centrality of this prayer gives it an importance which the "chain of witnesses" would have carefully watched.[11] We are, after all, historical creatures through and through. We are interconnected, always, it seems. From one side through witnesses; from our side, through our bonding with the tradition in which we live.

---

9. Martin, *Jesus*, 70–95. See Douglas-Klotz, *Prayers*, and Errico, *Setting*, for possible original Aramaic renderings. Thanks to Amy Hoppock.

10. Helpful on this is Levine, *Short Stories by Jesus*, 10–17.

11. See Bauckham, *Jesus and the Eyewitnesses*, esp. chapters 10–13, and 282, 286, 594, 601–2, for the original Aramaic forms. Bauckham places emphasis upon the role of eyewitnesses in the transmission of and control over the Jesus tradition; he thinks that New Testament criticism has ignored the role of eyewitnesses; they "drop out of the picture and the anonymous collectives of the early churches take control of the oral tradition, developing it more or less at will for the needs of the community. This picture is very implausible, because the eyewitnesses were certainly still alive and well long after the traditions originated, and many of them were very well known in the early Christian movement. They would have remained the authoritative sources and guardians of the Jesus traditions, a role that is common in oral societies, and they are the people from whom the writers of the Gospels are likely to have derived their material" (Bauckham, *Jesus: A Very Short Introduction*, 13–14).

We will see that much of the Prayer can be found in Jewish sources, but this does not mean that a practicing Jew like Jesus would not have used those prayers in formulating his own. An incarnational faith like Christianity would seem to expect that Jesus, rooted in his own historical context, would be greatly influenced by it, even while shaping it in his own Spirit-inspired way.

We humans are also narrative-oriented, seeing things and people and events in our own attempted frameworks of meaning or story forms, which blend events and narrative plot together.[12] We "see" events, and we may be profoundly focused on those events, but we see within and against the backdrop of our frame of meaning, our "story" as we know it in our culture and society. Good stories arise from within the events they narrate, and attempt to follow the curve of those events. We might, then, think of the Gospel evangelists as storytellers in this sense. They are not fabricating the story of Jesus and how the Lord's Prayer emerges within it; they are rather participating in the movement arising in the wake of Jesus, following its energy flow, guided by the testimony of the tradition, and each in their own way making their own contribution to the deeper meaning of dimensions of that testimony. Within that, we can expect heightening and intensification, selection, and breakthroughs to new insights along the line, along with obfuscation and distortion. The holy/unholy mix of an incarnational faith.

The Doxology

A very common experience of English-speaking Christians is a sense ranging from surprise to curiosity to puzzlement to maybe even a bit of prayer-xenophobia and sometimes to the question, "Why can't we pray this in the same way?" upon hearing an English version of the Prayer different from one's own. Of course, if people are acquainted with the various modern scholarly translations and variations among them in today's New Testament versions, these experiences might not be so intense. But even then they might reasonably ask, Why can't we agree on one version at least for our prayer in common? We will look at the most common variations of English translation in a moment, but before we do so, let us pause and take a look at the doxology ("word of glory"/"praise") sometimes attached to the Prayer's ending and commonly used by Anglicans, Protestants, and evangelicals. It is also commonly found in the many musical expressions in

12. See Thompson-Uberuaga, *Jesus and the Gospel Movement*, 48–49.

use for this prayer, even in churches, like the Roman Catholic, which do not typically use the doxology.

But the issue has perhaps become less of an ecumenical hurdle since the revisions of the Mass after the Second Vatican Council for Roman Catholics. For, following the example of some of the older eucharistic traditions, the doxology has been restored to the Prayer, but only after an intervening embolism (inserted prayer). So Roman Catholics are becoming familiar with the doxology as in some way connected to the Lord's Prayer, albeit not tightly.[13] It is also worth noting that the version of the Lord's Prayer given in the new *Catechism of the Catholic Church* includes the doxology.[14] The doxology is also found in the liturgies in use among Eastern Christians, albeit often it is the priest alone who expresses it.[15] Still, this lessens the inability to deal with the more common use of the doxology among others when that is experienced.

From the other side, it is notable that the 1979 revision of the US Episcopal Church's *The Book of Common Prayer* includes the version of the Lord's Prayer typically used by Roman Catholics in several of its rites, along with a slightly more contemporary version as well. In these versions, the doxology is not said. In typically Anglican fashion, reflecting the middle way (*via media*)—"Catholic but not Roman, Reformed but not Protestant"—this is perhaps a way in which Anglicans/Episcopalians might grow into a level of comfort with the "Roman" version, reflecting the "Catholic" side of their orientation.[16]

The *Didache*, an early (c. 100) Christian manual, seems to have followed Matthew's version of the Lord's Prayer, but then added the doxology (words of praise): "For yours is the power and glory for ever and ever." The

---

13. The current form of this embolism (inserted prayer), immediately following the Lord's Prayer: "Deliver us, Lord, we pray, from every evil, graciously grant peace in our days, that, by the help of your mercy, we may be always free from sin and safe from all distress, as we await the blessed hope and the coming of our Savior, Jesus Christ." The doxology immediately follows, recited by all: "For the kingdom, the power, and the glory are yours, now and forever." See Catholic Resources, "Embolism."

14. Vatican, *Catechism of the Catholic Church*, Part 4, Section 2, "The Lord's Prayer."

15. For example, the priest prays: "For yours is the kingdom and the power and the glory of the Father and the Son and the Holy Spirit, now and forever and to the ages of ages," and the people answer: "Amen" (Orthodox Page, "Divine Liturgy of St. John Chrysostom").

16. See Anglican Communion News Service for this saying. For the Lord's Prayer versions mentioned here, see, for example the Offices for Noonday, 106; Compline, 132–33; and The Great Litany, 153, in *The Book of Common Prayer*.

word "kingdom" was added to the Prayer later, perhaps drawing from the example of 1 Chronicles 29:10–11: David said: "Blessed are you, O Lord, the God of our ancestor Israel, for ever and ever. Yours, O Lord, are the greatness, the power, the glory, the victory, and the majesty; for all that is in the heavens and on the earth is yours; yours is the kingdom, O Lord, and you are exalted as head above all."

The addition of "Amen" would be a typical Jewish addition to prayer and would seem a natural conclusion for people influenced by the Jewish tradition of prayer.[17] Raymond Brown, PSS, wrote that "the Jews used 'amen' (doubled in Num 5:22) in corroboration and response, particularly to prayer, somewhat the way congregations respond to evangelical preachers." Its Hebrew root is *'mn*, meaning to confirm and support. From that also comes the meaning of "amen" as "truly," which we find in Jesus' "Amen, I say to you."[18] Bishop Stevenson supports the view that "amen" was originally part of the version found in the *Didache*.[19]

We will not find a doxology in Luke's version, nor will we find it in Alexandrian Greek manuscripts of Matthew. However, and this might surprise some, the doxology is found in some Byzantine Greek and Latin manuscripts of Matthew. It has been suggested that it was the use of Matthew's version in liturgy and worship generally which caused some manuscript scribes to add the doxology to the text. An allied question is that of why Matthew's version of the Prayer seems to have been the one to find its way into Christian liturgies and worship in the first place. Matthew, as one of the apostles, gives a special status to the Gospel under that name.[20] At the same time, early church writers like Eusebius, Irenaeus, and others commonly thought of Matthew's Gospel as the first Gospel.

We will come back to the doxology again, as we move into the more interpretive aspects of the Prayer in later chapters. At this point we are only surveying and introducing the "textual" tradition. But given the use of the doxology and "Amen" in Jewish prayer, it may not be going too far to suggest that Jesus himself and his disciples concluded the Our Father in this way now and then. We will be returning to the Prayer's origins with Jesus himself at a later point, and this may add some clarification.

---

17. See *Didache* 8.2, text in Stevenson, *The Lord's Prayer*, 19, who notes the presence of other doxologies in the *Didache* (21).
18. Brown, *The Gospel according to John*, 1:83–84; Blackman, "Amen," 18.
19. Stevenson, *The Lord's Prayer*, 20.
20. Ibid., 40.

The Jewish Background

Matthew's version of the Prayer "is especially Jewish," writes Jesuit biblical scholar Daniel Harrington. In comparison with Luke's version, he suggests a number of typically Jewish features. The address, "Our Father in heaven" (Matt 6:9b), is "a standard Jewish formula of address to God in prayer." Luke's more brief "Father" would be "a highly unusual one." The additional third "You" (Matt 6:10b) and "We" (Matt 6:13) petitions ("Your will be done . . . ; . . . rescue us from the evil one") are "typical of the flexibility of Jewish prayer." "The metaphor of 'debts' (6:12) as a way of talking about sins is characteristically Jewish."[21]

The general theological tradition of Judaism is also reflected throughout the Prayer. God's fatherhood is known, and God is addressed as Father in prayer (Hos 11:1; Isa 63:16; 1 Chr 29:10; Ps 89:27). The sanctification by people is a response to and manifestation in some ways of God's hallowed name (2 Sam 6:2; Jer 7:11; Ezek 36:23; Lev 11:45). The prayer for the coming of the kingdom can be said to reflect "God's rule with justice" (Ezek 20:33; Pss 46:7, 121:5). Anglican Bishop and scholar Kenneth Stevenson, whom I am following here, adds that "doing the will [of God] pervades the piety of the Psalter," and as we will see, as in the Psalter, so in the history of the interpretation of the Prayer, "there is a rich ambiguity that embraces God's will as both that with which we struggle in order to make sense of our lives as well as the final revelation of his will at the end" (Ps 119:27, 30, 32, 33; Isa 46:9).

As we move toward the second set of petitions of the Prayer, concerned with the human partners of the covenant, we likewise are within the midst of the Jewish theological tradition. Asking for bread or daily food is typically Jewish, and one also thinks of the manna in the wilderness (Ex 16:15; Num 11:6; Deut 8:3). We encounter the forgiveness of our sins by God (Exod 32:32; Pss 6:2, 18:35, 130:2), and the call to forgive our neighbor (Lev 19:18). The *Akedah,* in which Isaac is protected from sacrifice by Abraham, is a supreme example of being protected from trials (Gen 22:1–19), and oftentimes Israel and her people are delivered from evil (1 Sam 12:10; Ps 33:19).[22]

---

21. Harrington, *The Gospel of Matthew,* 97. The original Aramaic speech situation of Jesus gives this Jewish background added importance.

22. Stevenson, *The Lord's Prayer,* 24–25; see also Levine and Brettler, eds., *The Jewish Annotated New Testament,* at Matt 6:9–13 and Luke 11:2–4.

Texts and Versions

Harrington emphasizes, and Stevenson notes, the parallels between the Prayer and the *Amidah*, from the Hebrew root *'md* for "stand up." This is a prayer of eighteen (Stevenson says there are actually nineteen) benedictions, commonly recited while standing. Consisting of "three introductory praises, twelve petitions for personal and communal needs, and three concluding praises," it contains "practically every phrase in the Lord's Prayer." "Thou art holy and thy name is awesome . . . . Blessed art thou, O Lord, who desirest repentance . . . . Forgive us, our Father . . . . Behold our afflictions and defend our cause . . ."—these are some of the typical benedictions likewise reflected in the Lord's Prayer. Both the Lord's Prayer and the *Amidah* are roughly contemporary, combining praises with petitions, and were recited three times daily.[23]

Was the Lord's Prayer a "simplified version of the Eighteen Benedictions," perhaps even a Christian alternative to it? Harrington suggests this last possibility at least, given the polemical context of Matthew 6:1–18, in which the rabbis are roundly criticized for hypocrisy and ostentatiousness. "The terse and modest Lord's Prayer" would have been a way "for fostering the identity of the Matthean community vis-à-vis the early rabbinic movement." But in some ways, given the polemics, it would be an example of an unfortunate either/or alternative in Jewish-Christian relations, and an alternative quite foreign to Jesus' own use of the Prayer.[24]

Stevenson also finds merit in Birger Gerhardsson's suggestion that the threefold nature of the *Shema*—to love the Lord with our heart, soul, and strength (Deut 6:4–5)—may well be reflected in the Lord's Prayer. "The heart may be there in the hallowing of the name and daily bread; the soul in the coming of the kingdom and the gift of forgiveness; and strength in doing the will and protection from temptation and evil."[25]

The *Kaddish* (from the Aramaic for "holy"), a venerable Jewish prayer whose origins are earlier than the first complete text we have dating to the ninth century AD, certainly reflects much of the first part of the Lord's Prayer.

---

23. See Roberts and Donaldson, eds., *Didache* 8:3, for the thrice daily recitation of the Lord's Prayer.

24. Harrington, *The Gospel of Matthew*, 98–99.

25. Stevenson, *The Lord's Prayer*, 25–26, referring to Gerhardsson, *The Shema in the New Testament*.

> Exalted and sanctified be His great Name.
>
> In the world which He created according to His will, may He establish His kingdom
>
> in your lifetime, and in the lifetime of the entire House of Israel, speedily and soon.
>
> May His great Name be blessed forever and to all eternity.
>
> Praised, glorified, exalted, extolled, revered, highly honoured, and adored is the
>
> Name of the Holy One, blessed be He beyond all the blessings, hymns, praises,
>
> and consolations that are ever uttered in the world.

This is the "Half-Kaddish," for the "Full Kaddish" has additions, and that prayed for the departed has a special, final addition. Commonly the Half-Kaddish is prayed before the *Amidah*, and the Full after it in Jewish daily prayers. The festal prayer *Abhinu Malkenu* ("Our Father, Our King"), with its prayers of blessings, the gift of forgiveness, and protection from ills, and its repeated references to God as Father, also reflects the "world" of the Lord's Prayer.[26]

Hopefully these are a sufficient number of examples to bring home the thoroughly Jewish nature of the Our Father. As we move along, we can think about some of the special nuances which Jesus himself, and his followers, bring to this prayer. But our goal at this point is to underline the rootedness of this prayer in Jesus' Jewish formation. An earlier form of Jesus research, known as the "New Quest for the Historical Jesus," stressed as one of its criteria for assessing the historical authenticity of texts purportedly going back to Jesus himself, that of uniqueness or something utterly dissimilar to anything known before Jesus in the Jewish or Greco-Roman orbits. The more careful scholars of the New Quest, as for example, Ernst Käsemann, however, knew that as a Jew Jesus would have shared many of the practices and convictions of Jews. Humans are, after all, always a blend of the unique and the common, in varying proportions. Incarnation—rootedness in society and history—would seem to demand this.[27]

---

26. Ibid., 26–27.

27. See Käsemann, "The Problem of the Historical Jesus," 15–47; this essay was originally published in 1953, becoming something of a charter for the "New Quest," which was more optimistic about the ability to recover the original tradition of Jesus himself, after the somewhat pessimistic tendencies characteristic of the so-called "Old Quest." Today we also speak of the "Third Quest," referring to a loose consortium of scholars using diverse disciplines (anthropology, sociology, political science, literary studies, etc.)

Texts and Versions

English Versions Commonly Used in Worship and Prayer

Other than the use of the doxology, the other commonly noted difference in versions of the Our Father used for prayer, whether liturgical or personal, is the use of "debts/debtors," or its alternative, "trespasses/those who trespass against us." How did this difference in usage come about? It is really a fascinating story, going back to the beginnings of the Reformation in England, to the vernacular translations that were available at the time, to the need to provide a standard vernacular version in the kingdom, and to the preferences between the monarch, the parliament, and the bishops or other church authorities.[28]

Let us look at the two major English translations which were available at the beginnings of the Reformation in England, that of William Tyndale (c. 1494–1536), on the one hand, appearing in 1534, and that of Miles Coverdale (1487/8–1569), on the other, appearing in 1536. Tyndale's translation worked from the Hebrew and Greek, relying on Erasmus's text of 1516 in the original languages. Coverdale's translation worked from the (Latin) Vulgate, Luther's German version, and Tyndale's version. Tyndale, the reader may know, suffered martyrdom for his (at the time) illicit translation. Coverdale was more fortunate, for reformist pressure was building to force Henry VIII to have Bibles placed in all churches, the version being the so-called "Great Bible," which was largely Coverdale's work. Here are Tyndale's and Coverdale's versions:

Tyndale (1534)	Coverdale (1536)
	(variants only)
Our Father who art in heaven	
Hallowed be thy name.	
Let thy kingdom come.	Thy kingdom come.
Thy will be fulfilled	
As well in earth as it is in heaven.	Upon earth as it is in heaven
Give us this day our daily bread.	

---

beyond that of historical criticism in efforts of coming to know about Jesus in his original context and among his earliest followers. But there is a wide range of views here, from the more skeptical on the one hand, to the more optimistic (like Bauckham) on the other.

28. The best succinct treatment I have seen is in Stevenson, *The Lord's Prayer*, 172–86, which I will largely follow here.

And forgive us our trespasses,	And forgive us our debts,
Even as we forgive our trespassers.	As we forgive our debtors.
And lead us not into temptation:	
But deliver us from evil.	
For thine is the kingdom	
And the power, and the glory	
For ever. Amen.	

These versions were not "officially" sanctioned, of course. That would demand a lot of wrangling back and forth between the various church and government authorities. But these versions were the fundamental bases for any later official texts. The 1549 Prayer Book, issued during the reign of Edward VI, gives us the version which is so widely used among English-speaking Roman Catholics, Eastern Christians, Anglican/Episcopal, and Protestant churches:

> Our Father which art in heaven,
> Hallowed be thy name.
> Thy kingdom come.
> Thy will be done in earth,
> As it is in heaven.
> Give us this day our daily bread.
> And forgive us our trespasses,
> As we forgive them that trespass against us.
> And lead us not into temptation,
> But deliver us from evil. Amen.

This is largely Tyndale's version, without the doxology, but the doxology would finally make its way into the 1662 Prayer Book. The wide use and popularity of this translation seems to have insured its enduring vitality. Not even Queen Mary, with her restoration of the Latin Mass, dared to forbid this usage in prayer. On the other hand, a royally authorized "King James version" in 1611, coming out of the reign of James I, followed Coverdale and the Geneva Bible in using "debts/debtors," along with the doxology. But this translation, while royally sanctioned, was not that found in the Prayer Book, which was largely Tyndale's. Still, it is probably the authority of Geneva, the home of Calvin and the "Reformed" (Presbyterian) Reformation, which partly accounts for the "debts/debtors" and doxology in the Lord's Prayer among Christians of that heritage in English-speaking territories. Interestingly, as we noted at this chapter's beginning, the translation of Matthew 6:12 by "debts/debtors" is a preference of contemporary biblical translators. Such are the twists and turns of history![29]

The Lord's Prayer "Reflected" throughout the Rest of the New Testament

Before moving on to contemporary expressions of the Lord's Prayer, it will be helpful to look briefly at places in the New Testament other than Matthew and Luke in which we find the words and the theology of the Prayer. Some of these traditionally noted references are perhaps more convincing than others.[30] They illustrate how pervasive the Prayer's language and theology is. We have already noted this pervasiveness within the Hebrew Bible and Jewish tradition; now we are noting it within the New Testament as a whole. Some of these references—such as Paul's writings or Mark's—reflect the early, oral tradition of the Prayer; others reflect a later stage of the tradition, as it incorporates the earlier tradition or at least expresses it in equivalent ways.

<u>Mark 11:25:</u> "Whenever you stand praying, forgive, if you have anything against anyone; so that your Father in heaven may also forgive you your trespasses." Some manuscripts also add a verse 26: "But if you do not forgive, neither will your Father in heaven forgive your trespasses."

<u>Paul's epistles:</u> St. Paul's writings are our earliest New Testament texts. Their references to the language and theology of the Lord's Prayer illustrate its early origins. His important statement, "For I handed on to you as of first importance what I in turn had received" (1 Cor 15:3), illustrates our suggestion above, following Bauckham, about the role of witnesses to the Jesus tradition as forming a chain of transmitters. This would seem to intensify the argument for rooting the Lord's Prayer in the teaching and words of Jesus himself.[31] I will place the Lord's Prayer to the reader's left, and the New Testament echoes to the reader's right, in parentheses.

---

29. Henry VIII's *Royal Primer* (1545) changed Tyndale's "thy will be fulfilled" to "thy will be done." Edward VI's first Prayer Book (1549) changed the *Primer's* "Let us not be led into temptation" to "Lead us not into temptation," as we have seen above.

30. I am following Ayo, *The Lord's Prayer*, 241–44 ("New Testament Analogues").

31. See Bauckham, *Jesus and the Eyewitnesses*, 264–71.

Our Father in heaven ("Abba, Father"): Galatians 4:6

hallowed be your name ("the name that is above every name"): Philippians 2:9

Your kingdom come ("When all things are subjected to him, then the Son himself will also be subjected to the one who put all things in subjection under him, so that God may be all in all."): 1 Cor 15:28

Your will be done, on earth as it is in heaven ("that you may discern what is the will of God"): Rom 12:2

Give us this day our daily bread ("we all partake of the one bread"): 1 Cor 10:17

And forgive us our debts ("Blessed are those whose iniquities are forgiven, blessed is the one against whom the Lord will not reckon sin."): Rom 4:7–8

And do not bring us to the time of trial, but rescue us from the evil one ("God . . . will not let you be tested beyond your strength, but with the testing he will also provide the way out so that you may be able to endure it."): 1 Cor 10:13

John 17: Jesus' Priestly Prayer: This has traditionally been considered Jesus' "priestly prayer," for it presents us with a Jesus who, in priestly fashion, is praying for his people. If it is such, then, following Nicholas Ayo, CSC, and others, it would seem that the Lord's Prayer, much of which is echoed in this Johannine priestly prayer, finds a kind of mystical and deeply theological meditation here in the Gospel of John.[32] The more mystical prayer of the Jesus of the mystical Gospel of John perhaps gives us a mystic's laser beam insight into the Lord's Prayer of Matthew and Luke. Intriguingly, biblical scholar Raymond Brown, PSS, suggests that in the Gospel of John, the name to be hallowed is the "I am," echoing the sacred name of Exodus 3:14. "When you have lifted up the son of man, then you will realize that I am he . . ." (John 8:28), ". . . before Abraham was, I am" (John 8:58), says the Johannine Jesus in typical fashion (6:35, 51; 8:12, 24; 9:5; 10:7, 9, 11, 14; 11:25; 13:19; 14:6; 15:1, 5.[33] Would this name be the name referred to by Jesus in his Prayer? Let us look at the possible echoes between John and the *Paternoster*.

---

32. See Thompson-Uberuaga, *Jesus and the Gospel Movement*, 81–95; Countryman, *The Mystical Way in the Fourth Gospel*.

33. Brown, *The Gospel according to John*, 1:533–38; 2:755–56.

Texts and Versions

Our Father in heaven (God addressed as "Father"): 17:1, 5, 21, 24; ("Holy Father"): 17:11; ("Righteous Father"): 17:25

hallowed be your name ("I have made your name known to those whom you gave me . . ."): 17:6; (". . . protect them in your name . . . so that they may be one, as we are one."): 17:11; (". . . I protected them in your name . . ."): 17:12; ("I made your name known to them, and I will make it known, so that the love with which you have loved me may be in them, and I in them."): 17:26

Your kingdom come (". . . glorify your Son so that the Son may glorify you, since you have given him authority over all people . . ."): 17:1–2

Your will be done, on earth as it is in heaven ("I glorified you on earth by finishing the work that you gave me to do.")17:4; (". . . that they may be one, as we are"): 17:11; (". . . that they may all be one. As you, Father, are in me and I am in you, may they also be in us, so that the world may believe that you have sent me."): 17:21; (". . . so that the love with which you have loved me may be in them, and I in them."): 17:26

Give us this day our daily bread ("I am asking on their behalf . . . because they are yours."): 17:9

And forgive us our debts ("I ask not only on behalf of these, but also on behalf of those who will believe in me through their word . . ."): 17:20

And do not bring us to the time of trial (". . . I protected them that you have given me. I guarded them . . ."): 17:12

but rescue us from the evil one (". . . I ask you to protect them from the evil one."):17:15

<u>First Peter:</u> This letter is traditionally read in the Liturgy of the Hours (the "Office") during the days within the Easter Week following the baptism of catechumens at the Easter Vigil Service. These newly baptized Christians would have had the Lord's Prayer "handed over" (*traditio orationis*) to them as part of their initiation into the body of Christ.

Our Father in heaven ("Blessed be the God and Father of our Lord Jesus Christ!"; "If you invoke as Father the one who judges all people impartially according to their deeds, live in reverent fear during the time of your exile."): 1:3, 17 hallowed be your name ("... as he who called you is holy, be holy yourselves in all your conduct; for it is written, 'You shall be holy, for I am holy.'"): 1:15–16; ("... in your hearts sanctify Christ as Lord."): 3:15

Your kingdom come ("But you are a chosen race, a royal priesthood, a holy nation, God's own people, in order that you may proclaim the mighty acts of him who called you out of darkness into his marvelous light."): 2:9

Your will be done, on earth as it is in heaven ("For it is God's will that by doing right you should silence the ignorance of the foolish."): 2:15; ("For it is better to suffer for doing good, if suffering should be God's will, than to suffer for doing evil."): 3:17; ("... live for the rest of your earthly life no longer by human desires but by the will of God."): 4:2; ("... let those suffering in accordance with God's will entrust themselves to a faithful Creator, while continuing to do good."): 4:19

Give us this day our daily bread ("Like newborn infants, long for the pure, spiritual milk, so that by it you may grow into salvation—if indeed you have tasted that the Lord is good."): 2:2; ("Cast all your anxiety on him, because he cares for you."): 5:7

And forgive us our debts ("... maintain constant love for one another, for love covers a multitude of sins."): 4:8

And do not bring us to the time of trial ("Beloved, do not be surprised at the fiery ordeal that is taking place among you to test you ... rejoice insofar as you are sharing Christ's sufferings, so that you may also be glad and shout for joy when his glory is revealed."): 4:12

but rescue us from the evil one ("Like a roaring lion your adversary the devil prowls around, looking for someone to devour. Resist him, steadfast in your faith ... after you have suffered for a little while, the God of all grace, who has called you to his eternal glory in Christ, will himself restore, support, strengthen, and establish you."): 5:8–10

For thine is the kingdom, and the power, and the glory, for ever and ever. Amen. [For the kingdom, the power, and the glory are yours, now and for ever. Amen. (1979 *Book of Common Prayer*)] ("To him belong the glory and the power forever and ever. Amen."): 4:11

Texts and Versions

Examples of Other Versions

Our goal now is to sample some contemporary "versions" of the Prayer. I do not mean simply translations into English, but translations that are also in a very obvious way interpretations. Of course, it is probably true that all translations are also interpretations. The words we choose, based on the understanding we bring to the text to be translated, and also based on just what it is we are trying to do, offer a more "literal" translation, or try to go with the meaning and spirit: all of these go into our translations. And, of course, the words we choose to use are largely determined by the social and cultural milieu in which we live and/or in which our intended audience dwells.

We can see all of that very easily with translations of the Bible for children. Or maybe I should say, with pairing the Bible text with a more or less child-friendly retelling, which seems to be what usually happens. For example, in one retelling of the petition to give us our daily bread, we find the following retelling for children: It "means give us today all that we need. Keep in mind that these are things that we can't live without. We don't *need* video games and princess dolls . . . we need food, water and shelter."[34]

Another way to do this, for both children and older people, is to use pictures and art. The artistic rendering is a translation, and also very much of an interpretation. So, for example, one will find in a YouTube rendition of the Lord's Prayer for children the text below, and the artistic rendition, sometimes with words, above. This would be like the portrayal of the teaching of the Prayer on stained glass windows or in theater form in churches, or in the medieval woodcuts of the *Bibles of the Poor*. Such renderings are always interpretations. The Anglican Church of England has a beautiful rendering of the Lord's Prayer on YouTube, beginning with Justin Welby, the Archbishop of Canterbury, and moving through various scenes of people and nature that offer a "version and interpretation" of the prayer as the prayer is recited.[35]

Contemporary renderings—and musical renderings ought also to be included, the melody itself being an interpretive translation—are really a continuation of a long-standing tradition. They witness to the generative and inspiring character of the Prayer, and in some way represent a kind of

---

34. DLTK, "Bible Stories for Children."

35. YouTube, "The Lord's Prayer for Children"; Labriola and Smeltz, eds., *The Bible of the Poor (Biblia Pauperum)*; Church of England, "The Lord's Prayer." See Stevenson, *The Lord's Prayer*, 155, for the theater versions of the York Mystery Plays produced by the Pater Noster Guild.

"answer" or "response" to the "questions" of each day and place. They are something of a continuing dialogue between the Prayer and peoples of all generations. Stevenson notes examples through the ages: preaching on the Lord's prayer; expositions of it; paraphrases; metrical versions for use in catechisms or for singing (Martin Luther and John Wesley especially come to mind here); theatrical performances of the petitions; and allegorical interpretations, in which different petitions and verses are paired with the beatitudes of the Sermon on the Mount, or with virtues, or the gifts of the Spirit, or the various "ranks" of holy orders, for example.[36]

Here is a table offered by Stevenson: from the reader's left to right, we have the various holy orders, then the gifts of the Spirit, then the parts of the Lord's Prayer which are in correspondence, and finally the beatitudes:

Presbyters	Wisdom	Hallowing of name	Peacemakers
Deacons	Understanding	Kingdom	Pure in heart
Subdeacons	Counsel	Will	Merciful
Acolytes	Fortitude	Daily bread	Hunger for right
Exorcists	Knowledge	Forgiveness	Mourn
Readers	Piety	Temptation	Meek
Doorkeepers	Fear of Lord	Deliverance	Poor in Spirit

We have already mentioned Dante's rendering of the Prayer in his *Purgatorio*, which centers on the vice of all of us imperfect creatures, pride, or perhaps better, lack of trust in God as our sufficient Anchor:

> Our Father Who in Heaven dost abide,
> not there constrained but dwelling there because
> Thou lovest more Thy lofty first effects.
>
> And as Thine angels offer up their will
> To Thee in sacrifice, singing Hosannah,
> let all men offer up to Thee their own.
> Give us this day our daily manna, Lord;
> Without it, those most eager to advance
> Go backwards through this wild wasteland of ours.[37]

---

36. See Stevenson, *The Lord's Prayer*, 3–7, and passim (for the fuller evidence); the table, 126 (the gifts of the Spirit are at Isa 11:2–3); sometimes the gifts and the beatitudes are inverted. Where the Lord's Prayer is recited in liturgy, and how, is also something of an interpretation, and we will return to this in a later chapter.

37. Ibid., 149–50, citing Musa translation, Alighieri, *The Divine Comedy*, 2, *Purgatory*,

Texts and Versions

With Dante, we can see rather clearly how the translation is also an interpretation, and how the interpretation always expresses the horizon of thought of one's age. Liberation from hell, the *Inferno*, was very much of a late medieval preoccupation, and deliverance from purgatory as well. The chart above, listing the more allegorical pairings, is probably less convincing to us today, and the Reformers reacted strongly against them, seeing them as falling into those "empty phrases" against which the Sermon on the Mount warns (Matt 6:7). But a postmodern openness to allegory, which is really an appeal to a less literal and more imaginative participation in a text, may enable us to reappropriate these interpretations with a second naivete.

It is those more imaginative renderings which shine through in, for example, Hemingway's rendering, which we looked at in our introduction. We find another imaginative, but still more traditional, version in the Anglican *New Zealand Prayer Book*. Let us consider it now:

> Eternal Spirit,
> Earth-maker, Pain-bearer, life-giver,
> Father and Mother of us all,
> Loving God, in whom is heaven:
> The hallowing of your name echo through the universe!
> The way of your justice be followed by the peoples of the world!
> Your heavenly will be done by all created beings!
> Your commonwealth of peace and freedom
> sustain our hope and come on earth.
> With the bread we need for today, feed us.
> In the hurts we absorb from one another, forgive us.
> In times of temptation and testing, strengthen us.
> From trials too great to endure, spare us.
> From the grip of all that is evil, free us.
> For you reign in the glory of the power that is love,
> Now and forever. Amen.[38]

Again, translation and interpretation blend, with the interpretation becoming intense, reflecting the concerns of Anglican believers in the late twentieth century. From the introduction to this Prayer Book we learn of the concerns leading to this "new" version: ". . . an increasing awareness

118–19.

38. *A New Zealand Prayer Book*, 180, for Night Prayer.

of the delicate ecological balance within our country, interdependent with others . . . an increasing need to choose language which is inclusive . . . [and] affirms the place of each gender under God." Along with this is the stated desire to "close the gap between liturgical language and the words of everyday experience," and to reflect and affirm "the partnership between Maori and Pakeha." And all of this is reflective of a keen commitment to justice.[39]

"Eternal Spirit, Earth-maker," for example, seems reflective of the Maori and Pakeha tradition and of a new ecological sensitivity; "Father and Mother of us all," of gender equality; and the "way of your justice" and "Your commonwealth of peace and freedom" bring the commitment to justice into prominence, helping us to deprivatize the Prayer, hearing again its social and political dimensions. At the same time, there is something traditional about these themes as well. Not only do they nicely flow within the actual structure of the Lord's Prayer within the biblical text, but they also give currency to themes which are prominent in Scripture. Justice and peace and a "kingdom" characterized by these are especially emphasized by the prophets; the Eternal Spirit calls to mind the Holy Spirit; ecological attunement reflects a God of all created reality, of "heaven and earth"; and a Father who is also a Mother calls to mind the God who comforts her child Israel like a mother (Isa 66:13).

The use of both "Father and Mother" for the address to God seems a common way to express gender justice. Another interesting expression of this is the replacement of "kingdom" with "kin-dom": "May your kin-dom come." One could also use "reign" in place of "kingdom," but "kin-dom" avoids the unfortunate associations of dominating power expressive of many, most, or even all (?) kingdoms/reigns, at least the ones we know in human history. And "kin-dom" or "kindom" seems wide enough to embrace our entire family, human and all animates.[40] Praying for kindom's coming seems to express a yearning to refind in a new way our union with our earth, our cosmos, but also with those who are our kin, and yet we do not know them or even see them, persons certainly, but entire groups. A kindom is a decolonized phenomenon.[41]

---

39. Ibid., x–xiv.

40. McCall, "Versions of the Lord's Prayer"; Mary Magdalene Apostle Catholic Community, "May your kin-dom come." Also see Delio, *Making All Things New*, 76, 82, 85, for "kin-dom," but extending to all animates and all galaxies in Delio's work.

41. See Moore, *Empire and Apocalypse*, 12.

Let us end this look at new versions with Margaret Atwood's imaginative rendering, from her acclaimed dystopia, *The Handmaid's Tale*. For the moment we are primarily interested in offering a representative sampling of versions, not so much with offering an interpretation. Hopefully that will come in later chapters. But we are attempting to offer an ecumenical guide to the Lord's Prayer, and in our global world such a guide must move beyond the uses of more traditional believers and seek to learn from those "on the edges," so to speak, or "beyond the edges." Hemingway's version is wonderfully provocative in this regard. But Atwood's is as well.

Offred, the protagonist in the utterly patriarchal world of the novel, where women are valued as breeders, and little else; in the night, which seems to be her time, provided she draws no attention to herself; says, "Tonight I will say my prayers." But she remembers first the "anti-prayer" forced upon the women in this dystopia, the Republic of Gilead: "What we prayed for was emptiness, so we would be worthy to be filled: with grace, with love, with self-denial, semen and babies. Oh God, thank you for not creating me a man. Oh God, obliterate me. Make me fruitful. Mortify my flesh, that I may be multiplied. Let me be fulfilled.... Some of them would get carried away with this. The ecstasy of abasement. Some of them would moan and cry." We know today that there really are such places. In our own Western world, they are more hidden, and perhaps Atwood is exposing the shadow by way of intensification, taking patriarchalism to its ultimate conclusions.

Then comes her prayer, "sitting by the window"; open eyes. "Out there or inside my head, it's an equal darkness. Or light."

> My God. Who art in the Kingdom of Heaven, which is within. I wish you could tell me Your Name, the real one I mean. But *You* will do as well as anything. I wish I knew what you were up to. But whatever it is, help me to get through it, please. Though maybe it's not Your doing; I don't believe for an instant that what's going on out there is what You meant. I have enough daily bread, so I won't waste time on that. It isn't the main problem. The problem is getting it down without choking on it. Now we come to forgiveness. Don't worry about forgiving me right now. There are more important things. For instance: keep the others safe, if they are safe. Don't let them suffer too much. If they have to die, let it be fast. You might even provide a Heaven for them. We need You for that. Hell we can make for ourselves. I suppose I should say I forgive whoever did this, and whatever they're doing now. I'll try,

but it isn't easy. Temptation comes next. At the Center, temptation was anything much more than eating and sleeping. Knowing was a temptation. What you don't know won't tempt you, Aunt Lydia used to say. Maybe I don't really want to know what's going on. Maybe I'd rather not know. Maybe I couldn't bear to know. The Fall was a Fall from innocence to knowledge. I think about the chandelier too much, though it's gone now. But you could use a hook, in the closet. I've considered the possibilities. All you'd have to do, after attaching yourself, would be to lean your weight forward and not fight. Deliver us from evil. Then there's Kingdom, power, and glory. It takes a lot to believe in those right now. But I'll try it anyway. *In Hope*, as they say on the gravestones.[42]

In so many ways, this is a beautiful prayer because it seems so real, so authentic. "I wish you could tell me your name"; "I wish I knew what you were up to"; "I'll try, but it isn't easy." Can we ask for anything more? I cannot imagine any better attitude with which to approach the chapters to follow!

---

42. Atwood, *The Handmaid's Tale*, 194–95.

three

The Medium and the Message

"There's an old saying in biblical studies (I first heard it from Ben Witherington III) that a text without a context is just a pretext for making it say anything one wants," writes biblical scholar Amy-Jill Levine.[1] Texts do not come from nowhere, but from somewhere, might be another popular way of putting it. Texts are shaped by authors or groups who are shaped, knowingly and tacitly, by cultures, which are in turn shaped by traditions, whether literary, religious, political, social, tribal, familial, and the special talents of the authors themselves. These make up the thick "withness" of the text, that is, the "con-" (from the Latin for "with," *cum)* "text." Not even authors are always fully aware of how these contextual factors shape the capacity of their writings to convey meaning.

Thus, a good common sense rule of biblical interpretation, and indeed of any interpretation, is to pay attention to context. Not so much context in general, but the context that is likely most relevant to the text in focus. We have tried to practice this already to some extent, by noting how Jesus' own Jewish formation weaves its way through the entire Our Father. We have not yet attended to how his own special insights may have shaped the Prayer. That is more appropriate for later chapters.

We have also noted how the immediate context of the Prayer in Matthew and Luke discloses further insights into the Prayer. In Matthew it is the central core of the Sermon on the Mount, and so plausibly a key to how to make sense of that Sermon. But there is the reverse feedback, and so plausibly the Sermon—a kind of *magna carta* of Jesus' movement—helps us grasp how Jesus' Prayer is connected to his great work on behalf of the

---

1. Levine, *Short Stories by Jesus*, 8.

reign of God. It is the family prayer of the new family arising in the movement launched by Jesus. Similarly, Luke presents the Prayer as one of the central ways in which Jesus and his disciples keep themselves focused on the central journey of their lives, namely, the journey to Jerusalem. We make many journeys, we might say. But the journey to Jerusalem is to be the guiding journey working its way out in all our other "sub-journeys." These are what we might call aspects of the "theological" context, and we will explore these more fully in the chapters to come.

But allow me to register a bit of a caveat at this point. While I agree with what has been stated thus far, I also suggest that we do not lock the Prayer up into a special closet reserved only for biblical scholars. Sometimes the emphasis upon context becomes a pretext for reserving the Bible to the province of scholars alone. The scholars become the new "inquisition," blocking access to the Bible. When that happens, then typically church authorities in reaction go to the other extreme, locking the text up into their own "magisterium." We have seen this action-reaction syndrome repeatedly in the history of the Bible's reception. I would suggest that the deep down, perhaps the deepest, context of the text of the Prayer is the drama of humanity's relationship with God, and in God with others within the cosmos. Readers and prayers of the Prayer are already participating in this grounding and enveloping drama, or resisting that participation.

But this participatory drama is the context of contexts, the basic one, enveloping all the others and enabling our access to the Prayer's message. If you will, the Prayer prays us, in this great drama. Or we might say that our praying the Prayer reflects our participation in the Prayer's praying us.[2] We will need to explore this more fully, but for now let us wager that the Lord's Prayer reflects the basic movement of this grounding drama of our lives. That is why many saints and committed believers; even those with no "religious" affiliation; and especially those whose voices seem to remain unheard by those around them, all of the marginalized and oppressed; are quite capable of profound insights into the Prayer, even if they lack the sophisticated knowledge of the scholar. All the other "contexts" can enrich this founding context; they cannot replace it. Without it, at best we will have knowledge "about" the Our Father; we will not "know" the Father and his reign. It is because of this that I would wager that an Ernest Hemingway and a Margaret Atwood, or at least the protagonists of their writings,

---

2. Readers will perhaps notice the influence of Gadamer's notion of how the play plays us in his *Truth and Method*, 106–32, 503–6, 519–21.

The Medium and the Message

yield profound insights into our Prayer. And I would wager that others, especially including believers, teachers, and mystics of the great religious traditions of humankind, precisely because they are participating in this great drama of dramas in their own analogous ways, are to be heeded in any more integral ("ecumenical" tending toward "universal") approach to this Prayer. "In my Father's house there are many dwelling places," says the Johannine Jesus (John 14:2). This text from John takes on new meaning in a global age, and deserves to become more of a grounding principle of interpretation in today's biblical studies.[3]

One further thing worth noting here is the typical reading and hearing of the biblical text within the context of churches' liturgical gatherings, whether Eucharist, or other special "offices" and occasions. The Lord's Prayer is typically prayed within these contexts as well. In our introductory chapter we mentioned Pope Francis' praying of the Our Father with other pilgrims at the Anglican martyrs' shrine in Uganda. These church and liturgical gatherings provide a helpful lens through which the Scriptures can be appropriated, helping us become attuned to the wisdom of the churches with respect to various scriptural readings. In this way our capacities for hearing are widened and tutored by the rich heritage of the churches. This happens not only through homilies, but maybe especially through participation in the Eucharist. We hear the texts and pray the Prayer in the midst of the assembly as a family, not as isolated individuals. This attunes us to the familial dimension of the Prayer. And the Eucharist especially does this, focusing upon Jesus' own costly self-gift of sacrificial love. The Scriptures and the Prayer are to lead to that, or else they are being misunderstood.[4]

In this chapter, however, we would like to explore the literary context of the Prayer with a bit more serious consideration than it usually receives. We are going to do this because we have reasons to believe that the literary form or structure of the prayer shapes our ability to pray the Prayer. We are not exactly saying that the medium is the message, but that the medium is very tightly connected with the message, and that as we participate in the medium, we find ourselves being led into the thicket of the message. Here many of us have been helped by philosopher Paul Ricoeur's suggestion that literary genres need not simply be ways of classifying texts. For example,

---

3. See Thompson-Uberuaga, *Jesus and the Gospel Movement*, 160–68, 191–92, and Cox, *Many Mansions*.

4. For more on this see Wainwright, *Doxology*, and Thompson[-Uberuaga], *The Struggle for Theology's Soul*, 247–48.

the Lord's Prayer is in the genre of a prayer, which is distinct from a letter, or a song, or a poem, or a narrative/story, or a prophetic book, or a historical text, etc. It is a distinct genre—a prayer—but it is also the kind of genre which is productive and generative, because somehow it is peculiarly appropriate to the message of the Prayer, as well as actually enabling those of us who pray it to participate in the Prayer's message and to move more deeply into it.[5]

A Form of Biblical Parallelism

Perhaps the most immediate literary context of our Prayer would be the kind of parallelism we find in the prayer book of Israel, the Psalter. Jesus and his disciples were prayers of the Psalms.[6] John Dominic Crossan has especially turned to this technique of biblical poetry to elucidate aspects of the Lord's Prayer. Such parallelism, he notes, is "not a lazy redundancy in which the second part repeats the former . . . ." That would not really be parallelism, but simple repetition in other words or images. Crossan suggests that "what happens is that the parallelism creates a vibration of thought, a metronome in the mind." And that vibration becomes "a lure for meditation," or a way of spiraling deeper and deeper into insight. As the saying goes, the psalm becomes a balm. Remember that Matthew's version of the Prayer in the Sermon on the Mount is introduced by Jesus' warning not "to heap up empty phrases" (Matt 6:7), or vain repetitions, as it is sometimes put. I suppose that not every kind of repetition need be vain or empty, to be sure. Think of the beneficial results of memorization in learning, which often occurs through painful but necessary repetition. Biblical parallelism would be a rather potent technique by means of which falling into empty or vain repetition might be avoided.

Synonymous parallelism is perhaps the simplest example. The opening line of Psalm 23 might well qualify as an example: "The Lord is my shepherd, I shall not want" (23:1). Each part really says much the same thing, for if the Lord is truly one's shepherd, one would not be in want. The two halves parallel each other. In this example, redundancy is fairly well avoided. The second part has spiraled more deeply around the first part, or

---

5. Ricoeur, "Biblical Hermeneutics," 68.
6. Thompson[-Uberuaga], *The Struggle for Theology's Soul*, 33–63. The original Hebrew/Aramaic speech situation of Jesus heightens the importance of psalmodic parallelism.

meditated upon it more fully, and unlocked one of its meanings. Crossan offers an example that verges on redundancy, but still avoids it, from Psalm 8:4: ". . . what are human beings that you are mindful of them, mortals that you care for them?" Being mindful of and caring for are similar, but caring brings out a new dimension of how God is mindful.

Crossan suggests that the two halves of Matthew's version of the Prayer might be viewed as one big example of synonymous parallelism, as if the hallowing of God's name, the kingdom's coming, and the Lord's will being done find their parallel in the Prayer's second half. It is as if we have a kind of poetic syllogism: If the first half indeed occurs on earth as in heaven, then indeed we would have our bread, we would know the reality of forgiveness, and indeed we would not fall under the power of the evil one. Each of these disclose dimensions implied in the Prayer's first half. They are the fruit of Jesus' and/or his disciples' being lured into meditation on the Prayer's first part.

Another kind of parallelism is known as antithetical, and Crossan finds it in the end of Matthew's version of the Lord's Prayer: "And do not bring us to the time of trial, but rescue us from the evil one" (6:13). Here one part sets up a negative contrast with the second part, but notice that the second part really just unfolds a dimension of meaning proclaimed by the first part. For if indeed we are *not* brought to the time of trial, we will indeed be rescued from evil.

Finally, Crossan considers what is varyingly called stepped, climactic, or crescendo parallelism to be the most fascinating type, and he is convinced that the Lord's Prayer exemplifies it, in the way that it builds toward a climax, the final victory over the evil one. The kingdom's coming unfolds and builds, so to speak, toward its concluding victory. A commonly accepted example of this crescendo parallelism may be found in Habakkuk 3:17:

Though	the fig tree	does not blossom,
and	no fruit	is on the vines;
though	the produce of the olive	fails
and	the fields	yield no food;
though	the flock	is cut off from the fold
and	there is no herd	in the stalls . . .

The "though/and" examples offer us various parallelisms: fig and fruit, olives and fields, a flock and a herd. But the text also seems to build up from the "lesser" to the "greater" catastrophe, from no blossoms to no herd! Similarly, the Lord's Prayer, on Crossan's interpretation, builds in the form of a crescendo to a climax. What is "in heaven" reaches its earthly realization as God's will is accomplished on earth. For Crossan the Prayer "is both a revolutionary manifesto and a hymn of hope not just for Christianity, but for all the world." This moves us into biblical and theological interpretation, and we will hazard our own such interpretation in the chapters to come. But for now let us ponder Crossan's highly suggestive examples of how biblical parallelisms form the sinews of the Prayer, luring us into deeper insight. The image of spiraling comes to mind. A spiral is both a repetition and a going deeper.[7]

Primary Theology

We have grown accustomed to thinking of theology as a head trip, a cerebral and rational exercise that is at times far removed from the vibrant flux of living experience. We theologians frequently get raised eyebrows when we mention our craft, and maybe that is at times deserved. The creative theologians, however, have ways of breaking out of the straitjackets of rational systems removed from our experience, initiating ways of exploration that seem to make more sense of our faith experience. Recently some theologians have begun to refer to "primary" and "secondary" theology as a way of reminding us that "good" theology arises from experience and remains as close to the texture of experience as possible. Such would be "primary" theology, which the "secondary" theology of systematic thought strives to explore and organize into more conceptual categories.[8]

Primary theology finds its home in symbols, gestures, metaphors, prayer, poetry, song, ritual, myths, stories, and narratives, all of which remain relatively closer to the texture of our human experience and express it more vividly and suggestively. And likely these modes of expression arise from within the experiences themselves; they are experience in the act of disclosing itself. And of course these forms of expression typically have a long history in our various human and religious traditions. As we have just noted with respect to the Lord's Prayer, it seems to be in the form of

---

7. For these observations from Crossan, see his *The Greatest Prayer*, 4–6, 182.

8. See Wainwright, "Theology of Worship," 506, and Kavanagh, *On Liturgical Theology*. See Heath and Duggins, *Missional*, and Bass, *Grounded*, for parallel approaches.

the tradition of the poetic parallelism of the psalms. At the same time, old symbols can be given new meanings, if something new is emerging in experience. For example, the reign of God, while an older Jewish symbol, seems to be loaded with some new elements in Jesus' preaching, as we will see.

The Prayer is also brimming with symbols, not precise concepts: *Abba*, reign of God, hallowing, heaven and earth, bread, debts and sins, temptation and the evil one. Each of these symbols or metaphors gesture toward dimensions of our lived religious experience, but the experience remains too deep to be fully "captured." For example, *Abba* is Aramaic for "father." As one prays that word, all kinds of associations will spring up, depending upon one's experience of fathers, not only in one's family, but within one's tribe and society. Is the king addressed as a "father"? President Abraham Lincoln was sometimes spoken of as "Father Abraham" in the US Civil War period. And what kind of father is that king or president? Gentle, merciful, loving? Unbending, harsh, and violent? And now if this very familiar word is addressed to God, what then? What might that suggest? Can any of our earthly experiences fully express what God is? A similar exercise can be applied to all the other symbols too, from reign to the evil one.

Briefly, let us look at some of the other images. "Kingdom" or "reign," for example—"Your kingdom come . . ."—a symbol evoking our sociopolitical experience, and indeed it is partly rooted in the Hebrew experience of the kingdoms of Israel and Judah. The image makes us imagine our own social and political experiences and how they might, if at all, become vehicles for the coming in some way of another kind of kingdom, a kingdom rooted in the Father's act of reigning invoked by Jesus. How might this come about? Will it inevitably involve us who pray the Prayer in struggles within our own sociopolitical contexts? Will our kingdoms, if you will, always be in some kind of conflict with the kingdom of God? And what are we being asked to imagine? A kingdom in which the Sermon on the Mount is progressively realized? And what about the many who find themselves in varying ways excluded and violated in our earthly kingdoms? Is the Prayer suggesting that the conversion we need to undergo is one in which these exclusions and violations are overcome? And who are these peoples and groups who are left out? Do we even see them? Is one of the blessings of the Prayer the ability to really see them, maybe for the first time?

At a minimum, the image of the kingdom helps us deprivatize[9] the Prayer, sensitizing us to the sociopolitical dimension of our experience and faith, but also to the Prayer's early Jewish and Christian social and political dimensions. Within this context, the prayer for forgiveness alerts us to the social and political ways in which evil and sin express themselves. We need to own our sinful social and political blindness. In this way we begin to decolonize the Prayer, or rather, it begins to decolonize us. When we pray it, who is the "we"? Just our own tribe, our own fellow religious believers, our own circles of companionship? What about those we might tend not to include? If we are straight, what about the LGBTQ? If we are male, what about females? If we are white, what about those of other colors? If we are financially secure, what about those who are not? If we are Christian, what about those who are not? And on the questions go. The image of a Father of heaven and earth is equally provocative: this awakens us to the cosmos, and to the humble earth, and to all creatures. The new kingdom somehow extends to them too.

These primary symbols almost unendingly provoke questions, if we hearken to them. Our secondary reflections work best, it seems, if they continue to return to them. It would seem that it is that gesturing, suggesting, and always unfinished quality of the Lord's Prayer's primary soil and symbols that constitute its luring quality, its attraction, its seemingly neverending interpretations in the tradition, whether in its equivalent "primary" forms, like song (think of Albert Malotte's inspired 1935 composition, still widely sung today), theater (acting out the Prayer), picturing (as in children's portrayals), poetry (Dante's *Purgatorio*), or Hemingway's and Atwood's literary forms; or in its more "secondary" forms, like this book, for example, or other theological explanations of the Prayer. The better these secondary forms remain grounded in the primary forms, the better "map" they might offer us into the deeper, primary soil of the Prayer.

"Experience" comes from a Greek word meaning "to undergo something" or "to be tested" by what we encounter in existence (*peiraō*). "Empirical," for example, is derived from this word. Our experiences are the testings of life, from which we can learn. And "truth" in classical Greek tradition is originally the unveiling of reality, how reality manifests itself to us. Truth and reality are the same word, *alētheia*, in fact.[10] So we might say

---

9. One of the favorite terms of political theologian Johann Baptist Metz. See his *Theology of the World*. Cf. also his *A Passion for God*.

10. "*Aletheia*, with its double meaning of truth and reality, is Platonic-Aristotelian,"

that the more we are plunged into the experience of existence, the greater is the manifestation of reality, its truth. The biblical notion of truth is not so different, coming from a word for reliability. God is truth because God is reliable (Ps 31:5; Jer 10:10) for us in our lives. And God asks this same kind of reliability from us. We must walk in such a way that we reliably conform to what God is disclosing to us in our experience. Sometimes the Hebrew for "truth" (*emeth, emunah*) is translated as "faithfulness," which is another way of speaking about reliability. Reliability is fidelity to the lessons God is teaching us in experience. "Remember . . . O Lord . . . how I have walked before you in faithfulness with a whole heart . . ." (2 Kgs 20:3), prayed Hezekiah. Jeremiah teaches the same, but the translator has opted for the word "truth": ". . . see if you can find one person who acts justly and seeks truth . . ." (5:1). So it is this truth, the reliable truth of our faith experiences, that is primary and the foundation of all of our later, secondary thinking.

So first and foremost, we are suggesting that the Lord's Prayer is an experience we undergo. We "pray it," but it is "praying us" simultaneously, in ways too deep for precise understanding. But we strive to remain faithful to where it is leading us. We trust. And in the exercise of trust, we experience truth. Not so much a conceptual truth, which this book and other theological books strive to offer with more or less success. That depends, I believe, upon how well they remain close to our lived, primary theology. Rather, on the primary level, the truth we experience is that of our experience lighting up for us. The kind of *Abba* the Prayer has in mind we simply "know." Not so much knowing about. But knowing. Like the difference between the Spanish *saber* (to know about) and *conocer* (to know). The Jesuit poet Gerard Manley Hopkins would call this "inscape" and "instress": "I saw the inscape though freshly, as if my eye were still growing . . . ."[11]

Prayer

Of course, the primary theology that the Our Father is takes the form of prayer. What kind of "form" is prayer? How might this form or genre be said to be generative and productive? In a broad way, we might think of prayer as an exercise, in the manner of Ignatius of Loyola's *Spiritual Exercises*.

---

writes Voegelin, "Equivalences of Experience," 122; see for the biblical view, Blackman, "Truth," 269–70.

11. See his *Journal* for December 12, 1872, in *Gerard Manley Hopkins*, 214.

Exercises are activities, things we engage in. They require participation. Naturally prayers can be read or listened to, and each of these can be at a rather low level of energy and participation. But even hearing or reading can occur at high energy levels of participation. Sometimes really hearing at a deep level requires more of us than "saying" a prayer, silently or orally. This kind of "really hearing deeply" is like the kind of authentic silence which transforms "hearing" into "hearkening," if we follow philosopher Martin Heidegger.[12] But regardless, participation is a fundamental requirement of an exercise. We will not get far without this.

Composing a prayer, on the other hand, perhaps nearly always expresses high energy participation, a form of hearing becoming creative hearkening. Is this what we find with Jesus' own creative use of his Prayer, along with that of his earliest disciples? Is this hearkening what Paul is expressing when he writes about our crying "Abba! Father! . . . the Spirit bearing witness with our spirit . . ." (Rom 8:15–16)? In this concelebration of Spirit with human spirit taking place in a mutual hearkening a composition of prayer erupts. When Dante, or Hemingway, or Atwood compose their "parallel" Our Fathers, is this an analogous form of hearkening?

So we have a participation in which hearing turns into hearkening. An exercise like that. As Jesus prays "hallowed be your name," for example, he is hearkening to the Father's own hallowing of his "name" as it is occurring in heaven and now on earth. Jesus the human is not so much hallowing the Father's name, but listening in on the Father's own hallowing and being caught up in it. As we will see, this corresponds to the typically passive form of Hebrew prayer: the name is hallowed (by God). Going further, as we are caught up in this hearkening and discovering more and more of what the hallowing of the Father's name entails, we find ourselves longing for the reign and will of the Father, through which the hallowing occurs on ever more profound levels. We want to be fed by this (our bread), forgiven our failures to live in this hallowing, and delivered from falling away from this hallowing.

Traditionally the two large movements of prayer are elevation and conversation. The first "lifts" us up to the transcendent Mystery. "Lift up your hearts" (*sursum corda*), as the eucharistic preface commonly expresses it. This elevation is our responsive hearkening to the Holy Mystery, and in its depths it is God's gift, God's will being done within us and among us. For

---

12. Heidegger, *Being and Time*, nos. 163–65, 206–8.

no matter how much we might elevate ourselves, we could never "reach" God were God not already present, drawing us. The Lord's Prayer expresses this elevating dimension in its first part: the Father *in heaven*; the reign and will being done here *as in heaven*. When the doxology is added, as in the *Didache* and some New Testament manuscripts, then we have a resounding elevation toward the Mystery, the eternal reign, power, and glory. Here we can perhaps see how there was an almost natural impulse to move into the doxology, as we are caught up in the movement of elevation.

The two traditional forms of prayer called adoration and thanksgiving might be seen as parts of the continuum of elevation. Adoration is at the furthest edge of the transcending movement, focused as fully as possible on the divine Beyond. Thanksgiving is a bit more of a mixture between transcendence (giving thanks *to God*) and immanence/our earthly realm (we give thanks for *what we have been given*). The Lord's Prayer seems focused on the transcendent pole rather emphatically in its first part, although the Father remains here as well the Father of heaven *and of earth*. If it moves into thanksgiving, perhaps in its second part, that aspect remains more implied (it is clear that we are asking for what the Father *gives*) than expressed. But no matter how far toward the transcendent edge the person of prayer moves, he or she always remains human and not God. We do not turn into God. We are caught up in God's hallowing, not our own. Still, some of the mystic traditions, even in the Western religions, can resound with rather daring exclamations of the movement of elevation, as if God and human being nearly merge. Recall St. Paul: ". . . it is no longer I who live, but it is Christ who lives within me" (Gal 2:20).

The movement of conversation takes the form of a dialogue between God and human beings. It occurs, if it be prayer, while hearing and hearkening to the echo of the movement of elevation. We are speaking with *God*, after all. First, we acknowledge God's hallowing and pray within its energy. Only then do we speak with God about our very human and earthly concerns, personal but also social and cosmic, for it is a kingdom's coming on earth that we are speaking about: bread, forgiveness, protection from temptation and from the evil one. There is a powerful theological view of God's wanting to be a Thou for us at work in the conversational movement of prayer. The incarnation is perhaps the most emphatic expression of the conversational dimension of God. Perhaps more than anything else, however, this part of the prayer keeps our prayer humble and very human, personally and socially, and very earth-focused. It keeps our adoration and thanksgiving real, aware of our imperfection. That is why we pray for our needs, and perhaps most of all, for forgiveness. It is easy to see how the two traditional prayers of contrition (sorrow, asking for forgiveness) and petition or interceding for one another's needs are expressions of this human pole in our dialogue with God.

Occasionally or maybe even often we experience a tug of war between these two poles of elevation and conversation, of being lifted up ecstatically into a movement into transcendence, and of being brought back down to earth, if you will, by our very real human needs and imperfections. It is almost natural to think of oneself as more holy and pious during the ecstatic moments. "Ecstasy" comes from the Greek for "standing outside oneself," *ek-stasis*, and in moments of transcendence that may well be the sense or mood. But it is rather easy to be fooled, for we can be lifted up into an inflated self-absorption. This can even happen while we are supposedly listening to others or ministering to them. We would like to think the "I" that we are is going out to the "thou," when it is more likely that our "I" is simply finding more of its own "I" in the "thou." Tertullian and Origen, for example, were well aware of this, cautioning us in their commentaries on the Lord's Prayer that as we lift up or elevate our hands in prayer, we can do so as frauds.[13] The Lord's Prayer seems to want to keep us real, bringing us back to the earth: give us the bread we need, forgive us our sins, lead us not into temptation....

The mystic Teresa of Avila, in her humorous manner, invented a Spanish word for these delusional moments of pseudo-ecstasy: *abobamiento*. We might translate that as "being caught up into boobishness," staying close to the sound of the Spanish, or "foolishness." The Spanish word for authentic ecstasy would be *arrobamiento*, from the Spanish for "above" (*arriba*). We do not need to be too hard on ourselves. Such delusions are all too human. Keeping a sense of light humor about it all, like St. Teresa's verbal pun, is probably a healthy strategy. But it also seems that if we allow the Prayer to pray us—forgive us our sins ... lead us not into temptation—that we would be well on our way to avoiding such delusions.[14]

Perhaps the most important reason for keeping the two moments of elevation and conversation joined is the incarnation. The Lord's Prayer nowhere mentions this explicitly, yet its twin dimensions of "heaven and earth" point to it. We might think of the movements involved in the very

---

13. Tertullian, *On Prayer* 13, 50; Origen, *On Prayer* 2, 113.
14. Teresa of Avila, *The Interior Castle* 4.3.11, 490n13.

simple but very profound act of making the sign of the cross. The sign of the cross receives its Christian significance from the incarnation, especially the time of the Lord's being crucified. And as we make the sign we begin with the transcendent one (the Father, at our "top" or high point, the forehead). Then we move down, as the incarnate Word moved down, to our human depths (from forehead to chest), and then to the shoulders, as the Holy Spirit leads Christ to the Father's right hand (right shoulder) and the victory over the evil one (left shoulder). As with this sign, so in all prayer, transcendent elevation and dialogical interaction are present.[15]

Diptych, Triptych

Now might well be the appropriate time to compare the two parts of the Lord's Prayer to both of the two parts of the decalogue (Exod 20:1–17; Deut 5:6–21) and to the two parts of the great command to love (Mark 12:28–34; Matt 22:34–40; Luke 10:25–28). This will continue our theme of the twin dimensions of heaven and earth, elevation and conversation, divinity and humanity. I hope it will deepen this theme as well. The two tablets of the Law (Deut 10:1) might be compared to a diptych, hinged together. One cannot have them separately: they implicate each other. The one God of the Hebrew covenant is also the God of his people and their needs. If we attempt to separate these, we end up with a "god" other than Yahweh and a truncated people as well. As with viewing a diptych, we might contemplate them singly, but as we do so, one will lead inevitably into the other. Helpfully, as well, the decalogue of the Torah again deprivatizes our faith experience. The second tablet is focused upon our social covenant with one another. This helps us maintain this social focus, as we compare the two tablets of the Lord's Prayer to the decalogue, a comparison already made by the Reformer John Calvin long ago.[16]

Likewise, the great command to love God and neighbor is a condensed form of the new Torah, a new kind of double tablet hinged together. Loving God will certainly lead to love of our neighbor, and loving our neighbor will lead us into a deepened relationship with God. A new diptych, but

---

15. I have been stimulated by Andreopoulos, *The Sign of the Cross*, especially chapters 3 and 4. As we know, Eastern Christians move from the right shoulder to the left, and Western Christians from the left shoulder to the right. Andreopoulos offers various interpretations found in the Eastern and Western traditions.

16. Calvin, *Commentary on Matthew, Mark, Luke*, vol. 1, Matt 6:9–13/Luke 11:1–4.

one thickly informed by the Hebrew Covenant before it. The two "tablets" or "sides" of the Our Father, its "You petitions" and its "We petitions," can be imagined as a way of praying ourselves into the two tablets of the Torah and the two dimensions of the great command to love. And because of the union between heaven and earth, our praying the Prayer is its praying us. St. Augustine had suggested that the basic rule for interpreting the Bible correctly is to offer an interpretation that reflects the great command to love. Were a possible interpretation to violate that great command, it could not be an accurate interpretation.[17] Along these lines, a good way to interpret the Bible would be to do so with the guidance of the Lord's Prayer. Its two sides should foster an interpretation that does not violate the great command. This would be a good way, it seems, for us to begin our exploration of the You petitions and the We petitions in the following chapters.

But first let us think about the image of a triptych, a three-paneled rather than two-paneled object of contemplation. I do not think that this necessarily replaces our diptych image, nor that it is necessarily better than it. But it perhaps brings out a bit more clearly how the two panels are hinged, or how the one leads to the other. As we swing one way with the hinge, it will likely swing us back in the other direction. Let us imagine that the middle panel, connecting both sets of petitions (You and We), is that of the address, "Abba, Father." This address in a way lifts us up, but only because the holy Mystery has elected to be an "abba" for us. A "father," after all, has children. In this lifting, we are enabled to participate in the heavenly hallowing of the name, in the heavenly reign, and in the realization of the divine will. And as we do so, somehow we begin to realize what our real needs are, what is the true bread which will nourish us, what are the failures for which we need forgiveness, and what is the real vulnerability from which we need to be spared, what is the real shape of a reign/kingdom in which all, our earth and cosmos included, form a kin-dom.

****

Here is a prayer inspired by the Lord's Prayer—praying "like" (*houtōs*) the prayer of the Our Father (Matt 6:9)—which can place us in the proper frame of mind for the chapters to follow, chapters that are studying, after all, what we find in Scripture. It is a prayer evidently designed for Bible Study, and it seems to reflect the spirit of the great command just noted.

17. See Augustine, *On Christian Doctrine*, Book 3; cf. Nielsen, "St. Augustine."

The Medium and the Message

Our Father in heaven, sacred is your Word. Your kingdom come, your Words be heard on earth as they are in heaven. Give us today your sacred Word. Forgive our neglect of it in the past as we forgive those who neglect us. Lead us toward an encounter with You each time we search the Scriptures. For your presence, your power, and your glory are ever present among us now and forever. Amen.[18]

---

18. Catholic Prayers, "A Prayer before Reading the Bible."

four

Addressing the Holy Mystery

Matthew's version of the Prayer begins in typically Jewish fashion: "Our Father in heaven" (6:9); Luke's begins somewhat more directly: "Father..." (11:2). Here in the Prayer in Matthew and Luke, the word used for "Father" is the Greek for "father," *patēr*. Scholars commonly believe that this Greek was a transliteration from the Aramaic, *Abba*. We actually find the Aramaic *Abba* used three times in the New Testament, where it is followed by the Greek *ho patēr* (Mark 14:36: "Abba, Father, for you all things are possible ...," prays Jesus; Rom 8:15; Gal 4:6). And it is widely believed by scholars, but not without disagreement, that Aramaic was the street language or vernacular of Jesus' Galilee, for example.[1]

If we try to avoid locking up Jesus or his earliest disciples into praying straitjackets, there may have been variations in the Prayer's opening address. I believe we need to listen to the advice of Jewish biblical scholar Amy-Jill Levine: Jesus did not have "a set of three-by-five note cards or an iPad," inscribing his parables, or prayers for that matter, which could be cited "verbatim" on every occasion. Rather, he was a good teacher, a creative teacher. That is one of the reasons we are still listening to his parables today, and praying his prayers. Likely, then, like good teachers, he adapted his stories to the needs of his various audiences. I think the same might be said about his prayers. "He also likely honed his stories [and his prayers?]

---

1. See Knowles, "Which Language Did Jesus Speak?"; an alternative is that both Hebrew and Aramaic had become the vernacular in Jesus' time, not to mention some use of Greek and maybe even Latin, at least in Galilee. Levine and Brettler, eds., *The Jewish Annotated New Testament*, 605, seem to accept the view that Aramaic was the language of Jesus and his followers, for example.

Addressing the Holy Mystery

... until he knew what words worked best in what contexts."[2] I find Levine's advice appealing, not least because it is reflective of thinking of biblical criticism as an art, more than as a science. And also because it gives common sense a good name.

Take, for example, the form of the address given by Matthew: "Our Father." Do we really need to think that we have to choose between this "fuller" address, and the simpler "Father" of Luke's version? If we follow Levine's advice, the answer would seem to be "no." The "Our Father" is typical of Jewish prayers, for example, and those prayers reflect the communal nature of those prayers. "Our" seems a perfectly fitting word to add, particularly in a social context of prayer.

On the other hand, there may have been occasions when simply a more direct "Father" would be appropriate. Is Paul reflecting this in Romans 8:15, when he seems to be underlining moments in one's experience when the intimate presence of God breaks through, the Spirit enabling us to cry "Abba, Father"? As it did in Jesus' intimate moments, as, for instance, at Gethsemane (Mark 14:36), when he prayed, "Abba, Father, for you all things are possible . . . ." Some biblical scholars are inclined to think of Luke's more simple version as the original, following the view that simplicity indicates an earlier origin. And Luke is a work which reflects much of the "Q" material, the sayings that scholars think are the more primitive and form the basis for the common sayings of Jesus in Matthew and Luke. This may be so, but Levine's suggestion may also well be the case. The manuscripts of Luke which have the "our" may also be solidly based! In any case, as the Prayer proceeds to its second part, the We petitions, it is clear that God's Fatherhood embraces a communal, social dimension. And as we know, this is already clear from the Jewish tradition in which Jesus and his disciples were formed.

The major point seems to be that the Holy Mystery is approachable and accessible. We are told that the Mystery's name is hallowed, but not told precisely what that Mystery's name is in the Prayer (unless the invocation gives it), or whether there may be many names, "Father" being one of them. We recall that the esteemed biblical scholar Raymond Brown once suggested, in his commentary on the Gospel of John, that the name was the mysterious "I Am" (that is, YHWH), at least for that Gospel. At the least we may wager that the mysterious I AM is approachable and nameable as "Father" in Jesus' and his disciples' experience. And we may also wager that

---

2. Levine, *Short Stories by Jesus*, 14.

the versions of the address which we possess are representative of the kind of praying Jesus and his followers engaged in.

We have already suggested that with this greeting of the Prayer we are standing on the soil of Jesus' and his disciples' "primary" religious experience, a soil at home in image and symbol. So right away we might want to activate as much as we can our right brain, imaginative capacities. "Imagination" likes to work with images. "Father" and "heaven" would seem to be such images. We do need to open ourselves to the context of these images in the Jewish tradition, and we need to be on the lookout for any special twist Jesus or his followers might give to that contextual tradition. In that way, as we suggested, we might avoid reading anything we want into the images.

Context appreciation helps us avoid the pretext of uncritical interpretation, as we suggested in an earlier chapter. But still we are in the world of symbol rather than of narrowly precise concepts. At the same time, we do have our own primary experiences of the Mystery, expressed in our customary images, "Father" and "heaven" maybe being some of these. These experiences, while able and needing to be tutored by historical context, can serve as our own experiential bridge to and first guess in appropriating what the Lord's Prayer's greeting may mean.

We have also suggested that we are in the world of prayer, with its elevation and conversation. The Father *in heaven* would seem to express something of the moment of "elevating" ourselves toward the transcendent one in the heavenly heights; *the Father* in heaven, on the other hand, would seem to express the transcendent One's approachability and knowability. At a minimum we may suggest that Jesus is heir to the slow, perhaps three and counting thousand-year-old historical development of Israel's experience and understanding of the divine Mystery, the Yahweh, the El, the Adonai, the King, and at times the Father, among other primal names. Slowly this God, while remaining knowable, nameable, and approachable, has disclosed the transcendent nature of divinity: a God not just of this or that tribe, not just of Israel, but of all creation, as we finally find it in the later prophets: "I am the first and I am the last; besides me there is no God" (Isa 44:6). What is striking is that it is this transcendent One who wants to be accessible, a "Father." And perhaps this name is *the* name, as far as Jesus is concerned, along with his disciples, or maybe the preferred name. It does not seem to be the only name, however, and that may be significant.

ADDRESSING THE HOLY MYSTERY

"Father" in Jesus' and his Disciples' Context

Amy-Jill Levine, in an illuminating and provocative essay about "common errors made about early Judaism," lists as one of them

> the view that . . . God had become a transcendent, distant king, and that Jesus invented the idea of a heavenly "Father"; connected to this view is the still-heard claim that when Jesus addressed God as "abba" (Mark 14:36; see also Rom 8:15; Gal 4:6) that he used an intimate term meaning "daddy" that would have been offensive to his fellow Jews. These claims miss the numerous biblical and postbiblical uses of "father" for the divine, including Pss 68:5 [Heb 5:6], 89:26 [Heb 5:27]; Isa 64:8; Jer 31:9; Antiquities [of Josephus] 7.380, etc. . . .[3]

Levine is something of an apologist for Judaism, and she is a very fine one, challenging us where we need to be challenged. But she is not afraid to credit Jesus with a uniqueness not found elsewhere, so far as she knows. For example, with respect to the great commandment to love, she does not find Jesus' unique contribution to be in the combining of love of God (Deut 6:5) and love of neighbor (Lev 19:18), as many often still think today. But she does have this to say about Jesus' teaching on loving the enemy (Matt 5:44–45): "Only Jesus insists on loving the enemy: 'Love your enemies and pray for those who persecute you.'" She is quite nuanced, however: "In Jewish thought, one could not mistreat the enemy, but love was not mandated." Still she suggests: "He [Jesus] may be the only person in antiquity to have given us this instruction [to love the enemy]."[4] So while Jesus may be unique in some of his teaching, she does not find it in his use of the address "Father," or *Abba* in the Aramaic.

As we have happily suggested, Jesus is Jewish through and through. And if so, so too is his great Prayer. As with his Jewish heritage, his Prayer reflects a God both transcendent and lovingly intimate. Whether all strands of Jewish tradition reflected or came to reflect this trajectory may be questionable. But Jesus' great prayer does.

At the same time, when we zoom in with the lens, so to speak, we may sense some shades of nuance, or maybe a wider spread of color tones on the heavenly rainbow. For example, the name "Father" for God is known in the Hebrew Scriptures, as Levine has wonderfully reminded us. But while

---

3. Levine, "Bearing False Witness," 503.
4. Levine, *Short Stories by Jesus*, 82, 86.

the name occurs perhaps some twenty times—as here, for example: "I have become a father to Israel" (Jer 31:9)—it does not seem to be the most common name, among the many names which we find, whether El, Adonai, King, especially Yahweh, and many others. On the other hand, "Father" occurs some 250 times in the New Testament, a work which is much smaller than the Hebrew Bible. Something has happened to bring this image and name into greater prominence. It is this prevalence of the name in the New Testament that leads Christian scholars to give the name a kind of precedence on the part of Jesus and his earliest followers among names for the Holy Mystery. What is it which has happened to bring this about?

Using the name "Father" as a form of address for God occurs some fifteen times in the Hebrew Bible, and typically this occurs within the context of the Hebrew people as a people or as a whole. "You are Our Father, we are the clay . . ." (Isa 64:8; cf 63:16), for example. Of course it is this form which we find in Matthew's "Our Father," the "our" indicating the larger group of people embraced by the Father.[5] "Father" implies children, or at least a child, and Israel constitutes these children. As we suggested in the introduction, "Father" implies a "family." Maybe we could call this an example of an "I-We" relationship: We are addressing the divine Thou, or reversely, the divine I is approachable by the "we" of God's people.

Interestingly, Jesuit theologian Gerald O'Collins comments suggestively that it seems "puzzling" that the Hebrew Bible "readily speaks of the people as God's children but rarely names or addresses God as 'Father' or 'our Father.'" He goes on to suggest that "probably the [Hebrew Bible] avoids applying this title (or that of 'Mother') to Yahweh, because such usage could suggest the 'natural,' procreative activity attributed to El, Asherah, and other gods and goddesses of the Near East."[6] Despite this, however, there seems to have been something about Yahweh's approachability that occasionally broke through these hesitations. "Primal" or "primary" experience has a way of asserting itself over the objections of "secondary" reflection! O'Collins offers a particularly intriguing and surprising example of this from the Thanksgiving Hymns of Qumran: "For Thou art a Father to all [the children] of Thy truth, and as a woman who tenderly loves her babe, so dost Thou rejoice in them; and as a foster-father bearing a child in his lap, so carest Thou for all Thy creatures" (1QH 9, 34–5).[7]

---

5. As noted, some manuscripts of Luke also have the address, "Our Father."
6. O'Collins, *Christology*, 120; see 118–35, for some of my observations here.
7. Ibid., 121, changing "the Sons" to "the children."

Addressing the Holy Mystery

And perhaps it was Jesus' own primary experience that broke through those hesitations with an even more pronounced firmness. And it may be this which accounts for the veritable explosion of "Father"- or *Abba*-talk in the New Testament. As we noted earlier, we find this primary speech some 250 times in the New Testament. Jesus himself is presented as using some form of it himself some fifty five times, whether in personal prayer or when teaching others to pray, as with the Our Father in Matthew and Luke. This seems to have been quite untypical in the Palestine of Jesus or the early disciples. Even if not every instance of attribution of this speech originates with Jesus, John Ashton's conclusion still seems convincing: "The personal sense of the fatherhood of God was a typically Christian development of the Judaic tradition, and ... this probably originated in a recollection of Jesus' teaching and of the example of his own prayer."[8]

It is also interesting to see how the New Testament seemed to wrestle with the implications of this Father-talk for its growing understanding of Jesus and of his followers. Jesus' own special experience was special enough to initiate a new speech for God in some ways, or at least a newly typical speech for addressing God as Father in his ministry and prayer. And yet he also taught *us* to address God as "Father" or "our Father." O'Collins suggests that the New Testament is straining to express the specialness of Jesus, even while noting a kind of democratization of Father-talk for us all. Typically in the Hebrew Bible Israel is God's son; sonship language is much more common there than Father-talk. But the situation seems reversed in the New Testament. Father-talk is much more common, while Son-talk tends to be more reserved for Jesus, who is commonly addressed as the Father's or God's son (Matt 14:33; 16:16; Mark 15:39).

It would certainly seem that addressing God as Father implies that we somehow share in his sonship. And I believe we do, but perhaps O'Collins is correct to note that our sonship or daughtership is derivative from ("dependent on") Jesus' own sonship?[9] Thus we find Jesus portrayed as consistently speaking of—and distinguishing between?—"my Father" and "your

---

8. Ashton, "Abba," 7.

9. O'Collins, *Christology*, 124. O'Collins is doing Christology in this work, and so this brings a special sensitivity to the nuances of Jesus' possible specialness. The Lord's Prayer is Jesus' prayer, but does it imply a Christology? It nowhere mentions Jesus, nor does it develop a Christology, nor does it mention the Trinity, or the church, at least in any explicit way. These are questions worth returning to. It may be that the Prayer, as primary theology, shows us the way to do Christology and theology in the secondary sense, and in that sense launches us on our way. But maybe it does something more too.

Father" (Matt 11:27; 6:32). And following this thread, Paul will speak of our "adoption" as God's children or sons/daughters (Gal 4:5–7; Rom 8:14–15), Jesus being the "natural" son, while the Gospel of John refers to Jesus as God's son, and to his followers as God's "children" (John 1:12; 11:52; cf 1 John 3:1–2, 10; 5:2). Is the New Testament suggesting a distinction, between Jesus' Father-Son relationship, on the one hand, and our own "adoptive" participation in that, on the other? Again, we seem to be on the soil of primary theology/experience. Something is erupting into consciousness, and we may never achieve the kind of secondary theological clarity we would (perhaps too exuberantly) desire. Maybe we should keep in mind that we are praying the Prayer *with* Jesus in his Spirit, as Paul recommends (Rom 8:14–16). That may well be the primal, Spirit-formed, soil which will lead us toward the proper destination.

It is probably safe to assume that we need to interpret what Jesus means by "Father" by viewing it in the light of his core message of the reign of God and of his parables especially. Or, if we follow Levine's suggestion about God as a God of such radical love in Jesus' experience that he, it seems alone in antiquity, taught that God desires even love of the enemy, then "Father" is an image gesturing toward the source of this love. This kind of inclusivity coheres very well with Jesus' proclamation and practice of the reign of God. And its meaning in Jesus' teachings overlaps to some extent with the way in which the Fatherhood of God was understood in the Judaism of Jesus' time, for example in the prophets and in the Qumran texts. David Balch, for example, suggests that it may refer to (1) God as a refuge of the persecuted, (2) God as the one who assures us of the offer of forgiveness, and (3) God as a ruler whose providence guides us. He also notes the view of Mary D'Angelo that there is a critique of Roman patriarchal imperialism in the title as well.[10] We do know that the emperor, for example, was known as the *patēr*, a "father" quite different from that of Jesus' father.[11]

There is likely nothing sentimental in the title, although there is something remarkably personal and intimate about it. Love of the enemy, however, desentimentalizes it, for enemies can do painful things, including crucifixion. At one time it was thought that the Aramaic *abba* may mean "daddy," and perhaps this led to some sentimentalism in some interpretations. It need not. It points to an intimacy and trust, I would think. And

---

10. Balch, "Luke," 128, referring to 4Q372, 1, and 4Q 460, and to D'Angelo, "Abba and 'Father,'" 611–30.

11. Howard-Brook, *"Come Out, My People!"* 415.

perhaps many of us truly wish the word carried this meaning. But alas, it seems not to have meant that in the Aramaic of Jesus' time.[12] We are back with the second naïveté recommended by philosopher Paul Ricoeur!

At the same time, while personal and intimate seem appropriate ways to describe the meaning of "Father," we also need to add at a minimum two other qualifiers: familial–social–cosmic and transcendently holy. "Father" implies a family of children, and in Israel's history that family is Israel, with a kind of moving tendency also to include all nations and peoples and even all creatures within the Father's family. Just how all of these form the one family never achieved a full clarity, and in the New Testament and later times it still has not and perhaps never will. But this new family, one beyond tribalism and biologism, is conveyed by the primal or primary symbol of the reign of God, the kin-dom of a radically inclusive God, in Jesus' preaching. "Father" and "kin-dom" need to qualify each other. This kind of Father seems to break through barriers and blinders. It decolonizes us and those we would like to colonize, or maybe those we do not even know well enough, anyway, that we are colonizing.

Matthew's addition, "Father *in heaven*," which may well reflect Jesus' own usage at times, since it is very typical of Jewish prayer, is a kind of bridge from the social to the cosmic to the transcendent. If we let ourselves imagine this "heaven" as one of those primary images, then we might be free to attend to varied dimensions of its thickness.

Historically the "heavens" would have been the upper sphere, the skies, at a time when humans were more cosmocentric rather than humanocentric in their ways of thinking. "God sits in the heavens," and is even laughing (Ps 2:4)! We are told to "praise him in his mighty firmament!" This place is his "sanctuary" (Ps 150:1). "The Lord's throne is in heaven" (Ps 11:4). When the prophet Isaiah describes his prophetic call—"the seraph touched my mouth [with a live coal]" (6:6–7)—much of the imagery reflects a cosmocentric perspective. Isaiah "saw the Lord sitting on a throne, high and lofty." This high place was a "temple," and the "hem of [the Lord's] robe filled" it. Isaiah seems to be likening the heavens/skies to a great temple, with the Lord's throne at its apex. And "the whole earth is full

---

12. It is sometimes noted that, did *Abba* carry the meaning of "daddy," that the three New Testament texts citing the Aramaic would have followed with the Greek diminutive *pappas*, rather than with what we have, namely, patēr (Mark 14:36; Rom 8:15; Gal 4:6). Adding further confusion, apparently in modern Hebrew *abba* does carry the meaning of "daddy"! See Caruso, "Tag Archives: abba."

of [the Lord's] glory," reflected in the seraphs shouting, "Holy, holy, holy is the Lord of hosts" (Isa 6:1–3).

Here we can imagine that the Father's temple is the cosmos. This decolonizes us humans even more! In a way, this hearkens back to a time when all creatures, human, sentient, and animate, "spoke the same tongue," if I may paraphrase Chickasaw poet Linda Hogan. "In this kind of mind," she writes, "like the feather, is the power of sky and thunder and sun, and many have had alliances and partnerships with it, a way of thought older than measured time, less primitive than the rational present." I believe we need to "train" our imaginations to imagine these "heavens" anew, much as Hogan suggests here and in what follows, particularly as we attempt to move into a neo-cosmocentric age:

> . . . in spite of forgetting, there is still a part of us that is deep and intimate with the world. We remember it by feel. We experience it as a murmur in the night, a longing and restlessness we can't name, a yearning that tugs at us. For it is only recently, in earth time, that the severing of the connections between people and land have taken place. Something in our human blood is still searching for it, still listening, still remembering.

One almost thinks of Isaiah's seraphs shouting the triple "holy," as Hogan writes of the "first language" of our ancestors: "Anyone who has heard the howl of wolves breaking through a northern night will tell you that a part of them still remembers the language of that old song."[13] Our *"heavenly Father"* is an image we need to take much more seriously if we are truly to become cosmocentric again, but with a second naivete. Jesus' Prayer to his Father in heaven is "breaking through a northern night," and speaking that first language of the first people. But in a way, he is speaking it even more radically, for not even the cosmos, the Father's temple to be sure, can fully "contain" the holy Mystery. As Solomon prayed at the temple's dedication, "But will God indeed dwell on the earth? Even heaven and the highest heaven cannot contain you, much less this house that I have built! . . . Hear the plea of your servant and of your people Israel when they pray toward this place; O hear in heaven your dwelling place; heed and forgive" (1 Kgs 8:27, 30). The transcendent Father is truly transcendent. The temple is all of creation, and the light of the Father shines through all of it, because none of it can limit or stop it.

13. Hogan, *Dwelling*, 64, 19, 83, 63. See Thompson-Uberuaga, *Jesus and the Gospel Movement*, 168–74.

Perhaps that is why the Lord's Prayer immediately turns to the first You petition: Hallowed/holy be your name. Is this one of those biblical parallelisms? The heavenly Father and the hallowed name: the latter is saying the first, but with a twist. Jesus' theocentrism seems to embrace and widen both humanocentrism and cosmocentrism. We might want to remember that at Jesus' baptism the heavens were opened, the Spirit came down like a dove, and the Father spoke (Matt 3: 16–17).[14]

The Surplus of Meaning

"Surplus of meaning" in this work refers to the phenomenon that, among the multiple meanings which a text can generate, readers who "receive" these texts find themselves able to come upon "new" meanings not yet articulated in the text's tradition of reception. Sometimes, maybe often, even authors may not be aware of these possibly "new" meanings. But texts are rich realities, if we do not simply lock them up into a hermetically sealed box, but see them as forms of participation in the drama of human life, or in the case of the Bible, as forms of participation in the great drama of humanity's dialogue and struggle with God. As receivers of texts come to those texts, they bring with them their own levels of participation and learning in that drama. And as text and receiver interact—dialogue, if you will—depths of the divine-human drama may emerge that had remained unseen before, or less well seen. Sometimes the new meaning is more of a translation into one's vernacular; the newness is more or less thin in many cases. Reader and text, it might be kept in mind, are already one in this great drama. There is no artificial need to build a bridge between one and the other, although their interchange can be better or worse, depending upon one's readiness for it.

Actually the drama is not only between God and humans, but between God, humans, societies, histories, and the entire cosmos. A richly thick brew indeed. And so the Lord's Prayer has generated a long and potentially unending surplus of meaning. We already noted a bit of this in the Gospels, for Matthew's and Luke's versions already represent something of this surplus of meaning at work, and so, too, do Paul's letters, or the "priestly prayer" of John's Gospel, or the Easter Epistle of 1 Peter.

Pushing the envelope further, Hemingway's version or Atwood's version would seem to offer rich surpluses of meaning too. The Anglican *New*

---

14. Brockington, "Height, Highest, Hosanna, Heaven(s), Firmament, Throne," 105–6.

Zealand Prayer Book's version as well. At least this may be so, if we bring a hermeneutics of hospitality and generosity to these versions. And in an analogous way, musical versions (like Malotte's celebrated version) and pictorial versions might also offer us surpluses of meaning. These various versions bring up the question of "eisegesis"; that is, reading into a text whatever one likes. As opposed to "exegesis": going with and from the grain of the text. Philosopher Eric Voegelin wrote of the "sausage view of history" to describe a kind of mishmash of unregulated, arbitrary interpretations. Perhaps we can call this "sausagesis."[15] Most of us prefer not to know all the "things" going into a sausage! Perhaps the reader has heard of the GIGO acronym: "garbage in, garbage out."

All of this begs the question: How can we be discriminating? This is the phenomenon of discernment, and for this author, that is an art, a contemplative art, and not a "science." In the end it is a matter of making an argument for continuity between text and "surplus of meaning." And rather than issuing a grand view of it, I have tried and will continue to try to do this as we move along. The immediate example that comes to mind is the proposed reading of "heaven" just offered, from cosmocentric to theocentric/neocosmoscentric. The continuity resides in the cosmos; the newness in the way it is understood and appropriated. It is the same phenomenon (the cosmos) in the drama of existence, but as we participate within it, our consciousness of its various depths "deepens." Sometimes it does the opposite! The cosmos is a good example, for it may well be argued that we are just barely emerging from an era of having nearly "forgotten" our bond with it. I called this humanocentrism. Anthropocentrism might be another word.

Surplus of Meaning in Past Tradition

What might be typical features of the reception history of the address or invocation of our Prayer? We seem to find a fairly consistent range of interpretations of the invocation, "Our Father"—intriguingly called an "epiclesis" by Titus of Bostra[16] (d. c. 378)—in the early writers of East and West of the first thousand years. Interestingly, the interpretation almost always

---

15. Voegelin, *The Ecumenic Age*, 406. My own view of interpretation has been deeply informed by Voegelin, Gadamer, and Ricoeur. See my *Jesus and the Gospel Movement* for references.

16. Stevenson, *The Lord's Prayer*, 54.

focuses upon those of us who are invoking the Father: We are manifesting that we are his children, that we have undergone the baptismal regeneration (citing John 1:12, 3:5) enabling us to make this invocation, that we have been given the gift of sonship or adoption. Perhaps much of this has to do with the use of the Prayer in baptismal catechesis in the early period, for here the focus naturally falls upon what the Father is doing for us. I do not believe that this is a kind of subjectivism, as if the early writers were simply focused on themselves. It strikes me that it represents a more holistic atmosphere, in which the newly baptized is related to the Father, and in invoking the Father discovers his or her own dignity as son or daughter, mainly through faith and baptism.

In St. Maximus the Confessor (d. 662), we find the invocation of the name discussed in the context of the typically Eastern spirituality of deification: praying the name becomes a form of deified contemplation and entry into the real meaning of "theology." Deification is also linked to the theme of image and likeness: baptism deepens the disciples' likeness to the divine image. In his observations on Cyril of Jerusalem's *Mystagogic Catecheses* (4th century), Bishop Stevenson notes Cyril's teaching that "We call God our heavenly Father, because we are his adopted children, and are a 'heaven,' because we bear his likeness—an important theme in mystagogy, because of its stress on imitation."[17]

While baptism seems to be a common basis for praying and interpreting the invocation—there was the tradition of "handing over" the prayer to the newly baptized, as for example in the *Mystagogic Catecheses*[18] of St. Cyril of Jerusalem (d. 387)—at the same time the early creeds remind us that God is also our creator, and so in some way we are children of the Father in virtue of our created nature. "Creator of heaven and earth," the creeds commonly confess. This aspect of the matter, something like a universalization of the invocation, is a theme very dear to our attempted ecumenical approach in this book, and something which still awaits a fuller exploration. Matthew's version of the Prayer may well reflect this more universal

---

17. Ibid., 46. Unless otherwise noted, Stevenson's book, chapters 3–8, is the key source for my observations on the tradition. It is *the* place to begin. For access to some of the major Eastern Fathers' commentaries on the Our Father, go to Orthodox Prayer, "The Lord's Prayer."

18. Cyril of Jerusalem, *Lectures on the Christian Sacraments* 5.11, 75. On the "discipline of the secret," whereby the Lord's Prayer was kept secret from the non-baptized, see Stevenson, *The Lord's Prayer*, 63. The issue is rather unclear.

orientation.[19] The mission of the disciples is to the entire world, and the Father is the Father of heaven and of earth.

In the early writers we also find a focus upon the communal, ecclesial dimension of the Prayer's invocation: We are one family with one Father; we are in fellowship. There is a celebrated text in Cyprian (d. 258) which well may be the most acclaimed expression of this dimension, which can truly be said to represent the thinking typical of East and West:

> Before all else, the teacher of peace and master of unity desires that we should not make our prayer individually and alone, as whoever prays by himself prays only for himself. We do not say: "My father, who are in the heavens," nor "Give me my bread this day." Nor does anybody request that his debt be pardoned for himself alone, nor ask that he alone be not led into temptation and delivered from the evil one. Our prayer is common and collective, and when we pray we pray not for one but for all people, because we are all one people together. The God of peace and master of concord, who taught that we should be united, wanted one to pray in this manner for all, as he himself bore all in one.[20]

The following from St. John Chrysostom (d. 407), commenting upon Matthew 6, perhaps merits equal acclaim with Cyprian:

> He teaches . . . to make our prayer in common, in behalf of our brethren also. For He saith not, "my Father, which art in heaven," but "our Father," offering up his supplications for the body in common, and nowhere looking to his own, but everywhere to his neighbor's good. And by this He at once takes away hatred, and quells pride, and casts out envy, and brings in the mother of all good things, even charity, and exterminates the inequality of human things, and shows how far the equality reaches between the king and the poor man, if at least in those things which are greatest and most indispensable, we are all of us fellows . . . for to all hath He given one nobility, having vouchsafed to be called the Father of all alike.[21]

At times we also come across some observations on the invocation's qualification of the Father as "heavenly," or "in heaven." On the one hand, heaven is the place where God dwells. On the other, as the saint lives there,

---

19. Stevenson, *The Lord's Prayer*, 228, suggests this.
20. Cyprian, *On the Lord's Prayer* 8, 69.
21. John Chrysostom, "Homily 19 on Matthew 6" (no. 6).

heaven also becomes the saint's own heart. This double-edged interpretation—place and heart—is that of St. Augustine (d. 430), and it establishes the two sides of the reception of the churches of East and West. For example, John Cassian (d. 430?) will write about the soul's ascent to God as one of the meanings of invoking the heavenly Father. The more virtuous the soul becomes, the more heavenly. On this view, heaven almost becomes a cipher for the sanctified soul.

Heaven as the place where God dwells, on the other hand, does suggest not collapsing "heaven" into a merely allegorical expression of the sanctified soul. It is a "place" in some way, a "space" where the saint is with God and with other saints. The "communion of saints" of the creed would also lend authority to this perspective. In this way, the image overlaps with the social, communal perspective just noted. Again, we are in the territory of primary images, where conceptual borders are leaky. When secondary theological precisions are attempted, they sometimes become suffocating. For example, when Origen (d. c. 254) attempts to explain this part of the Prayer, he writes that those who give "heaven" a spatial sense are employing a "degraded conception of God." He is worried about reducing God to a form of corruptible matter.

Still, the words of the Prayer force Origen to go further. Basically he opts for an allegorical meaning, in which "heaven" indicates the distance between God and creation, "Christ" represents the Father's throne, and may "allegorically be called 'heaven' while his church should be termed 'earth' and a 'footstool for his feet.' Still, he hesitates and does not want to remove God completely from the locative dimension of the heavens/skies. For "there comes a certain glory from God, and power from him, and, so to speak, an outflowing of divinity." Origen is fascinating, for he illustrates the move beyond cosmocentric thinking to a more transcendent spiritualism, as in the earlier Platonists. Still his hesitation and comment on God's outflow gives us a bridge to a new form of cosmocentrism.[22]

One final comment on this first millennium of the tradition. Tertullian seems to claim that the name of "Father" had been revealed to no one prior to Christ. Origen, his contemporary, seems more nuanced, arguing that he had searched the Old Testament, finding God referred to as "Father," but nowhere actually addressed as "Father." Origen's comment is surprising, given his reputation for biblical expertise. But it is perhaps the witness of these two writers that began a tradition of interpretation that at times

---

22. Origen, *On Prayer* 3–5, 163–65.

endures even into our own times, as we have seen biblical scholar Amy-Jill Levine noting. To note another two names of this unfortunate tradition, we find St. Thomas Aquinas (d. 1324) citing St. Augustine as his authority that addressing God as "Father" was unknown to the Jewish people: "Yet do we never find it taught to the children of Israel to address God as 'our Father' . . ."[23]

The later writers of East and West before the Reformation and Renaissance periods continue the common themes noted above with respect to the opening address. Perhaps there is more attention to the trinitarian dimension, "Father" naming more precisely the first person of the Trinity, although there was some of this in the earlier period (Maximus the Confessor, for example). We can also see something of a greater drive toward conceptual precision, typical of a scholastic trend. For example, the transitional figure Moses bar Kepha (ninth century) gives us six reasons for why God is called "Father," a sort of amalgam of much that we have seen, according to Stevenson.[24] Unsurprisingly we will find this in the medieval scholastics, which is not to say that we will not discover intriguing insights here. Hugh of St. Victor (d. 1142), or Richard of St. Victor (d. 1173), for example, will offer a virtue approach: "Father" brings us benevolence; "our" excludes falling into pride; "heaven" fosters reverence.[25] Aquinas in one place lists five virtues we learn by invoking God as "Father": these words "instruct us in our faith"; they "raise our hopes"; they serve to stimulate charity"; they lead us "to imitate God"; and lastly they lead us "to humility."[26] Some of this is a continuation of the tendency toward allegorization of the Prayer, which goes back to Augustine particularly, and which we noted in our second chapter.[27]

Martin Luther (d. 1546) and John Calvin (1509–64), of course, introduce many new accents, and we will be seeing more of this in later chapters. Both are a mix of early tradition, medieval times, and then the something "new" of reformation. The critique of medieval allegorization is

---

23. Aquinas, *Catena aurea*, Matt 6:3, lectio 3, citing Augustine, *Sermon on the Mount* 2.8, 25. Augustine seems to have been the first to use the title "Sermon on the Mount" (Stevenson, *The Lord's Prayer*, 77).

24. Stevenson, *The Lord's Prayer*, 112.

25. Ibid., 123, citing the *Allegories on the New Testament*, now thought to be by Richard of St. Victor.

26. Aquinas, *The Lectures on St. Matthew*, 456–58.

27. For Augustine on this, see Stevenson, *The Lord's Prayer*, 80; Augustine, "Sermon on the Mount" 1.4.11, 6–7.

a well-known reformatorial element, although, as mentioned, a postmodern sensitivity may see the matter with a new, second naivete. Luther is described as "existential" oftentimes, perhaps meaning that he brings out the participatory nature of faith. The Prayer prays us: We are in Christ, married with him in a mystical union. He writes that the "grace of faith . . . unites the soul to Christ, as the wife to the husband, by which mystery . . . Christ and the soul are made one flesh." The Father really is *my* and *our* Father, and our praying it in faith is his grace, a form of the Spirit witnessing with our Spirit, as Paul teaches in Romans 8. When we were baptized, Luther teaches, Christ "incorporates" us in himself, and when the Father "gives us His Holy Spirit . . . by His grace [we] lead a godly life . . . ." He continues: "God anticipates us, and Himself arranges the words and form of prayer for us, and places them upon our lips . . . that we may never doubt that such prayer is pleasing to Him . . . ." Calvin also accents the faith dimension of the invocation: praying it frees us from distrust. "By the great sweetness of this name [Father] he frees us from all distrust, since no greater feeling of love can be found elsewhere than in the Father," wrote Calvin.[28]

One senses in these Reformers, and in the Roman Catholic and Anglican reformers as well, a yearning to return to the primary theological experience of the faith in an age that had perhaps swung rather far over into faith's secondary, doctrinal conceptualizations. Anglican bishop Jeremy Taylor (1613-67) used spousal imagery in his devotional writings, and viewed the Prayer from this perspective. It was the prayer of intimate union.[29] Teresa of Avila (1515-82), in her many works, is a wonderful example of the return to primary, originary spiritual experience. We have already noted how her *The Way of Perfection*, much of which is a commentary on the Lord's Prayer, seeks to teach her sisters and their disciples something of the way back to the originary springs of faith experience. Archbishop Rowan Williams referred to this book as "perhaps [her] most consciously mischievous book." A passage like the following is part of the reason:

> Take careful note of interior stirrings, especially if they have to do with privileges of rank. God, by His Passion, deliver us from

---

28. Luther, "The Liberty of a Christian," chapter 3; "The Lord's Prayer," second petition, *The Small Catechism*; *The Large Catechism* 22; Calvin, *Institutes of the Christian Religion* 3.20.36, 899.

29. Stevenson, *The Lord's Prayer*, 183, citing *The Great Examplar* (1649). We will return to this in the next chapter, with full references.

dwelling on such words or thoughts as, "I have seniority," "I am older," "I have done more work," "the other is treated better than I."

That passage, while certainly applicable to Teresa's convents, easily implies a critique of a church infested with a rather clericalistic notion of hierarchy. As Teresa writes about the Prayer's invocation, for example, in calling God Father we are recognizing Jesus as our brother and one another as equals. Nuns or others who are concerned about their lineage should be the least to speak about the Father. The disputes between people over their supposed status "in reality amount to nothing much more than a debate about whether the mud is better for making bricks or adobes."[30]

The Catechism of the Roman Catholic Council of Trent (1566) sees in the invocation an affirmation of divine creation and providence, along with redemption, echoing the traditional scholastic theology of nature, grace, and glory. God is the Father and Provider of all creation, "the Father of all . . . also of the unbelieving," and so this widens our view beyond the baptized.[31] That narrower focus might be the danger in the Reformers' stress upon faith, although the Bible's teaching always included the wider, less narrow perspective. But it still awaits a fuller unlocking, some of which we sought to introduce in our comments on "heaven" above and on decolonizing the Prayer.

Contemporary "Transitions"

Because the material for the contemporary period is so vast, and because we are still within its midst, I will simply note a number of major transitions, seeking to raise their implications for the Prayer as I survey them. Hopefully, the reader will appreciate that I am not an historian, but a theologian, albeit one historically trained, and that even if I were an historian, anything like a "full" grasp of the entire sweep of tradition is beyond probably anyone's grasp. We are truly all amateurs when it comes to the entire sweep of anything. At best anyone of us may have historical patches in which we can hope to claim some special expertise. Beyond that, we stand upon the shoulders of others.

---

30. Teresa of Avila, *The Way of Perfection* 12.4, 83; 27.2, 138; 27.6, 139; Stevenson, *The Lord's Prayer*, 170; Williams, *Teresa of Avila*, 101–102.

31. Catholic Apologetics, "The Lord's Prayer," *The Catechism of the Council of Trent*.

We may helpfully think of the following transitions: modernity, late modernity, postmodernity, and globalization. Because they are transitions, we can be said to be undergoing them, and as we do, we do not simply leave each behind, but bring each with us, striving, at our best, to integrate them all when that is possible. At times it is a ragged journey. Roughly these transitions begin with the eighteenth century period of the Enlightenment (the beginnings of modernity), and extend into approximately the middle of the twentieth century (late modernity), the late twentieth century (postmodernity), and then on into our contemporary period. Globalization can be said to be the most recent transition occurring, but it has been happening in spurts since modernity at least. And globalization is the force which is spreading and will spread all the other transitions worldwide, with more or less acceptance, resistance, or even outright rejection.

The turn to contemporary science, and to human experience understood largely through that scientific lens, or at least with that lens greatly in mind, may be said to be the defining characteristic of modernity. The use of the historical method in biblical studies is one example of this, and we have used these historical studies extensively in our approach to the biblical witness in these chapters. Of course, biblical exegesis has gone through these various transitions, and as it has done so, it has complexified in some ways, but also hopefully it has improved in its craft. As theology has struggled with the challenges of this transition, it has sought to make its case by some form of appeal to our growing understanding of human experience understood in its historical, cultural, and scientific dimensions.

For this author, perhaps the key question for theology is what is the range of human experience? Christianity witnesses to a tradition of divine revelation. Is our view of experience ample enough to include the Holy Mystery? Do we shrink that Mystery to our own view of experience, however ample, or do we widen our view of experience to an ever growing openness to the Mystery? Or perhaps better, does that Mystery widen us? That is a rather stark way of putting it, but in the end it more or less comes to that. We can study the Bible, or in our case here, the Lord's Prayer in its historical and cultural dimensions, availing ourselves of the best historical and other human and even scientific studies. We may learn a great deal with respect to "data." Information, if you will. Voegelin had this informational overload in mind when he invented his colorful notion of "the sausage view of history." In many ways it does remain like a sausage, if there be no divine Mystery. God-talk and Father-talk remain, if not babble, at best projections of the human speaker, if we fit the Mystery to our own limitations. We may know much (information). But we will not be wise in the sense of the traditional religions, for we will lack the one thing necessary.

Let us suggest that the Mystery is probably best not thought of as an item of information, nor as something that we can "prove" like we might prove dimensions of the data we uncover in our studies. The Mystery might better be approached as the presupposition of our ability to ask questions, to explore, to keep ourselves open and learning and loving. This is a very Pauline approach: "O the depth of the riches and wisdom and knowledge of God! How unsearchable are his judgments and how inscrutable his ways!" (Rom 11:33) But this is also very ecumenical, for it is more or less the wisdom of the great religious traditions. This openness is also the way toward relativizing our own egos, so to speak, and so keeping ourselves self-reflective and critical. It is also the way toward relativizing our intellectual systems, our social and cultural accomplishments and systems, and even our religious conceptualizations, dogmas, and systems. Relativization does not mean saying each is equal, or each is unnecessary, but rather that each is not ultimate, but is to be judged by how well each advances us all toward the Mystery.

The Lord's Prayer, in this perspective, might be viewed as a way in which Jesus tutors us in the art of growing openness to the loving Mystery — the Father—that guided his life and that of his followers. The Mystery was not an "It" for Jesus and the Jewish tradition from which he came, but more like a "Thou": a loving, caring, personal, and even dialogical "Father." So the Prayer helps us process the transition from ego to a self in relation, from subjecting the "all" to our own limits (our ego), to opening the ego to the "all" (a relational self). In that openness, our egos are not dissolved; we remain free, thinking, and loving beings. But our egos are expanded, into a journey of openness to others (the "thous" and the "we," and the "its" of the cosmos). Self-hood moves outward into relationships and connectivity. Its energy is ecumenical and "catholic," moving always toward the universal.

John Wesley (1703–91) might be noted here as an example of the "Romantic" wing of modernity, which attempted to recover the role of affectivity and the feelings as against a simply intellectual or physicalistic view of human experience. His "methodism" was something like a recovery of the traditional means by which the religious affections could be cultivated, the "heart strangely warmed," to use his famous phrase from his *Journal*.[32] He is

---

32. Wesley, *Journal*, May 24, 1738.

recovering the "language of the heart," as he puts it in his *Explanatory Notes Upon the New Testament*. In his commentary on the Lord's Prayer within a sermon on the Sermon on the Mount, he uses one of his favorite expressions in referring to the invocatory "Father," namely, "uncreated night." This nicely expresses the depths of the loving Mystery guiding and luring the awakened heart.

Wesley is one of the prime examples of modernity, along with John Keble (1792–1866), F. D. Maurice (1805–72), and Evelyn Underhill (1875–1941), each writing upon the Lord's Prayer. Keble, along with John Henry Newman, were Anglo-Catholics seeking to reclaim the rich, catholic inheritance of Anglicanism, not unlike John Wesley. One senses in Keble's commentary on the Lord's Prayer an attempt to reclaim its trinitarian and ecclesial dimensions, along with its value as an aid to fostering "union in Christ," such as we find it in the Gospel of John and the early Fathers. This author is reminded here of the echoes of the Lord's Prayer in the priestly prayer of John's Gospel noted in our second chapter. We might say that the Anglo-Catholics, and the Anglican become Roman Cardinal Newman, are deeply attuned to the ecclesial and patristic dimensions of the religious and Christian quest.

Underhill, along with her friend and mentor Baron Friedrich von Hügel, returned to the rich mystical tradition, in which they found an openness to the "many mansions" of religious and Christian experience which might well resonate with and yet broaden the modern "turn to experience." Her exposition of the Prayer echoes much of the mystical tradition: The Prayer expresses

> the most mysterious and yet the most certain reality of our experience; the intercourse of the Transcendent God with fugitive man and of fugitive man with the Transcendent God . . . . This is a conception of prayer which we easily forget; for the cheap fussiness of the anthropocentric life has even invaded our religion. There too, we prefer to live upon the surface and ignore the deeps. We seldom pause for that awed recognition of pure Being, so steadying and refreshing to the soul, which is the raw material of the interior life . . . the seven clauses of the Lord's prayer . . . become seven moments in a single act of communion, seven doors opening upon "the world that is unwalled."

Maurice, on the other hand, because of his attunement to the social dimension of the gospel, noted throughout his own exegesis of the Prayer, is a good bridge to our next transition, that of late modernity.³³ Late modernity, as we are understanding it here, refers to a psychological, sociological, and political broadening and critique of modernity, hearkening back to thinkers like Freud, Jung, Durkheim, Weber, Vico, Marx, and others. Partly this represents an awareness of the sources of personal and social pathology, of a more or less "subconscious" and "unconscious" nature: Why and how do we humans fall victim to irrationality personally and collectively, and in what way are the passions, along with subtle cultural, political, and economic ideologies, involved in this? Theologians attuned to this in varying ways apply the critiques provided by the psychosocial sciences to the religious and Christian contexts. We might think of political theologies, theologies oriented to providing a social or political critique or perspective, and theologies which analyze victims of subjugation (feminist, womanist, African liberationist, liberation, LGBTQ, postcolonial theologies, etc.). Obviously the many horrors of modernity—world wars, nuclear devastation, the continuing problem of slavery and slave trafficking, victimizations of all types, colonizations, the Holocaust, sex and gender victimization, etc.—are the key factors giving rise to the "sciences" of late modernity.

That is a very fruitful, challenging, and provocative area of thought, with potentially rich benefits for the study of the Bible, for theology, and for religious studies in general. We have attempted to express some of this by our attention to the larger social (including ecclesial/church) and political dimensions of the Lord's Prayer, by our admittedly brief but hopefully helpful use of postcolonial sensitivity (the ways we colonize and are colonized), and to some extent by attending to the even larger dimensions of ecological devastation and our newly emerging neocosmocentrism. This of course overlaps to some extent with globalization, which likewise awakens us to some of these issues just noted, but also widens our religious perspective toward a new and even wider kind of interreligious ecumenism. The religions are increasingly aware of one another, and will increasingly need to enter into dialogue, or, failing that, colonize themselves into zones of isolation.³⁴

---

33. Underhill, *Abba*, 1–3. See Stevenson, *The Lord's Prayer*, chapter 8, for references to John Wesley, Keble, Newman, Maurice, and Underhill. For Von Hügel, see his *The Mystical Element of Religion*.

34. For more on these transitions, see Thompson-Uberuaga, *Jesus and the Gospel Movement*, 27–36.

Addressing the Holy Mystery

The "Father" with a Second Naivete?

In the light of those transitions, let us conclude this chapter with some thoughts on the name "Father," or *Abba*. If we want to be tutored by the modern turn to experience, we might say that the invocation of God as "Father"/*Abba* represents the experience of the Jewish people to some extent, and very emphatically of Jesus and his followers. There is no question that it is an experience shaped by culture, by Jewish and even other cultures. Experience seems to work through cultural formation. But we need not say Jesus' *Abba* experience is simply *determined* by culture, as if he did not have other choices of expression and cultural formation available to him. He clearly did, and so did his disciples. The many other primary images for God available in ancient times attest to this. But more importantly, the ever greater Mystery is the grounding lure, keeping Jesus and his followers in postures of fidelity and openness to the holy Lure, sometimes against their first tendencies. Let us suggest, then, that we need to distinguish between cultural *conditioning* and cultural *determinism*. The "ever greater" holy Lure can break open our cultural conditioning, as the great prophets have constantly shown us, helping us to avoid the slide into cultural determinism.

The postmodern turn, which might be described as an emphatic attunement to cultural formation and the ways in which cultural narratives shape us, can lead to forms of cultural determinism. These have existed in the past: Think of the many forms of colonial oppression. But postmodernity—radically attuned as it is to our many cultures and diverse histories and narratives—might breed even more forms of this, if it surrenders to radical forms of cultural relativism. For this reason, I suggest the important distinction between cultural conditioning and cultural determinism. For all of us who are "noninvasively" lured by the holy Lure, so we trust, determinism can be breached.

Having said this, it still seems that the name "Father" enjoyed and enjoys a kind of priority as a primary form of expression with Jesus, his followers, and on into our ongoing tradition. It "conditions" us, even if it does not, hopefully, "determine" us. We sought to unpack a bit more fully some aspects of this primary image. But it is a matter of imagination, albeit a shaped one, and not a matter of precise conceptualization.

Many of us share with our spiritual ancestors broad similarities of formation with respect to our God-talk. And this can serve us as our experiential and symbolic bridge to Jesus' prayer experience. Although we know we need to be broadened by Jesus' and his disciples' experience and symbolization, and at times this can be very difficult. If our experiences of our own "fathers" (personal, social, and political) are abusive, we will likely encounter much resistance to the invocation of the Lord's Prayer. Owning this resistance, achieving a reflective distance from it to the extent that we can, might be said to be aided by the kind of late modern analysis of pathology earlier noted. Recognizing the pathology can be the first step toward healing. But Christians and others speak of "grace" as even more crucial in this regard; this might be another way of gesturing toward the ever greater lure of the holy Mystery breaching our pathologies. Likewise, our resistance need not mean that we are only striving to overcome something. In some ways, befriending, listening, and asking what it all means might be a bridge to a theological breakthrough of a quite surprising kind.

The recovery of other primary images for the Divine—"Mother," other female and male images, and images derived from nature—can be placed within this context of breaching cultural determinism, and recognizing that even our beloved Jewish and Christian traditions of revelation are subject to the subtle but real slide from cultural conditioning to cultural determining. Whatever else "heavenly Father" may mean, it cannot mean determinism. The "Father" known by Jesus not only recognizes but grounds our personhood, and without freedom, a person becomes depersonalized. Instead of seeing the Father image as an obstacle to a more inclusive range of symbols and images for God, perhaps we might see it as part of that holy Lure toward a greater range of inclusive images. As we participate in and with this kind of Father, we sense this attraction, even against great odds. It is not just a more inclusive range of symbols to which we are drawn, but toward a more inclusive way of living.

It seems plausible to me that in Jesus' very patriarchal context, a male like him witnessing to a heavenly "Father" who seemed to act with a radically inclusive love, was rather beyond the cultural norms of the day. It was the exception, although it was hinted at here and there in the tradition. What is primary, I suggest, is the primary experience of the lure toward loving inclusion in the family of God. We need not, and probably should not, think that this "primary experience" was not expressed at all times through a range of symbolic images derived from Jesus' cultural formation, chief among them *Abba*. But what I do think we might argue for is that Jesus' primary experience was one of radical detachment or non-clinging to all forms of cultural and social determinism and colonialization. He did not cling to any one symbol, thus running the danger of making it rather than the holy Lure our guide. We need the symbol, truly; but we must breach the clinging, as the mystics have taught us down the ages, through not clinging.

Fascinatingly, we might recall that the risen Jesus said to Mary Magdalene when she recognized him, "Do not hold onto me . . ." (John 20:17). Here I would recommend a more mystic-informed approach to this provocative text from John: not clinging as one of the forms that ego detachment must take. Magdalene becomes a paradigm of the call to move to a wider, more expansive mode of consciousness, which in a way is a mode of participating in Jesus' movement from earthly life, to resurrection appearances, to ascension and the sending of the Spirit.[35]

So we might consider several options. We might argue that "Father"-talk was primary for Jesus, and so it should be likewise primary for us. All other images become secondary. "Father" imagery becomes the "unnormed norm," and all other images and concepts become "normed" by it. In response I would suggest that this is to detach the "Father" image from its primary experiential context, which is one of non-clinging freedom and openness to the holy Lure. In doing this, that image becomes a kind of dogmatic concept—a form of absolutized "secondary theology." Jesus, I think, tried to avoid this tendency through the imaginative and playful use of his parables, and their wonderful range of images. Remember that his disciples asked him why he spoke to the crowds in parables (Matt 13:13). If he did not, he said, citing Isaiah 6:6–13, they would be like those who see and yet do not perceive, or hear, and yet do not listen, or like those who do not understand. Jesus was, I think, trying to lure his hearers toward their originary, primary experience, the soil of imagination and openness to the Mystery.[36] At the same time, Jesus may have suspected that the symbols and language that we use can be greatly manipulated and controlled by the ruling powers in one's society. "You know that among the Gentiles those whom they recognize as their rulers lord it over them, and their great ones

---

35. "In telling her not to hold on to him, Jesus indicates that his permanent presence is not by way of appearance, but by way of the gift of the Spirit that can come only after he has ascended to the Father," writes Brown, *The Gospel according to John*, 2:1012. Not holding or clinging makes me think of Paul's comment: "where the Spirit of the Lord is, there is freedom" (2 Cor 3:17). Unsurprisingly, the mystic St. John of the Cross comes close (?) to this interpretation of John 20:17 in his *The Ascent of Mount Carmel* 11.12, 184.

36. See Thompson-Uberuaga, *Jesus and the Gospel Movement*, 48–49, for more on this. I have been goaded into these comments partly by O'Collins' wonderful thoughts on "saving 'Abba'" in his *The Lord's Prayer*, chapter 2. I think one direction his thoughts *may* lead to is the one offered here.

are tyrants over them," said Jesus to the twelve, in response to James and John, who shared the same kind of view of leadership as that of the tyrants (Mark 10:42). Jesus was trying to teach them another, servant form of leadership. He knew how powerful social elites could be.[37]

Another option would be to propose that as one journeys on the spiritual scale, so to speak, one moves toward a state of radical ego-less detachment, including detachment from all images, however treasured they may be. One simply dwells in a state of imageless experience. On this level of "pure" experience, more or less uncontaminated by any culturally conditioned or determined images or conceptualizations, one has entered into a level of radical freedom. And at this level a form of oneness with all creatures and even between all religions becomes possible. Images, however well intentioned, always more or less have elements of human and cultural projection in them, and then run the danger of anthropomorphizing the Divine.[38] This need not mean that one does not recognize the partial validity of all other images and expressions for the Divine, however!

My suggestion, on the other hand, is the one proposed in earlier comments: Our primary experiences have a primacy because they are primary, and are likely always co-mediated by images and symbols. The goal is not one of moving beyond these primary experiences and symbols, if such be possible, but rather one of not clinging to them. A dimension of the primary experience is one of non-clinging, or, from the other side, of radical openness to the Mystery. It is as if the many depths of the primary experience break through all pretensions of mastering it. "Deep calls to deep," prays the psalmist (Ps 42:7). "Abba, Father, for you all things are possible; remove this cup from me; yet, not what I want, but what you want" (Mark 14:36), prayed Jesus in Gethsemane. In this space of inclusive openness, we discover more and more—eschatologically—just how universal is our divine family.

This space of inclusivity—something perhaps like the *nada* of a mystic like John of the Cross—is one of clinging to no-thing, or from the other side, of openness to all. John of the Cross wrote:

---

37. Helpful on this is the notion of "power analysis," well known in political and social studies; a good pastoral approach to this can be found in Law, *The Wolf Shall Dwell with the Lamb*, chapter 6. My thanks to Bishop Brian Thom of the Episcopal Diocese of Idaho for recommending this book to me.

38. Something of this seems to me to be a possible implication of Wilber, for example, in his wonderfully helpful and provocative *The Integral Vision*, chapter 5 especially. But I am not sure. We may actually be in agreement.

Addressing the Holy Mystery

> To reach satisfaction in all
> desire satisfaction in nothing.
> To come to possess all
> desire the possession of nothing.
> To arrive at being all
> desire to be nothing.
> To come to the knowledge of all
> desire the knowledge of nothing . . .
>
> And when you come to the possession of the all
> you must possess it without wanting anything.[39]

Particularly with that last sentence we link up with Paul's teaching of kenosis/emptying: "Let the same mind be in you that was in Christ Jesus, who, though he was in the form of God . . . emptied himself, taking the form of a slave . . ." (Phil 2:5–6).

Hemingway may or may not have had this in mind when he wrote his parodic (?) "Our nada who art in nada . . . ." But I would suggest that it is a possible and even plausible surplus of meaning, which turns back upon his parody. A parody typically is comical. And so the parody makes a joke of itself! Which in some way is what all mystics do, and in doing so, a space of openness clears. Hearing can become a hearkening. In this space of inclusivity, can we not find the supplications of agnostics and atheists, who after all, do not wish to make idols of any-thing. Might their no-thing-to-be-worshipped have its own legitimacy? Yes, it may be only a partial legitimacy, like all things created. The desire to know with clarity and proof, perhaps, is yet to be breached, in some forms of agnosticism and atheism. On the other hand, perhaps their *nada* might be understood as a protest against a too easy "faith," which can be manipulated by all kinds of powers. This might be a form of prophetic agnosticism and atheism.

Our suggestion is that praying the Prayer might well bring us to this inclusive space of solidarity with the "non-believer." Such non-believers, who are perhaps believers in the all by way of the no-thing, to echo John of the Cross, form part of the family of the Our Father too. Putting this in other terms, the Prayer may well decolonize us "normal" believers. This

---

39. John of the Cross, *The Ascent of Mount Carmel* 13.11–12, 150–51. See Thompson, *St. John of the Cross*, 190–91, and Thompson, *From Dark Night to Gentle Surrender*, especially for keen insights on letting go.

kind of decolonization is a process in which multiple forms of solidarity might yet emerge, between the so-called "normal" believers and the many who remain somehow outside of our imaginations of what constitutes the Father's family.

All of this would seem to be implications of what it means to pray to a Father of heaven and earth, which I take to be a way of witnessing to the universal outreach of the Holy Mystery. From our side this probably can only be worked towards: The catholic or ecumenical is always on the way toward the universal. For the universal, to be such, must include the "all": all creatures of the past, of the present, and of the future, and all within the infinite womb of the Mystery.

One last thought: All of this raises questions about the religions and their interrelations. The "many mansions" of the Father (John 14:2) may well carry as one of its surpluses of meaning a new perspective on the religions. Perhaps it has only become possible to imagine this with any force because of our relatively new experience of globalization, and because of our many past failures of achieving it without much violence and discord and fear. But it is a hope of this author that our perspective on the depths of the primary experiences of the Mystery, in which non-clinging is an intrinsic dimension, might provide a space in which we can begin to recognize these religions as parts of our own family, precisely because they each have their own integrity within the primary field of human existence. They are not parts of our family because they conform to our "clung-to" image of what that family is. It is *their* family too. The primary field of existence *is* one of many mansions. As we learn non-clinging to our own images and practices, perhaps we can sense our connectivity with these "others," and learn that they are not simply "other." We need not and cannot know fully where this will lead. But if it leads us further into the holy Mystery, it will lead us in the right direction.

five

The "You" Petitions

Widespread agreement exists that the Lord's Prayer is twofold, one section seemingly more focused upon God the Father; the other, more upon ourselves and our world. These sections are connected, if only because the God whom we have just invoked is *our* God, the God of heaven and earth. But the Prayer does begin with God, with the moment of prayerful elevation, and that is worth pondering. In this chapter we will explore the first tablet or panel of the diptych, treating the petitions as a piece, because we want to get a sense of the biblical parallelism involved, each petition perhaps crescendoing more and more, and each meditatively surfacing dimensions of the preceding petitions. Like the tablets of the Law, or like the two great commands to love, we begin with the beginning: God the Father, the holy Mystery. As Augustine expresses it, "earth [that is, the concerns of the We petitions] is fruitful from the heaven [the concern of the You petitions] fertilizing it."[1] How many You petitions are there? Matthew offers us three; Luke, two. Matthew's three is a constant in the later tradition as well, although at times the invocation will be counted with Matthew's first.

. . . hallowed be your name (Matt 6:9; Luke 11:2).

How can we possibly hallow the already all-holy God? That was a question often in mind in the earliest tradition of commentaries on the Lord's Prayer. The name of God the Father, wrote Tertullian, is "that name whose hallowing we beseech, not because it is fitting for people to give God our good wishes . . . or as though he might be in trouble did we not wish him

---

1. Augustine, "Sermon on the Mount" 2.6.24, 41.

well . . . ." Likewise, Cyprian wrote: We are "not wishing that God should be made holy by our prayers, but asking the Lord that his name should be hallowed in us." He then cites a text much noted in the tradition of commentary on this petition: "Be holy, as I too am holy" (Lev 20:7).[2] Our hallowing, if you will, is a recognition of God's holy being. And we are able to do that, because God has hallowed us, making us sharers in the divine holiness. Our God-given holiness enables us to recognize God's holiness. Like recognizes like. Another source called upon for understanding this would be John 17:1: "Father . . . glorify your Son so that the Son may glorify you . . . ." We might say, following this, that as we are caught up in the divine holiness—glorified by the Father—we are enabled to recognize and honor that divine holiness. In that way, we are able to glorify the Father.[3] In this regard we might note here that a similar understanding might well be brought to the use of the doxology at the end of the Lord's Prayer. That is, our giving praise is a form of our reflecting the divine glory in which we participate and which we are then able to recognize and honor in the Father.

It seems that our recognition of God's holiness, a holiness emanating from God, and not from us, although we are enabled to participate in it, is a very biblical and indeed Jewish way of thinking of God. Jesuit theologian Gerald O'Collins thinks that this first petition is possibly the most Jewish of all the invocations. He offers four reasons in support. First, it is common in the Jewish tradition and Hebrew language to use the reverent passive voice. Thus, as we pray, "hallowed be your name," we are prayerfully recognizing that God's name is hallowed *by God*. If you want, our hallowing is a manifestation of God's own hallowing and a participation within it from our side. So, maybe it would be more appropriate to say that we are hallowing in actuality, but it is a participatory event fully enabled from God's side. Might we speak of a form of "nonsymmetrical" participation? This would be similar to the Son's being able to glorify the Father, because the Father has first glorified the Son (John 17:1). As we likewise participate in the Father's glory and holiness, we are enabled to give glory to God, for giving glory is a way of recognizing the divine glory.

---

2. The NRSV translates this as: "Consecrate yourselves therefore, and be holy; for I am the Lord your God."

3. Tertullian, *On Prayer* 2-3, 43-44; he refers to John 12:28 ("Father, glorify your name."); Cyprian, *On the Lord's Prayer* 12, 73. Vatican, The *Catechism of the Catholic Church*, Part 4, Section 2, "The Lord's Prayer" notes that "hallowed be thy name" is to be given an "evaluative sense: to recognize as holy." It is not to be taken "primarily as causative (only God hallows . . .)."

The "You" Petitions

O'Collins refers to two New Testament examples of the reverent passive use: Jesus has been raised on the third day from the dead, Paul tells us (1 Cor 15:4), it being implicitly understood that this was done *by God*. Likewise, when we are told that the stone of Jesus' grave has been rolled away (Mark 16:3), it is understood that this was done *by God*. A further common example from the Hebrew Bible might well be Ruth 4:14, "Blessed be the Lord . . . ."[4] This prayerful, passive use in Ruth may well be a very close example of the reverent passive use here in the Prayer.

Secondly, O'Collins notes the utter reverence with which the Jewish believer approached the traditional divine name, the Tetragrammaton (YHWH), revealed at the burning bush (Exod 3:1–16). As is well known, *Adonai* (in Hebrew) or *Kyrios* (in Greek) would be substituted for the divine "name." Thus, if YHWH was the divine name being hallowed—we recall that Raymond Brown suggested that this was the case at least in the Gospel of John—this would intensify the reverence being expressed in this petition. As we earlier noted, there are grounds for thinking that *Abba* was the name of priority in Jesus' and his disciples' lives. Nonetheless, by way of a process of symbolic "transference," so to speak, we might at least argue that something of the reverence accorded the Tetragrammaton would be transferred to *Abba*.

Thirdly, O'Collins notes the constant linking of the name of the Lord with the themes of praise and salvation in the psalms. "From the rising of the sun to its setting the name of the Lord is to be praised" (Ps 113:3). "Then I called on the name of the Lord: 'O Lord, I pray, save my life'" (Ps 116:4). Psalm 79:9 combines the two themes: "Help us, O God of our salvation, for the glory of your name; deliver us, and forgive us our sins, for your name's sake." Whether the name was *Abba*, or YHWH, or another primary symbol, likely these themes of praise and salvation would have attached themselves to those names, again by way of a process of symbolic transference.

Finally, suggests O"Collins, we know that holiness was one of the central features of Yahweh in the Hebrew Bible. The "Holiness Code" of the Book of Leviticus (17—26) emphasizes the refrain: "You shall be holy, for I the Lord your God am holy" (Lev 19:2; cf. 20:26). By way of transference, this attribute would have likely been attributed to the divine

---

4. See, for example, Simon et al., *The First Hebrew Primer*, 343; cf. 184–45; chapter 28; a further example: Hahn, "Matthew 5:1–48."

name (s).[5] Here, it seems, something of the otherness of God from the gods of the other nations and peoples is being pointed to. In time, this otherness would be recognized as utterly singular: there is only one God, as we noted in Isaiah. "I will sanctify my great name, which has been profaned among the nations . . . and the nations shall know that I am the Lord . . . when through you I display my holiness before their eyes" (Ezek 36:23; cf. Isa 45:5–6).[6]

Your kingdom come (Matt 6:10; Luke 11:2).

This is the very heart and central message and work of Jesus: ". . . Jesus came to Galilee, proclaiming the good news of God, and saying, 'The time is fulfilled, and the kingdom of God has come near; repent and believe in the good news'" (Mark 1:14–15; Matt 4:12–17; Luke 4:14–15). With much confidence, this theme can be attributed to Jesus himself, given its multiple attestation in the New Testament. Interestingly, although God was known as "king" (1 Sam 12:12; Pss 74:12, 84:3, 95:3), and we find an expression like "the kingdom of Israel" (1 Sam 24:20; 1 Kgs 21:7), the expression "the kingdom of God" is relatively rare until Jesus' time.[7]

"Kingdom" or "reign" can be a way of referring to God's *act* of ruling, and many frequently understand it in this way. But the symbol—for it is arguably a primal symbol, with multiple meanings—suggests a meaning even more concrete than one of God's "acts." Kingdoms come from social and political life and suggest various forms of sociopolitical organization. A kingdom, then, would be an action whereby God brings about some kind of social and at least "political-like" order. We offer the suggestion here that Jesus believes that his *Abba* is about the work of establishing a new and alternative way of living together in community, a community in which all are sons and daughters of this one Father, and in which this community is characterized by the inclusive love and care asked for by this Father. And that is what makes it an *alternative* community, for where has such a community of inclusive love yet been found? And that is what also makes it

---

5. O'Collins, *The Lord's Prayer*, 57–59; besides the notion of symbolic transference, I have added the ambivalence with respect to the "name," whether YHWH, *Abba*, or other names. See chapter four, above, for more on this.

6. Balch, "Luke," 1128.

7. See Dulling, "Kingdom of God, Kingdom of Heaven," 49–69. He notes that only the extra-biblical Psalms of Solomon 17:3 actually uses the phrase "kingdom of God" (51).

appropriate to refer to this community as a "kin-dom." This neosymbol is not a way of being cute, but of giving expression to the radicality of the inclusivity being imagined.

It also seems important to note here that in this alternative community, people are not treated as "blobs," to be subjected to some kind of abstract "common good," which is really not good, although it may be all too "common." A creed of protecting the "individual" might not be the best way to express this, however, if by "individual" we end up falling into an absolutized individualism. Some have suggested that we think of a movement from being an "individual" to being a "self," likening this to a journey of growing in love, whereby one's own tendencies toward egocentricity are transformed into sharing and loving. Many of Jesus' parables, for example, like that of the good Samaritan (Luke 10:29–37), or those of the lost sheep, the lost coin, and the lost/prodigal son (Luke 15), illustrate the regard for the person in the alternative community of the Father. "[N]ot a hair of your head shall perish . . ." (Luke 21:18), Jesus tells his followers. It seems as if in this kind of community our egos learn a new, inclusive, and loving way of living and acting that transcends the divide between individualism and social domination. This perspective may also be extended beyond humans to all creatures: no creatures are to be mere throwaway commodities. This theme has yet to be explored with great depth, but it seems implied in the kind of reign of a God who is Father of heaven and earth, that is, of all creation.

By placing the kingdom theme here among the "You petitions," the stress falls upon the fact that this reign or new community is *Abba's* community, rooted in *Abba* and based on *Abba*. The setting of this petition within the beatitudes of Matthew's Sermon on the Mount intensifies this suggestion that the Father's community is a new kind of community. The Sermon is the social charter of that new community. Without the Father, the beatitudes of the reign would be a form of hopeless utopianism; with the Father's grace, they become vivid possibilities and even realities, happening even now in Jesus' and his disciples' words and deeds, but of course only fully when the Father's name is truly sanctified by all. We are still praying, as in this prayer, for the kingdom's coming, but we also know that the "kingdom of God has come to you" (Matt 12:28; Luke 11:20). For Luke, the kingdom's coming is of a piece with Jesus' journey to Jerusalem with its impending rejection and crucifixion. This also removes it from utopian daydreaming. This kind of community will come by way of crucified love.

Perhaps here it may be appropriate to underscore the "temporal" and even the "geographical" or spatial coordinates of the kingdom, which we have not yet alluded to, except perhaps implicitly (the geographical dimension) or softly (the temporal aspect). In the New Testament, there are series of texts that underscore both the kingdom's presence and yet its futurity, its "already" and "not yet" character. These are themes that are well known and often debated by biblical scholars and historians. For example, the Lord's Prayer would seem to exemplify both dimensions: In praying for the kingdom's coming, there is the implication that it has yet to manifest itself fully. Yet it would seem to be a futile exercise of prayer, if in the petitions of the Prayer there were not the gifts of hallowing, doing the Father's will, of being nurtured by the holy bread, forgiveness, and deliverance from temptation and evil at least somewhat being given on earth even now. Each of these gifts are various aspects of the promises of the reign of God, well expressed in Jesus' teachings and actions. The Lord's Prayer, then, exemplifies the futurity of the reign of God explicitly, and its presence in some way in a more implicit or soft way.

So, if you will, the temporality of the reign of God is an in-between kind of temporality: on the way, and yet incipiently established. It has come to us in Jesus' exorcisms (Matt 12:28), and it is in fact among us (Luke 17:20); and yet it is also on the way, as we pray for its coming (Matt 6:10; Luke 11:2). The coming in glory of the king is yet to be (Matt 25:31–46). This in-between character keeps it on the move and at best always on the way. In this sense, it is not a utopian daydream without regard for the constraints of history, sin, and imperfection. But it is a reality at work, and under grace, it can break through our stubborn resistances. As such, it is the lure toward continual change and reformation. Paul's conversion is perhaps a paradigmatic example of this. The enduring presence of the church as a sign of hope, despite its evident failures, is another. Our own praying the Lord's Prayer is in fact a testimony to and even a sign of the reality of the reign of God in our midst as well.

The dynamics of the kingdom's temporality are thickly layered as well. A sense of urgency or nearness runs through the texts referring to the reign of God (Mark 1:15; Matt 22:3; 24:33; 25:13); there are even some few texts that can almost give the impression that the reign of God in its fullness will happen relatively soon (Matt 10:23; Mark 9:1; 13:30). "The kingdom of God has come near (*ēggiken*)," Mark writes (1:15). "Keep awake . . . for you know neither the day nor the hour" (Matt 25:13). It is as if the future reality of the reign is actually breaking through, in the sense that a form of participating in its *fullness* in some way were occurring, or at least a glimpse of its fullness were taking place. "Here is the bridegroom! Come out to meet him!" (Matt 25:6). The way Matthew uses the Greek aorist tense in his version of the Lord's Prayer, as we saw, is likely also a way of bringing out some of these eschatological tones.

The many healings and exorcisms of Jesus might likewise be seen as anticipatory manifestations of the full reign of God. We might, from a much later time, think of the mystical experiences of union written of by Teresa of Avila, or John of the Cross, or Jeremy Taylor, or mystical experiences of deification and divinization, explored by a hesychast like St. Gregory Palamas (d. 1359).[8] Here the future reign exercises a pull, like a gravitational energy.

The time of the kingdom, a temporality that an older cosmology thought of as absolute, is more like the relative time sketched by quantum physics or relativity theory. This is what theologian and Sister Ilia Delio, OSF, describes as the "'wave' dimension of our relatedness," as the particle aspect of life breaks down. The energy at work is now a wave creating a new form of relatedness. Another, more traditional way to put this is to say that the passage of time is not simply a *chronos* but a *kairos*: a call and pull toward inclusive relatedness. In a way, this helps us reimagine the notion of the reign of God as God's *act* of reigning. It is a dynamic, wavelike relatedness, in which we are caught up.

But that is also a place, a new kind of community which occupies space. In a wider sense, it occupies land. In another sense, it is matter, or the cosmos, or at least within the cosmos. As we noted earlier, this is at least tacitly evoked by the image of a Father of heaven and earth. Following Ilia Delio again, who is seeking to integrate theology with contemporary cosmological and quantum theory, we need to honor not only the wavelike nature of energy, but the particle nature of it all too. "Wave-particle duality . . . is the basis of quantum physics." The energy pull toward relatedness pulls us toward a new kind of space, one which makes room for all. Here space can become a home, but a very wide home, in which all life not only lives but thrives. Because scriptural studies have for so long been dominated by the historical sciences, more attention has been given to the temporal than to the spatial dimensions of the reign of God, I believe. Colonial studies, with its attention to the land and to whom it belongs, but also newer

---

8. Palamas, *The Triads* 3.9, 106: The saints "contemplated that uncreated light which, even in the age to come, will be ceaselessly visible only to the saints . . . ."

cosmological studies, such as we find it in thinkers like Delio, are widening our perspectives, so that we attend to matter, space, and energy as well. So as we pray for the coming of the kingdom, we are praying for a new kind of kin-dom, of inclusive relatedness. Time and space are two dimensions of a continuum, like waves and particles, the energy of each bending toward relatedness.[9]

Let us now explore a theme that may help us gain an insight into how these You petitions are intertwined. A classic text from Isaiah will get us started. "For as the rain and the snow come down from heaven, and do not return there until they have watered the earth . . . so shall my word be that goes out from my mouth; it shall not return to me empty, but it shall accomplish that which I purpose, and succeed in the thing for which I sent it," Isaiah 55:10–11 tells us. This very Jewish notion of the "word" seems to come from primary theology/experience, in which language, name, and vividly actual experience and action are united. The primary word erupts from within the manifold of living experience; it is not an abstract concept detached from that living experience, but a form of actually participating in it and recognizing it on deeply affective levels.

It might be helpful to look at the movement from (1) hallowing the name, to (2) praying for the kingdom's coming, to (3) praying that the divine will be done from within this perspective of the word as primary experience and symbol. In this case, the "word" is the name being hallowed. Within this primary experience, name, action, and affective awareness form an undifferentiated whole. That is why this name leads on to its realization in a new community and actualization in people's wills. We might compare this to a deeply affective experience of intimate love, as with engaged couples. The very calling to mind of a lover's name, or perhaps of the "special" names lovers give to each other, vibrates on deep levels of the lovers' beings, changing their behavior and altering their will. As these little love experiences are shared, the two become as "one." They constitute a new kind of community of shared wills. This kind of love is a paradigmatic primary experience, helping us to understand what we mean by "primary theology," or the theology manifested in such primary experiences. Another such paradigmatic primary experience would be that of the conversion of Saul in Acts 9. A key dimension of this is the calling of the name, "Saul, Saul, why do you persecute me?" (9:4) This name is the personal recognition of Paul (Saul) by the Lord, which in turn initiates the turnaround of

---

9. See Delio, *Making All Things New*, 37, 42, 84.

The "You" Petitions

Paul's life. Later, through Ananias' instrumentality, Paul will be initiated into the discipleship of another name, that of Jesus: "I myself [Jesus] will show him how much he must suffer for the sake of my name" (9:16). This new name, decisively changing Paul, will bring about the new community of shared wills of Gentile Christianity. In Acts the "name" of Jesus functions as the "word" noted by Isaiah, which does not return to the Lord empty.

This may also help us understand Tertullian's later textual variant, whereby doing the Father's will actually precedes the kingdom's coming.[10] These elements—name, kingdom, and will—form a united whole in the primary experience. We also find another later variant: namely, the coming of the Holy Spirit, rather than that of the kingdom, is prayed for, by some writers, Gregory of Nyssa, for example, and Maximus the Confessor knows this variant. In the primary experience, symbols are fluid, unlike precise concepts.[11]

The hallowed name (word) is like the snow and rain that has come down from heaven, and its becoming a new community (kingdom) of people's changed wills (through the Spirit's coming) is its watering of the earth, its not returning empty. Crossan's view that we are experiencing a form of biblical crescendo parallelism is another way of saying this. As one dwells within the hallowed name of the Father, one becomes a daughter or son of a new family, and one's will is thereby changed. We are learning to love the Lord with all our heart, soul, mind, and strength (Mark 12:30).

Your will be done,
on earth as it is in heaven (Matt 6:10).

Jesuit biblical scholar Daniel Harrington helpfully suggests that this petition expresses "a perfect harmony between the way in which heaven and earth run." If we look at it in this eschatological sense—now is the special time of the realization of the heavenly kingdom on earth, going along with the aorist verb tense in Greek used by Matthew—it brings out what is already implied in the second petition for the kingdom's coming. This third petition also is already anticipated in the invocation to the Father in heaven, and that invocation finds it realization here.[12] Crossan's view of crescendo parallelism fits very well here: What begins with the Father in

---

10. Tertullian, *On Prayer* 4, 44; Stevenson, *The Lord's Prayer*, 30.
11. Stevenson, *The Lord's Prayer*, 48.
12. Harrington, *The Gospel of Matthew*, 95.

heaven reaches its earthly climax now upon earth in doing the Father's will in the way it is done in heaven. If this interpretation is accurate, it may also represent a bridge petition, leading on into the We petitions, which take place upon earth.

However, there is an older cosmocentric view which may also be hinted at here. And upon it we might build a neocosmocentrism. The heavens, as we saw, were the higher sphere, the skies, rather than the more purely transcendental region of God. In these skies, there were higher powers at work, not all of whom were good. We find something of this in the Pauline view that "our struggle is not against enemies of blood and flesh, but against the rulers, against the authorities, against the cosmic powers of this present darkness, against the spiritual forces of evil in the heavenly places" (Eph 6:12). So perhaps part of what is being recognized here is the "earlier" defeat of the evil powers in the heavens through Christ, and its extension now to the regions of the earth as well. Something of this older "cosmology" may also be found in Revelation 12:13, in which after a heavenly battle "the dragon saw that he had been thrown down to the earth." If this is the case, then the Lord's Prayer is asking for the full defeat of the dragon even in the sphere of the earth, just as it had earlier been done in the heavens through Christ.

Surplus of Meaning in Past Tradition

The hallowing of the Father's name is typically thought of as a glorifying of the Father's name, along the lines of the Gospel of John. As we are caught up in the Father's glory, we are able to acknowledge the profundity of the Father's glory. But this renders us like the angels in heaven who give glory, and simultaneously manifests our own growth in baptismal grace and the knowledge of love. Interestingly, Tertullian universalizes the hallowing: It calls us to pray that everyone, even our enemies, will be able to hallow the name. In this way, we are obedient to the Lord's command to love even our enemies (Matt 5:44). "Consequently . . . we do not say 'Let it be hallowed in us,' but manage to say: 'in all people.'"[13] Thomas Aquinas offers a kind of synthesis of these two sides, which is typical of his synthetic thought: God is sanctified in others "through us insofar as we are sanctified by him . . . . For he himself said (Lev 11:44): 'Be holy because I am holy.'" And in accordance with the medieval exaltation of the saints, he argues that "Among

---

13. Tertullian, *On Prayer* 3, 44.

the different signs which manifest the holiness of God to human beings, the most evident sign is the holiness of those men and women who are sanctified by the divine indwelling."[14]

The implication in the early tradition, then, is somewhat similar to the reverent passive in Jewish prayer. Our own hallowing of the name is a manifestation within us of God's own holiness. As God's name is hallowed *by God*, so we also are enabled *by God* properly to acknowledge God's holiness. We become in this sense like the angels, manifesting the holiness of God. "You shall not profane my holy name, that I may be sanctified among the people of Israel: I am the Lord; I sanctify you . . ." (Lev 22:32). In a particularly compelling way, Aquinas writes, "'We do not mean that God's name is not holy; but we ask that [people] may treat it as a holy thing . . . .'"[15]

Luther, I believe, represents a return to the stress upon the reverent Hebrew passive: We add nothing to God's own holiness, but our lives must manifest it nonetheless. Luther is reacting against a one-sided view in which our own human manifestation of God's holiness might be thought of as our own autonomous possession. God is indeed to be sanctified among us, as Leviticus teaches, but only because God has sanctified us, thus enabling us to sanctify (Lev 22:32). This is, of course, a way of thinking through the petition of hallowing in the light of the Reformation teaching of justification by faith through grace. What God gives is "without condition . . . pure grace," Luther teaches. God's name is "holy in its nature . . . but in our use it is not," he writes. But through being incorporated in him in baptism, we are enabled to give the name "its proper honor." Calvin teaches a similar view, but nicely adds in a later part of his commentary on the Prayer "that we need not only the grace of the Spirit, to soften our hearts within and to bend and direct them to obey God, but also his aid . . . ."[16]

From the Roman Catholic side, the Council of Trent displays a sensitivity to the churches and the great upheaval of the Reformation occurring in its time. John Calvin, from the perspective of a pastor overseeing churches in Reformed territories, also has an eye toward the common good of the

---

14. Aquinas, *Compendium theologiae* 7, in Vollert, 349-50, 199.

15. Aquinas, *Summa theologica* 2-2.83.9.1, 1544. Aquinas's sources are quite representative of the tradition: Tertullian, Cyprian, Gregory of Nyssa, Chrysostom, Augustine, and others.

16. Luther, *The Large Catechism*, 93, 36, 38; Calvin, *Institutes of the Christian Religion* 3.20.46, 913. At 41, 904: "Now since God reveals himself to us partly in teaching, partly in works, we can hallow him only if we render to him what is his in both respects, and so embrace all that proceeds from him."

churches in his commentary on the Lord's Prayer. Trent suggests that we must pray for the conversion of unbelievers, so that the divine name may truly be hallowed. The implication for both Calvin and Trent is that our prayer will only properly or fully occur when it does so within the church itself, as each understands that. This seems to be the approach taken by Teresa of Avila as well, for she counsels that the reason why the petitions for hallowing God's name and the coming of the kingdom are placed together is that we are really unable to properly hallow and praise the Father apart from the help given us in the kingdom of the church. Within the church, as we make our way to the eternal fullness of the kingdom, God sends us moments of profound praise, as in mystical experiences of prayer and quiet.[17]

The Anglican divine[18] and bishop Jeremy Taylor, echoing Teresa of Avila's prayer of mystical surrender and quiet, suggests that our hallowing of the name is an experience in which "the soul puts on the affections of a child, and divests itself of its own interest, offering itself up wholly to the designs and glorifications of God." But also like Teresa, the next petition for the kingdom's coming is one in which this child "puts on the relations and duty of a subject to her legitimate prince, seeking the promotion of his regal interest." The child must grow up, Taylor seems to say, by being guided by and in the kingdom. But he goes on beautifully, again echoing much of Teresa of Avila's mystical teaching, to suggest that the petition for the Father's will being done means that the child and subject will be transformed into a "spouse," united with the Father, "loving the same love and choosing the same object, and delighting in unions and conformities."[19]

The petition for the kingdom's coming takes various accents in the tradition: an accent falling upon its heavenly, future realization; upon its partial, but real present realization on earth; upon its personal realization in the hearts and souls of persons, as they struggle with the devil and various temptations; upon its more ecclesial, social realization in the churches, a theme which is more accented in the later medieval period and the Reformation times; sometimes a combination of these; and sometimes simply upon Christ or the Holy Spirit in their coming. One has the sense that when

---

17. Teresa of Avila, *The Way of Perfection* 30.4, 150–51. For Calvin, one can find his commentary on the Lord's Prayer in *The Institutes of the Christian Religion*, Book 3, 20.34–52, with references to the church and the community of believers at 20.42 especially. See Catholic Apologetics, *The Catechism of the Council of Trent*.

18. This is an Anglican way of referring to a theologian.

19. Taylor, *The Great Exemplar* 2.6, 468; his book was the first devotional life of Christ in English, published in 1649; see Stevenson, *The Lord's Prayer*, 182–83.

the kingdom is identified with Christ, that it is the "whole" Christ, head and members of the church together, that is in mind. As Augustine writes, "Sometimes the title Christ appears in Scripture in reference to the Word equal to the Father.... Sometimes in reference to the Mediator.... Sometimes in reference to the head and the body... for the body with its head is one Christ."[20]

Thomas Aquinas also offers the rather liberating perspective that we are praying for our freedom, or for the time when we will all be monarchs, as we petition for the kingdom's coming. This is a perspective which anticipates modern times, and which is something of a counterpoint to Jeremy Taylor's stress upon our praying for the kingdom as a sign of our being subjects to our heavenly monarch.

> In fact, not only will all be free, but all will be kings ... inasmuch as all shall be of one will with God, and God shall will whatever the saints will, and the saints shall will whatever God wills. Hence, in the will of God shall their will be done. And thus all will reign, since the will of all shall be done, and God shall be the crown of all (Isaiah 28:5): "In that day the Lord of hosts shall be a crown of glory and a diadem of splendour for the remnant of his people."[21]

Teresa of Avila, perhaps even more daringly, thinks of the petition for the kingdom somewhat subversively as asking for the place in which we understand "by experience" that if we try to grasp everything, we lose everything. "As the saying goes, whoever tries to grasp too much loses everything...."[22] This can be read on two levels: that of the individual person, striving for mystical transformation; and more indirectly but truly, that of the church, which needs to learn that too much grasping ends in losing. At a time when the church tended to identify itself with the kingdom, Teresa's description of the kingdom was quite counterintuitive and courageous. But she realistically knew that the church could only come to this realization through its mystics and reformers.

The Council of Trent, interestingly, opens up the perspective even further in some ways, inasmuch as it recognizes God's kingdom not only in grace (the church on earth), but also in nature (creation) and glory (cosmos and church in full splendor). The traditional recognition of nature as an aspect of the Father's kingdom points ahead to and awaits its honoring in a

---

20. Augustine, *Sermo* 341.12, 240. See Mersch, *The Whole Christ*.
21. Aquinas, *In Orationem*, 1056, 226; Murray, *Praying*, 49–50.
22. Teresa of Avila, *The Way of Perfection* 31.10, 158.

neocosmocentrism for our times. Prophetic thinkers like Jesuit Teilhard de Chardin and Franciscan Ilia Delio are helping us break new ground here.

The petition that the Father's will be done on earth as in heaven is missing in Luke, we perhaps recall. That invites the possible implication that it is already implied in the petition for the kingdom's coming. Our comments upon biblical, poetic parallelism, go along with this, for such parallelisms are more or less an uncovering of dimensions implied in earlier verses. This also coheres with our thoughts about primary theology and experience: In that experiential manifold, symbols and insights are fluid and very compact, because our experience is so crammed. As the kingdom finds its realization among us in action, so, too, are our wills correspondingly transformed. That is what is happening on the level of lived experience, and it takes a bit of poetic or reflective distance to express that in symbols and perhaps even more limited "concepts." That is why it seems that when we look at the early tradition of interpreting this petition that the Father's will be done, what we find is more or less a "doubling" or "echo" of what has been said about the prior petition for the kingdom's coming. Some writers will stress the work yet to be done, through struggle, detachment, and commitment, in this new sphere of the kingdom; others, placing the accent upon the goal, write of our transformation and becoming as the angels, or they write of the spousal union as we find it in Bishop Taylor and Teresa of Avila.[23]

But this is a "doubling" or "echoing" with a difference, for it seems that biblical parallelisms always uncover something "new." The accent upon the "will" points to a deepened insight into the interiority of the persons making up the kingdom. This is something like an echo of the great command to love, which speaks of loving with our hearts, souls, and minds (Matt 22:37), and with all our strength (Luke 10:27). This is why we might want to think of this kingdom as a new or alternative "community." It is something more than an organizational structure. Interestingly, the petition in the Lord's Prayer is referring to the *Father's* will, and only indirectly to our own. The tradition in grappling with this petition has found itself emphasizing our response to the Father's will, making that will our own. The tradition may have been drawn to this because the Father is the Father of heaven *and of earth*, of the place where human wills are operating. The Father's will needs to be implemented here, on earth, as it is in heaven. This

---

23. Unless otherwise noted, the original sources can conveniently be found in Stevenson, *The Lord's Prayer*, chapters 2—7.

The "You" Petitions

is all quite biblical too. Jesus' parables are filled with references to our acting responsibly (the watchful servants, watchful householder, and faithful manager [Luke 12:35–38; 12:39–40, 42–46]). "Not everyone who says to me, 'Lord, Lord,' will enter the kingdom of heaven, but only the one who does the will of my Father in heaven," says Jesus (Matt 7:21).

The relationship between our human wills and the divine will is one of those great and contentious theological issues much debated in the tradition, from Augustine against the Pelagians, to the Reformation in the debates concerning grace and faith and free will, and unto now. The Lord's Prayer, dwelling in the region of primary experience and theology, does not and thankfully need not wander into this issue. Like good primary theology, it avoids sharply binary thinking in many cases. What we tend to imagine as two realities—God's will and our own—primary theology imagines and experiences as one. It leaves to forms of secondary, conceptual theologies the task of providing conceptual models of how these wills can be both one and yet two. As with the petition for hallowing God's name, our hallowing reflects God's own hallowing. We are to be holy as God is holy and enables us to be holy: "I am the Lord; I sanctify you" (Lev 22:32). So too with respect to our wills: "For who can resist his [God's] will?" (Rom 9:19) "What do you have that you did not receive?," asked Paul (1 Cor 4:6). And yet, somehow, like Jesus, our own will is God's will: "My food is to do the will of him who sent me and to complete his work" (John 4:34).

If we desire a sample of fine, "secondary" theology, offering a more conceptual reflection on this matter of the relation between the divine and our human wills, these thoughts of Nicholas Ayo, CSC, deserve attention. He is referring to the union between the human Jesus' will and that of his Father, and drawing implications from that for the way to think of how all human wills can be in union with the divine will.

> . . . let us argue for both the will of God and the will of Jesus united in the recognition that the human heart's desire at its depth is precisely the will of God for the salvation of all flesh. The greatest miracle of God's sovereign will is the conversion of the human heart. Greater even than creation from nothing is the transformation of human free will from sin to grace. God works our salvation without denigrating the integrity of our freedom.[24]

Perhaps a bit more of an insight is to be found in the fact that we are *praying*, for this is a petitionary prayer. Are we first asking of God, and then,

24. Ayo, *The Lord's Prayer*, 46.

secondly, because of that, God is granting? Or is our asking already God's granting, simultaneously? There is a difference between simply asking and *prayerfully* asking. The latter implies a prior, interpersonal relationship of reciprocal but nonsymmetrical love. The seeking arises from within that love manifold and is made possible by it, it seems.

Contemporary Transitions

The petition that God's name be hallowed might appropriately be considered in relation to our "modern" transition, which at least in the developed West is one of grappling with the challenges of the modern turn to experience and the modern sciences it has generated. Archbishop Rowan Williams suggests that this petition alerts us to the temptation to manipulate God, using God as a tool for our own purposes.[25] This is a very subtle temptation. And much of the "modern" reaction to religion and theology stems precisely from the charge that the theistic religions have fallen into this manipulative tendency. If this be so, it would seem to mean that we are not praying very well, that is, we are not hallowing very well. Can the Lord's Prayer be one of the central ways in which we are tutored in the discipline of remaining open to the holy Mystery, or in the discipline of not clinging, even to our most cherished dogmas?

In this respect, the way the mystics pray this prayer—or are prayed by it—is perhaps the most relevant response to the charge of manipulation. As John of the Cross wrote, "And when you come to the possession of the all, you must possess it without possessing anything."[26] In our consumerist atmosphere, in which we are taught to possess, consume, possess some more, and consume some more, unendingly, so that we think we are freely desiring even while we are being manipulated into desiring our "desires," it is hard to believe that we do not end up turning God into one more satisfaction of our own desires. Hallowing the name in this atmosphere might consider taking the form of "possessing while not possessing." Our consumerist atmosphere might also heighten our attention to the potential relevance of the petition for doing the divine will, for it is only as our own wills are operating out of that depth from which they are in union with the divine will that they can truly find the freedom from compulsion and domination for which they yearn. A will that possesses without possess-

---

25. Williams and Beckett, *Living the Lord's Prayer*, 32.
26. John of the Cross, *The Ascent of Mount Carmel* 13.12, 151.

ing is a will hallowing the divine name, a will attuned to the ever present dangers of manipulating and being manipulated.

The possessive temptation is especially subtle for the religions, which believe they are inspired by the Divine. This gives a transcendental charge to their beliefs and doctrines, which can seemingly raise them above criticism. Of course, we know enough today to realize that the secular ideologies that have rushed in to replace the religions have all too easily given a transcendental surcharge to their own ideologies, as a way of responding to and replacing our orientation to the holy Mystery. If you will, the authentically transcendental has been transferred to the inauthentically transcendental. I believe that this is one of the central reasons for the emergence of the late modern and postmodern transitions. The first has discerned the pathologies hidden, not only in the religions, but in the modern ideologies that have arisen in their place. The latter likewise has discerned the hidden "absolutism" in modernity's various "isms," and is seeking to find the little plants that might grow in those in-between spaces.

But the petition that the name be hallowed also challenges the late modern and postmodern transitions and all possible critiques, even while overlapping with their concerns. For critique would seem to be a derivative phenomenon: We critique in the name of something, on behalf of something. The evil is a parasite on the good, actively damaging the good. The ugly is a parasite on the beautiful, damaging it. The false is a parasite on the true, distorting it. Could it be that the good, the beautiful, and the true are the summons from the holy Mystery, from the name which is hallowed? Once the Mystery ceases to be Mystery, and therefore the ever present summons to surrender and love, it ceases to be truly Mystery. Truly hallowing and truly healthy critiques seem only possible in the presence of true Mystery.[27]

The petition for the kingdom's coming seems particularly relevant to the late modern critiques of pathologies social, political, economic, and psychological (with its exploration of distorting, more or less unconscious passions). These critiques do help us maintain in focus the sociopolitical dimensions of the kingdom. In this way we deprivatize it, which is not to rob it of its need to be appropriated by human persons, but which reminds us of our call to instantiate the reign of God socially. The new reign of God does, of course, challenge us all to a profound change of heart and mind, but

---

27. Even now, the most compelling exploration of the theme of the divine Mystery which I have found is Rahner, "The Concept of Mystery in Catholic Theology," 36–73.

it also challenges us to new forms of social togetherness and community. In doing this, it will challenge us to unearth the "unconscious" ideologies by which we inhibit true community for anyone and every creature.

The new community of inclusive love will likely always be in tension with various forms of political "order" and "disorder." The various critiques help us appreciate the important connections between the kingdom and the churches, but they also alert us to the dangers of simply identifying those churches with the kingdom. The kingdom cannot be colonized by our various little colonies, regardless of our imposing empires, ecclesial, religious, or secular. It is of earth and heaven, and it is of *Abba* and *Abba's* inclusive love. It is ecumenical, but it is more than that, stretching the ecumenical into and toward the universal. Echoing Aquinas, as long as one creature is not truly free, not a "monarch," then the Lord of hosts is not yet able to be a "crown of glory and a diadem of splendor for . . . his people" (Isa 28:5).

Gestures toward Trinity, Incarnation, and Interreligious Hospitality

Occasionally writers in the tradition have made references to the Trinity in their explorations of the Lord's Prayer. As the trinitarian nature of God gained more clarity in the early churches, it would be natural that its influence would make itself felt in approaches to the Lord's Prayer. Stevenson mentions several writers in the earlier tradition in this regard: Gregory of Nyssa, who makes mention of the Trinity somewhat; Hildefonsus of Toledo (d. 667) and Euthymius Zigabenus (twelfth century), who think of the prayer as addressed to the entire Trinity; and Maximus the Confessor, who thinks that the revelation of the Trinity is one of the "mysteries . . . of more general importance . . . [which] lies hidden within the Lord's Prayer." And these mysteries constitute theology in the proper sense.[28] But these are hints, and they remain largely unexplored. This again draws us into the question of the surplus of meaning of texts, or into the many possible meanings which texts can generate. And it also draws us into the questions of the possible limits of drawing multiple meanings from texts.

I can only ask the reader to revisit my suggestions on this in earlier chapters as a kind of preface to the comments to follow. All too briefly: I believe that texts are results of authors' participating in the complex flow of reality, a reality which includes the divine Ground, the cosmos and all its

---

28. Maximus the Confessor, "On the Lord's Prayer," 285–305, at 287, 291; Stevenson, *The Lord's Prayer*, 48, 60, 91–95, 108.

creatures, societies, and humans in remarkably rich relationships. We, that is, we later interpreters of the text, in this case, the Lord's Prayer, are participating in the same flow of reality as Jesus and his disciples, and our own experiences and vantage points at times give us insights that come from our "later" experiences from within the flow of those relationships making up our primary field of existence. One such later experience is that of the emergence of the trinitarian belief. That colors and hopefully enriches our perspective. If you want, we wager that the Trinity is tacitly "present" in the Lord's Prayer, or so "compactly" present that it awaits more "articulate differentiation." And something of that is what we are gesturing toward here.

In a "speculative" way, Nicholas Ayo, CSC, suggests: "Can we compare the first thou-petition with the Creator, the Father-almighty; the second thou-petition with the kingdom of his only Son, our Lord Jesus Christ, and the third thou-petition with the gift of the Holy Spirit that tunes our will to the will of the Father?"[29] I do not think we will be too surprised by the first comparison. The hallowed name, whether "Father" or "YHWH," for example, is certainly referring to the holy and divine Mystery. And in line with another of Ayo's suggestions, it seems more reflective of the Gospel of John. We do know that the theme of glorifying the Father is emphatic in John (17:1, 4).

Again, we know, especially in the Synoptics—which Ayo also notes —that the theme of the kingdom or reign of God is closely associated with Jesus the Lord. It is the Father's kingdom, but Jesus is its central mediator and agent, and it forms the core of his message and work. "But if it is by the Spirit of God that I cast out demons, then the kingdom of God has come to you" (Matt 12:28), says Jesus. And as well, again following up a suggestion by Ayo, the gift of the Spirit's "sanctification and transformation congenial with Paul's writing" would seem particularly associated with the third Thou petition, for sanctifying transformation finally would seem to have to do with the "deification" of our wills. And Paul especially associates this with the Spirit, from whom we "reap eternal life" (Gal 6:8).[30]

That the mystery of the incarnation is tacitly present is to some extent bound up with Jesus' role as the mediator of the reign of God. For that reign comes through his message and work, that is, through his very life. We

---

29. Ayo, *The Lord's Prayer*, 52.

30. Ibid.: "Moreover, is the 'hallowed name' more Johannine, the 'kingdom' more the Synoptics, and the 'will be done' more sanctification and transformation congenial with Paul's writing?"

cannot and should not want to isolate Jesus from his companions and followers. With Augustine, we might want to think of the "whole" Christ, head and members. But the mystery of the incarnation means that we need to give full affirmation to what being the "head" of the body of Christ means. Another way to look at this is from the perspective of the name of God as *Abba*/Father. A "father" implies at least one child, and perhaps many. That Abba is *our* Father implies that there are many children and even all creatures, for this *Abba* is the Father of heaven and of earth, that is, of the very cosmos. But, following up the various ways in which Jesus' own relationship with the Father seems very special and unique, there would seem to be a unique Father and Son relationship in his case, a relationship in which the rest of us share. We have received "a spirit of adoption"; and this grants us a share in Jesus' own relation with his Father, by which we become "joint heirs with Christ" (Rom 8:15, 17). As we pray this prayer, then, we are caught up in the flow of this Father and Son dynamic through the Spirit. We are experiencing incarnation. In this sense, the "our" of the Our Father might be said to reflect both the trinitarian "our" of Father, Son, and Holy Spirit, and the "our" of the family of God, which embraces the churches, all peoples, and the world (all of creation). Through our adoption in the Spirit, the latter "our" is grounded in the first trinitarian "our," something helpfully suggested in Abbot Jeremy Driscoll's superbly eucharistic meditation on the Lord's Prayer.[31]

In primary theology and experience—our primary "field"—these mysteries are all in some way one. Dualistic or separatistic thinking is not a typical feature of primary experience and theology. The layers of primary experience are thick, and a multitude of symbols, punctuated by awe and silence, are characteristic of it. Praying this Prayer, or being in the flow if its praying us, is a good way to reroot our secondary, more conceptual theologies of Trinity and incarnation (or Christology) in their originary soil. Echoing and citing St. Maximus the Confessor, it is within this soil that the "mystery of deification" is happening, in which "through participation by grace in the Holy Spirit," we "share in the divine nature (2 Pet 1:4)." As we bring "the [Lord's] prayer to fulfillment through our actions," we come to a "wisdom" out of which true "theology" comes. For "mystical theology teaches us, who through faith have been adopted by grace and brought to the knowledge of the truth, to recognize one nature and power of the Divinity, that is to say, one God contemplated in Father, Son and Holy Spirit."

---

31. Driscoll, *What Happens at Mass*, 110–11; see the entire meditation, 107–18.

For this is "what the self-emptying of the only-begotten Son through the flesh has now made us...."[32]

Finally, tacitly present in the Lord's Prayer is a recognition of a unity in diversity of the one family of the Father of heaven and earth. The unity is apparent in the recognition that there is one Father of all. The diversity is less apparent, but implied in the recognition of heaven and earth as the locus of the Father's family. For heaven and earth, or the very cosmos itself, is made up of very diverse species, although united in a vastly complex ecosphere. It seems appropriate to note this here in connection with Trinity and incarnation, although because these are the "unique" features of the Christian faith, the unity in diversity of all creatures under the Father challenges us to an ecumenical on the way to becoming truly universal understanding of just what it is that we profess while we pray the Prayer. Today's new global horizon, although in the making for many centuries, has stretched and perhaps exploded our previous understandings of what the ecumenical really is.

At the time of the Oxford Movement, in the mid-nineteenth century, the Anglo-Catholic priest, theologian, and professor of poetry John Keble (d. 1866) wrote a paraphrase of the Lord's Prayer that is still very valuable and inspiring, and this book is within its trajectory. Keble's paraphrase comes at the conclusion of his preface to a collection of his sermons. In it he suggests "that at one time or another in our daily devotions we should offer up our Lord's Prayer, as a prayer, in special, for Church union; if so He may graciously accept it, remembering His own Eucharistic petition, 'that they may be one, as we are.'" He then goes on in the opening invocation and in each petition to accent the prayer for unity. Hallowed be "Thy Name One." In praying for the kingdom's coming, we are praying to be made "both visibly and invisibly one in Thee [the one Father]." God's will "is to gather together in one all things in Christ . . . in Heaven . . . on earth." As we pray for our daily bread, we remember that "we being many are one Bread and one Body." As we seek forgiveness, we think of those who need it because of "rending Thy Blessed Body: forgive us the many things we have done to mar the unity of Thy mystical Body." We pray to be led away from any temptation "to cease from being one in Thee," and to be delivered "from whatever might disturb Thy Church, and cause it to be less one in Thee."[33]

---

32. Maximus the Confessor, "On the Lord's Prayer," 304, 287, 295–96.
33 Keble, *Sermons*, Preface, lxx–lxxiii.

Your Kin-dom Come

The emergence of the World Council of Churches in 1948 as one of the more important beginnings of the modern ecumenical movement, along with the earlier Oxford Movement, deserve to be noted as inspirers of our ecumenical guide to the Lord's Prayer.[34] Each of these are manifestations of the global, ecumenical horizon that has emerged with such force in our modern times. We are quite consciously drawing from the riches of all the Christian churches in our little work here, as we noted in our introduction. But today's global horizon stretches us beyond only focusing upon Keble's concern for the unity of the church, the mystical body, understood as the Christian church. We are trying to imagine that mystical body along the lines of the interreligious and cosmic mystical body.

Again we may suggest that if we keep in mind the lessons of primary experience and theology, we can remain hopeful and resist any utopian pretensions. For the consciousness of primary theology tends to avoid binary thinking, because it emerges from within the soil of primary experience, where realities are dimensions of one great whole. The Lord's Prayer is a prayer from within this primary manifold. In praying it, we are returning in a more conscious way to this manifold; we are returning to our roots, if you will, or to our native soil. In a way we are not really "returning," because we are always within it, even if we may not remember that. One of the blessings of letting the Prayer pray us, releasing our imaginations to its primary images and symbols, and resisting the temptation to "control" the prayer by limiting the range of the prayer's primal symbols, is that our amnesia regarding our primal habitat within primary experience can be transformed into a new, global anamnesis. We *re*-member that of which we are already *members*.

If we view that in this way, then it becomes possible to imagine that the various religions, and indeed all creatures, are participating in one, vast ecosphere. Of course we say this from a posture of faith, or perhaps better, from a posture of fidelity to the multiple depths of the reality within which we dwell. That fidelity turns into a consciousness that in varying ways and shades is attuned to all the partners in the communion of reality. That consciousness is within, not outside. It is a participatory consciousness. Just as we know our Father because we are within our Father's family, so we know by experience, indwelling, communion, and symbolic imagination tending

---

34. See World Council of Churches, *The Church*; would that this hope-inspired document could be implemented; see "Historical Note," 41–46, on the history of the ecumenical movement. For the Oxford Movement, and Keble's part in this specifically, see Chandler, *An Introduction to the Oxford Movement*.

toward various kinds of understanding and more limited conceptualization, ourselves and our partners within the cosmic ecosphere within which we dwell.

Our various symbols, then, might be said to have a kind of roughly equivalent significance, when they arise from our conscious experiences of the same partners in the communion of reality.[35] We are always coparticipating in the same vast reality somehow, so we trust in fidelity. But we do so in varying modes of experience and symbolization. We have enough unity to assure us that we are truly one. We have enough diversity to assure us that we may challenge and enrich one another. This might be another way of thinking about Jesus' words in John's Gospel, that "in my Father's house there are many dwelling places" (14:2), an insight noted by others, as we have seen. We are all in that house. Many religions do use some of the same symbols to express this Father. The texture of the experience and the shades of evocation of the symbols likely vary, however. But there would seem patently to be a oneness in diversity. The historical experience of Jesus' *Abba* undoubtedly gives the dominant shading to the Christian loading of its symbols for the divine Mystery, but Christians do believe that this Father is universally present to all and in some way communicated to all consciousnesses through the Spirit, the "wind" or "spirit" sweeping or hovering over the waters of creation (Gen 1:2). And in that Spirit, who is one with Jesus Christ, all creatures are participating in Jesus too, in ways too profound for most of us to understand. He is "the image of the invisible God . . . and in him all things hold together" (Col 1:15, 17; cf. 1 Cor 3:3), writes Paul of what the tradition calls the "Cosmic Christ."[36] That gives us Christian prayers of the Lord's Prayer hope that we are all, regardless of religious perspective, truly one in diversity, and can be even more consciously and experientially one. Hopefully we will all get better at understanding this oneness and expressing it in ways which do not coopt "others."

But we need to remain modest, even if in hope. Teresa of Avila, echoing John 14:2, wrote of the soul that it is "like a castle . . . in which there are many rooms, just as in heaven there are many dwelling places." Importantly

---

35. See Voegelin, "Equivalences of Experience." I have been deeply influenced here by Voegelin's inspiring preface and introduction to *Israel and Revelation*, 19–24, 39–50.

36. See Maloney, *The Cosmic Christ*; interested readers might also find the following helpful: Thompson[-Uberuaga], "Thomas Merton's Transcultural Christ," 250–76.

she goes on to add: "It is impossible that anyone understand them all since there are many."[37] It is well to keep that in mind.

---

37. Teresa of Avila, *The Interior Castle* 1.1.1, 3, 283–84.

six

The "We" Petitions

In the West, Tertullian's and St. Augustine's view that the Lord's Prayer consists of seven petitions—three heavenly and four earthly—tended to rule supreme, until perhaps Thomas Aquinas with some others began to question that in the thirteenth century. Luther, however, returned to a sevenfold structure for the prayer. The Eastern Christian tradition by and large opted for six petitions. Stevenson states that "this scheme rules supreme, without any distinctions of earthly and heavenly, throughout the East, right down to the present day." Interestingly, John Calvin opts for this Eastern pattern of six petitions, although he would make a distinction between the first three, which focus on God's glory, and the final three, which focus upon our earthly needs, as long as we do not lose sight of God's glory, he cautions. Bishop Stevenson himself prefers the approach of the East and Calvin, "because it better reflects the linguistic structure of the prayer, memorably described as 'three aspirations' and 'three petitions' by Austin Farrer."[1]

Whereas Western writers like Tertullian and Augustine, when they come to the first We petition, that for our bread, tend to write that the Prayer is now moving from the divine or heavenly to the human or earthly, Eastern writers tend not to write in this way. However, even the very "spiritualist" Eastern writer Origen, influenced by the "other-worldly" tendencies of an evolving Platonism as he is, knows that the later petitions concern our needs. And this is very strongly noted in many of the Eastern writers.

The Eastern tendency of not noting any break between the "heavenly" You petitions and the "earthly" We petitions accords well with its deification theology. That is, because of the incarnation, created reality is being

---

1. Stevenson, *The Lord's Prayer*, 222–23. Calvin, *Institutes* 3.20.44.

transformed or deified through participation in Christ (2 Pet 1:4). Our earthly petitions through deification are transforming us in a heavenward direction, so to speak. The deifying glory of God is shining through the earthly even now. And this results from our adoption in our brother Christ. His humanity is distinct but not separate from his divine Word, and that divine Word is transforming his humanity, not by destroying it, but by releasing its God-given human potential to be the image and likeness of God. So, too, we by adoption and in our own ways are distinct but not separate from God. Our earthly concerns, reflected in the Prayer's second part, are in a way being transformed day to day, so that we are enabled to come to the realization of our full potential as made in God's image and likeness. If we follow this Eastern pattern, we might say that the two parts of the Lord's Prayer are distinct but not separate. This formulation would reflect the teaching on the incarnation of the Council of Chalcedon (451), which is one of the glories of Eastern Christendom, and indeed of the united Christian churches of the first millennium.

This Eastern pattern of deification might be compared to an icon. When we contemplate one of these beautiful images, we see figures—Trinity, Christ, Mary, the other saints—as if transformed by a glowing light. The transformation is so great that oftentimes the figures appear strange and even distorted to us, at least from our more "ordinary" human perspective. Is this to suggest that somehow what we typically see on our level is an illusion or distortion, and that if we could only learn to see correctly, through our adoption in Christ, these illusions would vanish? Likewise, from this vantage point, the final petitions (whether four or three) look like requests for one thing when contemplated apart from our adoption in Christ, and requests really for something quite different (namely, in fact, for the realization of the first three petitions in us!) when contemplated from within our deifying adoption in Christ.

That may be more typical of the Eastern approach to the Lord's Prayer. It is a hauntingly beautiful approach, and an icon-based theology of beauty is in many ways typical of the East. The first three petitions are celebrations in a way of the divine glory or of that glory attracting us through beauty. As we move to the second set of petitions, are we praying that the beauty of the first set transfigure the realities of the second set? St. John of Damascus wrote that "the icon is a hymn of triumph, a manifestation, a memorial inscribed for those who have fought and conquered, humbling the demons and putting them to flight." Is that what we are doing as we pray this second

The "We" Petitions

set of petitions, namely, are we slowly fighting and conquering, putting the demons to flight? And as we do, do we become a hymn of triumph?[2] I have also noted among Eastern theologians a tendency to treat of the Lord's Prayer within the context of the Divine Liturgy of the Eucharist or of the offices of the church (Matins, Vespers, etc.). This liturgical infrastructure would tend to add even more emphasis to this iconic, deification interpretation of the Lord's Prayer.

But that approach is not without its dangers. Do we honor the earth because it has been transformed into heaven, or because its being earthly is precisely its blessing for us? Must the tree be cut down and turned into an icon before it is a reflection of the divine beauty? Or is its deifying splendor somehow resident in its being a tree? Of course, sound Eastern Christian theology would agree about the dangers of extreme spiritualism. I am speaking only of a danger. Still, it might be appropriate to say that the East has had a tendency to stress the Divine *in* the earthly and human, and the West perhaps the earthly and human *as* the locus of the Divine. The East is more Johannine; the West, at least somewhat more than the East, more in the footsteps of the Synoptic Gospels. Earthly bread, quite apart from manna or eucharistic food or the spiritual "bread" of feasting on God's word, is quite simply holy. As we pray for forgiveness and freedom from evil, we are praying not only that creatures be transfigured but that they be truly themselves as well. Evil distorts our reality, while grace restores it, even if with Christ grace brings blessings even greater than creation could be without Christ.

Perhaps matters are even simpler. Thinking in an incarnational manner, maybe we should avoid the kind of dualistic, left brain thinking that pits heaven against earth, deification against humanization and cosmification. That is to render God and creatures competitors, whereas incarnation breaks through that kind of dualism. In this way the two sets of petitions, the You and the We, are two in one, like Jesus in his divinity and humanity. At times this perhaps helps us to glimpse the divine in the cosmic and human in ways we could hardly imagine. This might be the typical Eastern icon. But at other times it enables us to glimpse the human and cosmic in the divine in ways we could also hardly imagine. The stunning Coptic icon of friendship, which portrays Christ and a friend holding each other up as friends, with the friend supplying Christ's feet on earth, might well be an

2. John of Damascus, *On the Divine Images*, 59.

example of this kind of icon.³ The reader may want to revisit our earlier thoughts in chapter three about how the Prayer is structured, the medium in relation to the message. These thoughts here are a further amplification of that.

> **Give us this day our daily bread (Matt 6:11).**
> **Give us each day our daily bread (Luke 11:3).**

Luke Timothy Johnson suggests that the most difficult matter in interpreting these texts is the phrase shared by both Matthew and Luke, *ton arton ton epiousion*, which is translated here by the New Revised Standard Version as "daily bread." That word *epiousion* so far has not been found anywhere else in Greek literature, so the interpreter is left solely with its etymology and context here as a guide. Origen (d. c. 254) and Jerome (d. 420), who was influenced by Origen, translated this word as "supersubstantial." In Origen we find a very spiritual (more in the sense of not being material or flesh-like) view of the bread for which we ask; that bread becomes something nourishing our rational natures, and for Origen that is most fittingly "the Word who was with God in the beginning" (John 1:1). As we are nourished by this Word, we are in fact praying "to be made divine." Origen comes to this interpretation by way of a conviction that the term *epiousion* is related to the word *ousia*, which means "essence," which in some Greek philosophy was the incorporeal "principle underlying reality." The Word in the beginning is, of course, this principle. The reader will be able to see here in Origen's interpretation one form of the Eastern view of deification: As we are nourished by the divine Word, we become divine.[4]

Origen used only Matthew's version of the Lord's Prayer,[5] whereas Jerome noted both Matthew's and Luke's versions, following Origen's interpretation of *epiousion* as *supersubstantialem* only for Matthew's version. Jerome gave the meaning of "daily" (*quotidianum*, in Latin) to the word in Luke. Perhaps Jerome was disposed to follow Origen's use of "supersubstantial" for Matthew because of his belief, following a line begun by Papias, that Matthew was originally written in Hebrew. Hence Jerome looked to Semitic influences for Matthew, among which was the word *ma-*

---

3. See "Icon of Christ and His Friend."
4. Origen, *On Prayer* 7–13, 178–84.
5. Ibid., 21, 159.

har (either Aramaic or Syriac for "tomorrow") found in the lost *Gospel of the Nazarenes*, a word that Jerome thought gave a more eschatological (the age to come) interpretation to *epiousion*.[6] Incidentally, it is not clear that Jerome and Origen necessarily mean entirely the same thing when they use the word "supersubstantial." Perhaps we might suggest that the term gives a more "spiritual," otherworldly tone to the bread for which Matthew asks, and in that sense Origen and Jerome overlap.

What do today's exegetes say? Luke Timothy Johnson thinks the term "'supernatural bread,' favored by some patristic writers," is "the least likely" way to translate *epiousion*. "The three likely options are: 1) 'daily,' 2) 'future,' and 3) 'necessary.'" Since he is interpreting Luke's version, however, he favors the third option, "necessary," given "the narrative context which emphasizes going without provisions and depending on hospitality for provisions." In essence we are praying for "the bread we need." The context in Luke 10, just prior to the Lord's Prayer, is the story of the good Samaritan, who risked his possessions to help another, and the hospitality shown Jesus by Martha and Mary. Presumably "supernatural bread" (this likely refers to Origen's and Jerome's *supersubstantialem*) would give too much of an otherworldly, spiritualist emphasis to a much more this-worldly context.[7]

But biblical exegesis is not an exact science. Johnson prefers "necessary," at least for Luke's version of this petition, but he recognizes other possibilities. We are back with the challenge of multiple meanings. Sometimes one or more may be central, and others more "softly" present. Another interpreter, David Balch, notes that "interpreters typically ask whether [the bread] is ordinary bread or the eschatological bread of the messianic banquet (Isa 25:6–8; see Exod 16:8)." This seems similar to saying that the bread may be "daily/necessary" or "future," using Johnson's categories. Balch likewise thinks that there is "an irreducible economic component that some interpreters try to eliminate," found in the first beatitude (Luke 6:20) as well as in this petition (Luke 11:3). "If we interpret the Lord's Prayer in light of Jesus' first beatitude, 'Blessed are you beggars, for yours is the kingdom of God,' the petition for bread is also eschatological." These beggars, the

---

6. See sources in Stevenson, *The Lord's Prayer*, 74. Origen, *On Prayer* 13–17, 183–86, for his views on eschatology; it seems to be a very realized eschatology, whereas Matthew has a more already/not yet perspective, although the not yet dimension may be very near. For Jerome: "In the Gospel that is called 'according to the Hebrews,' for the words, 'bread to sustain our lives' I found the word 'Mahar,' which means '[bread] for tomorrow.'" (Jerome, *Commentary on Matthew* 6:11, 205.)

7. Johnson, *The Gospel of Luke*, 177–78.

"'poor,' that is laborers and artisans, lacked the 'necessities of daily life.'" Quite helpfully, however, this "economic" perspective leads him to suggest that we may be dealing with "a false alternative" in these interpretations. As reminiscent of the beatitudes, the bread seems eschatological. But as evoking the poors' lack of daily necessities, that bread seems very ordinary and necessary.[8]

Harrington, in interpreting Matthew's version of this petition, renders *epiousion* as "coming"; hence we are asking for bread for the coming day. But as he works out what this means, he seems to try to avoid dualistic alternatives. "Coming" as the translation "might refer to the eschatological Day of the Lord (as the previous petitions suggest), or as a morning prayer it could allude to the food necessary to survive for the rest of the day." Recall that Harrington had suggested that the Lord's Prayer may have functioned as an early Christian shortened and eschatological "version" of the Jewish Eighteen Benedictions (the *Amidah*) prayed daily. Harrington even seems to open up some room for the "supersubstantial" interpretation, "which is connected with the eucharist in Christian piety, [and] may carry an allusion to the manna provided for Israel in the wilderness."[9]

Whereas Matthew writes that we are praying that we be given "this day" or "today" (*sēmeron*) our *ton arton ton epiousion* (daily/tomorrow's/necessary/supersubstantial bread), Luke prays that this bread be given "each day" or "day by day" (*kath' hēmeran*). Luke is using the present tense imperative, meaning something like "keep giving us," whereas Matthew, as we have seen, is using the completive aorist tense in Greek. That seems to give his thought a more eschatological tone: now is the limited time for the receiving of the bread promised in the final days.

Gerald O'Collins suggests reading these texts along the lines of the Israelite exodus experience, given Jesus' and his disciples' Jewish formation. As God provided the Jews with their daily manna (see Exod 16:8, 12), so now will he continue to so provide. This would seem to cohere with Luke's emphasis upon being given our bread "each" day. But it may also be thought of eschatologically: that is, the bread is the sign that we are now with Jesus' kingdom entering into the time of the final promises (see the "heavenly banquet" theme: Matt 22:1–14; 25:10; Luke 14:15–24). The Gospel of John explicitly links the bread of life which Jesus brings with the heavenly manna

---

8. Balch, "Luke," 1128.
9. Harrington, *The Gospel of Matthew*, 95.

(John 6:25–40). This more eschatological slant would then cohere with Matthew's version as well. And both Luke and Matthew describe Jesus as saying not to worry about what we are to eat and drink . . . God will provide (Luke 12:22–28; Matt 6:25–34).

The use of the apparently rare word *epiousion* begs for some interpretation. It almost seems similar to the choice of another rare word in Greek writing, namely *agape*. Did Matthew and Luke think that Jesus was pointing to something very special and unique in his preaching and work? If so, it would make sense again to come back to the eschatological dimension: now is the uniquely special time of the realization of the promises. At the same time, this special time of the "now" continues on, it seems. We are in an in-between, already and not yet special time, in which we experience anticipatory moments of the future fullness we await. The last supper may well have been one of those special moments. Jesus' resurrection was of course *the* paradigmatic moment of that fullness making itself felt.

A eucharistic resonance, then, is also not far away, which John 6:25–71 seems to suggest in the discourse on the bread of life which the Son of Man brings. The link between the Passover and the eucharistic final meal of the disciples with Jesus also hints of a reference back to the manna (Mark 14:14, 22–25; Matt 26:18, 26–29; Luke 22:15–20).[10]

If we put all of this together, then, it would seem that the bread for which this petition asks is thickly layered: necessary and daily, if we are to continue building the reign of God; coming, both every day as we work our way through the day and "definitively" or eschatologically, with the "Last Day's" arrival; eucharistic, as we are nourished in this new Passover time; and more "softly" but possibly also supersubstantial, inasmuch as this word points to the eschatological and transcendental dimension of the reign of God. But it is supersubstantial without being anti-earthly or antibodily, pace Origen and his line of interpretation.

And forgive us our debts, as we also have forgiven our debtors (Matt 6:12).

And forgive us our sins, for we ourselves forgive everyone indebted to us (Luke 11:4).

In the rich manifold of our primary experience, where life's many dimensions are united, sometimes blessedly and pleasantly, and sometimes

---

10. See Cranfield, "Bread," 37–38, and O'Collins, *The Lord's Prayer*, 85–90.

in tension and friction, being nourished (the prior petition for bread) and being forgiven as well as forgiving (this petition)—or at least asking to be forgiven—often go hand in hand.[11] Our families feed us, our earth supplies us, our animals are sacrificed for us, but at times, even within the same family or clan, some are not so well nourished, while others seem over-nourished. And among the over-nourished are those blithely unaware of their neighbors' plights, and worse, those who are actively exploiting some for their own narcissistic benefit, including our animate fellow creatures. In other words, creation and the yearning for liberation because of evil and sin go hand in hand. That is how a more conceptual, "secondary" theology would put it. Another way to put this is to say that history seems to follow a threefold very general pattern: from (1) creation to (2) evil and sin to (3) liberation and salvation (at least in hope). At least this is typically how the Semitic religions of Judaism, Christianity, and Islam think of it in roughly equivalent ways. And perhaps in today's global world we will notice more and more a similar pattern of thinking in other religious traditions.

So perhaps we have another instance of Crossan's biblical crescendo parallelism at work here in the movement of these petitions. Remember how such parallelisms reflect how various things are "contained" in one another, like smaller boxes in larger boxes, or circles within larger circles. But as we take each box out or concentrate on each circle, we find something a bit different and new. So as we strive to realize the reign of God and to do its will by aligning our lives and wills with it, and as we hallow the divine name and resist trying to "manipulate" God, we recognize that we need the nourishment of "bread" in all its senses, and we also, in the light of the hallowing of the name and in the light cast by the various realizations of the holy kin-dom, recognize our own need for either forgiving or being forgiven. Our primary experience is a kind of crescendo parallelism, and the Lord's Prayer, emerging from the soil of that experience, manifests that simple but complex reality.

Matthew uses a Greek word for "debts" (*opheilēmata*), whereas Luke uses the word for "sins" (*hamartias*), while retaining "debtors" in the second clause. The image of "debts" is sometimes a Jewish way of referring to offenses against God and others: "The wicked borrow, and do not pay back,

---

11. The writings of Baron Friedrich von Hügel are a good place to go for thinking through the tensions and frictions of primary experience. See Kelly, *Baron Friedrich von Hügel's Philosophy of Religion*. Hügel, *The Mystical Element of Religion*, is probably the key work to consult.

The "We" Petitions

but the righteous are generous and keep giving" (Ps 37:21). In other words, "debt" functions as a metaphor for "sin."

The image of "debt" is ambiguous, however. Are all forms of debt sinful? Psalm 37 seems to have in mind debts that remain unpaid. There is something not quite right about the debt situation. Perhaps, from the side of the debtor, resentment and anger might be involved, not to mention simply ignoring one's obligations to repay, which can lead to sinful actions. And from the side of the one who places someone in debt, forms of anger, haughtiness, and other dispositions might arise that sinfully complicate the debt situation. Attention to anger and resentment is a noted theme in Matthew's presentation of Jesus. "If you are angry with a brother or sister, you will be liable to judgment" (Matt 5:22). Origen, in his commentary on the Lord's Prayer, seems to be aware of this ambiguity regarding the symbol "debt," referring to "unpaid" debts rather than all debts as "sin." And insightfully Origen notes that we are all in a debt to God that can never be repaid. This is not necessarily sinful, although it may lead us to resentment and anger, and in that way there may be a sinfulness about it.[12]

The image of debt also evokes our social obligations, suggesting the possible social dimension of our sinning, when sin occurs. The use of the word "our" also goes along with this. In this way it deprivatizes our sense of sin. It pressures us to think of how we treat others, of our mutual obligations within society. This is true, both from the side of the one who loans, and from the side of the one in debt. In a way, living in society as we do, we are all in various ways in debt to others, often in ways we will never clearly understand. If we do not recognize that, what does that suggest about our moral behavior? Those who only believe others are in debt to them might well want to ponder this. Likewise, from the perspective of those in debt, perhaps they have obligations—to family, perhaps—making it impossible for them to repay their debts. Not all unpaid debts need be sinful. And perhaps something of this is implied in the seventh Jubilee Year of the remission of debts (Deut 15:1–2). This last aspect of the Jubilee Year seems especially relevant to Jesus' master theme of the reign of God, a new kind of inclusive community and of relationships. Perhaps, if we are all truly one family, all debts may be forgiven? Luke's Jesus, we might recall, invokes the theme of the Jubilee Year as an aspect of the new reign of God (Luke 4:18–19).

---

12. Origen, *On Prayer* 28, 187–92.

We can see, then, that the symbol "debt" is many-layered indeed. Did Matthew's Jesus have all of this in mind? Luke seems to focus on sinful forms of debt here in this petition for forgiveness; although, maybe not? He does note in the second clause that we seek to forgive anyone "indebted" (*ophelonti*) to us. In other parts of his Gospel we certainly come upon the theme of debts and forgiveness (Luke 7:41; 16:5, 7; 17:10) in a wider sense as well. So perhaps Luke's Jesus, too, along with Matthew's Jesus, is somewhat ambiguous. Are we speaking only of sins, or also of sinful forms of debt, or of all forms of debt, sinful or not? This is a good example of the surplus of meaning at work.[13] It is also a good example of the thick stew which our primary experiences and symbols are.[14]

However, this petition is not only about debts or sins, but perhaps more importantly it is about forgiveness, our being forgiven by the Father, and our own forgiving of others. Matthew's Jesus tells the story about a person who is forgiven his debt by his lord but refuses to forgive another's debt in turn (Matt 18:21–35). The lord, summoning him, said: "I forgave you all that debt . . . should you not have had mercy on your fellow slave, as I had mercy on you?" (Matt 18:32–33). O'Collins' comment on this is illuminating, bringing out "the magnitude of God's prior forgiveness towards us." "Over against the mind-boggling debt owed to the king . . . nearly 4 billion US dollars, anything that might be owed to us is as small as the debt owed to the unmerciful servant . . . US $9,000."[15] Luke's Jesus, similarly, models forth the image of forgiveness (1:77; 3:3; 5:20–21). Note O'Collins' view that our forgiveness follows God's *prior* forgiveness of us. We will see that this issue emerges in the later tradition.

---

13. See Saldarini, "Matthew," 1018, and Balch, "Luke," 1028.

14. Crossan, *The Greatest Prayer*, chapter 7, 143–62, makes a very strong case for reading "debts" literally, and not as a metaphor for "sins," but argues that in the present context of the synoptics, it needs to be read as both "debt" and "sin." "Indeed, the ultimate challenge may be to ponder their interaction. And, at least for the biblical tradition, when debt creates too much inequality, it has become sinful" (160).

15. O'Collins, *The Lord's Prayer*, 94–95.

The "We" Petitions

And do not bring us to the time of trial, but rescue us from the evil one (Matt 6:13).

And do not bring us to the time of trial (Luke 11:4).

Matthew and Luke have Jesus introduce the very Jewish notion of being tested or tried in some way by God, along with the notion of asking that we be rescued from it. "The Lord tests the righteous and the wicked" (Ps 11:5); "Prove me, O Lord, and try me; test my heart and mind" (Ps 26:2). The word used is *peirasmos*. Both Matthew 4:1–11 and Luke 4:1–13 had earlier given great attention to the trials or "temptations" of Jesus, and thus apparently we disciples can expect nothing different. Jesus, like those who pray this petition, asked his Father to spare him the "coming trial" of crucifixion (Matt 26:39; Mark 14:35–36). "Pray that you may not come into the time of trial (*peirasmon*)," Jesus likewise tells his disciples at Gethsemane (Luke 22:40, 46). The ongoing story of the early church as narrated in Acts by Luke illustrates over and over again the many trials and struggles of Jesus' disciples: Peter (Acts 11:2–3), Stephen (Acts 7:52–54), and Paul (Acts 21:21–22; 22:21–22).[16]

Again, within the manifold of primary experience, trials and struggles are there aplenty, but so too is the felt experience and realization that all is in the hands of the divine Mystery, and that somehow the Mystery permits and guides us throughout. This is all very dimly "understood," and the Scriptures and later tradition manifest a long and circuitous history of grappling in a more conceptual manner with what all of this confusing mix of realities means. Do we always merit our trials? Why are some spared, and others not? Why would God allow such things in the first place? Is our testing something to build our character, or something more in the line of a punishment for our misdeeds, or a mix of these? Paul manifests much of this in a more reflective way here and there in his writings. Here is a particularly relevant text: "No testing has overtaken you that is not common to everyone. God is faithful, and he will not let you be tested beyond your strength, but with the testing he will also provide the way out so that you may be able to endure it" (1 Cor 10:13; cf James 1:13).

Matthew's version adds at this point the plea for rescue from the evil one, using the very ambiguous word *ponēros*, which might be translated, as here in the New Revised Standard Version, more "personally" or anthropomorphically as "the evil one," or more abstractly, on the other hand,

---

16. Balch, "Luke," 1128.

as simply "evil in general." If we read "the evil one," then this would easily evoke "Satan," which may well be what Matthew has in view, given his likely eschatological sensitivity. For the end time is the time of the final battle with Satan: "But if it is by the Spirit of God that I cast out demons, then the kingdom of God has come to you" (Matt 12:28). As Jesus was "led up by the Spirit into the wilderness to be tempted by the devil" (Matt 4:1), so throughout his ministry and that of his disciples the battle with Satan and his demons is taking place (Matt 12:24).[17] If we follow Crossan here, which I do on this point, we need to treat Matthew's petition as one whole in some way, for it is another example of climactic and synonymous parallelism, but "in negative/positive format" (also known as antithetical parallelism): "do not bring us to the time of trial" (= the negative), "but rescue us from the evil one" (= the positive). "Those two lines are mutually interpretive," like all forms of biblical parallelism.[18]

It is at this point that some later Latin and Greek manuscripts of Matthew add the doxology, "For yours is the kingdom, and the power, and the glory, forever. Amen," perhaps echoing 1 Chronicles 29:11–12 and early Christian liturgical practice, as well as Jewish liturgical practice, which "seals" prayers in this manner. The reader may want to revisit chapter two, where we studied the doxology more fully.

Surplus of Meaning in Past Tradition

With respect to the fourth petition, that for our bread, it will come as no surprise that all or nearly all of the views expressed by our biblical study above surface. We probably ought to note that it is not always possible to tell whether a particular author in the postbiblical tradition wants to offer an "exhaustive" interpretation or not. Sometimes we have occasional explanations directed toward concrete pastoral needs. However, writers like Augustine and Thomas Aquinas, given their width of interests or pastoral concerns, and at least in Aquinas' case, a wonderful talent for synthetic thinking, offer all or nearly all of the biblical views we have already mentioned. And both of them had some knowledge of the Eastern Christian tradition as well, which makes them more representatively ecumenical.

---

17. See Schofield, "Adversary," 17–18.
18. Crossan, *The Greatest Prayer*, 167.

The "We" Petitions

More specifically, an early Eastern theological trend, seen in Gregory of Nyssa and John Chrysostom,[19] for example, thought of the bread as the material food or materials in general we need for survival, and Luther and Calvin, along with some early Anglican writers, followed them in this matter. Luther is quite fascinating on this, making a point of including our need for the "nourishment" provided by government a part of this petition's meaning. In this way he offers something of a "political" dimension to the petition.

> And there is, indeed, the greatest need to pray for temporal authority and government, as that by which most of all God preserves to us our daily bread and all the comforts of this life. For though we have received of God all good things in abundance, we are not able to retain any of them or use them in security and happiness, if He did not give us a permanent and peaceful government. For where there are dissension, strife, and war, there the daily bread is already taken away, or at least checked. Therefore it would be very proper to place in the coat-of-arms of every pious prince a loaf of bread instead of a lion, or a wreath of rue, or to stamp it upon the coin, to remind both of them and their subjects that by their office we have protection and peace, and that without them we could not eat and retain our daily bread.[20]

The Latin or Western writers, on the other hand, tended to think of the petition as one of asking to be nourished by the eucharistic bread. And as suggested, Augustine, Aquinas, Jeremy Taylor and some others opted for multiple meanings: the bread is normal food, it is also God's word nourishing us, and it is in a very special way the eucharistic food. "We are praying for the needful daily bread for the body, and the consecrated visible Bread, and the invisible bread of the Word of God," wrote Augustine in his commentary on the Sermon on the Mount.[21]

Aquinas echoes Augustine's breadth of interpretation, but also brings some fresh accents. We are praying for "sacramental bread and for the bread of God's word." We are asking that "it may profit us unto salvation." And he writes that consequently "we derive the happiness which is a hunger for justice." Is this an echo of a more Matthewlike eschatological thrust, which places this petition and the entire Lord's Prayer within the context of the

---

19. Stevenson, *The Lord's Prayer*, 47–51.
20. Luther, *The Large Catechism*, 73, 75.
21. Augustine, *Commentary on the Lord's Sermon on the Mount*, 135.

beatitudes? In connection with this, in his collection of patristic writings, he cites a text which emphasizes how the Eucharist is already a foretaste of resurrection joy. It is "that bread of everlasting life . . . . [Whoever] has a wound seeks to be cured . . . . The cure is the heavenly and [awesome] sacrament. If you receive daily, daily does 'Today' come to you. Christ is to you Today, Christ rises to [you] daily."[22]

Discussions on the fifth petition for forgiveness, so far as I can tell, either assume that "debts" is but a metaphor for "sins," or simply concentrate on "sins" of various types. The Council of Trent puts these offenses within the general context of the cross that all Christians are called to bear, and that might offer an opening to a wider consideration of "debts" as also needing to be considered.[23] That is, as we noted above, are our human debts within society something we seek forgiveness for, or should we narrow this to only the kinds of debts that are in some way sinful? In any case, human debts would seem to fit under the general category of the crosses which we humans have to carry.

When it comes to the second part of this petition—"as we forgive . . ."/"for we forgive . . ."—we find some diversity and debate. Is this second clause expressing a condition, that is, will the Father only forgive us if we forgive others? Or is it unconditional in some way? That is, God always offers forgiveness, whether we forgive others or not. And when we do offer forgiveness to others, we are in some way reflecting God's own prior grace of love and forgiveness to us. Gregory of Nyssa had suggested that God imitates us, that is, as we forgive others, then God manifests the same kind of forgiveness to us. Bishop Stevenson considers this to be an "exaggerated view of forgiveness." Gregory had written: ". . . God wants your disposition toward the good to be an example to him! The order of things is somehow reversed!"[24] We would need to place this observation of Gregory's within the entire context of his theology of the incarnation and grace, however, to bring a balanced perspective to it. That is, is Gregory expressing something of the "exaggeration" of the incarnation in his sentiment, that is, God's humbling of God in becoming human for us?

The sinful woman who kissed and anointed Jesus' feet was forgiven much, since she loved much (Luke 7:36–50). Here we have a sequence

---

22. Aquinas, *In Orationem Dominicam*, 1079, 230; *Catena Aurea*, on Luke 11:1; Murray, *Praying with Confidence*, 70.

23. Stevenson, *The Lord's Prayer*, 169.

24. Ibid., 48; Gregory of Nyssa, "Fifth Homily."

similar to this fifth petition of the Lord's Prayer: She was forgiven *since* she loved. Biblical scholar Luke Timothy Johnson comments: "In line with Jesus' argument, the 'since' is to be understood not as the basis for the forgiveness but as the demonstration of it. Only this reading makes sense of Jesus' extended exposition of her deeds. And the trailer makes it clear: the one who is forgiven little loves little."[25] Part of the context has to do with Jesus' mentioning the story of a creditor who forgave the debts owed him by two debtors, one owing much more than the other. The one owing much more Jesus likens to the woman who anointed his feet, for she would love him more, since he had forgiven her more (Luke 7:41–43). This offers us a biblical way to understand our fifth petition's second clause, I believe.

We might also want to go back to O'Collins' appeal to a lord forgiving his slave's debt, in our explanation of this petition above. We recall that that slave in turn refused to forgive what his fellow slave owed him, to which the Lord said: "I forgave you all that debt . . . should you not have had mercy on your fellow slave, as I had mercy on you?" (Matt 18:32–33). O'Collins makes the important observation that God's forgiveness was the "prior" reality. These stories from Luke and Matthew seem to reflect the biblical pattern: first is the Lord's forgiveness; ours follows from that.

My sense is that the various texts in the early commentators are ambiguous, but that they can be read in the sense suggested by the biblical pattern above. The great Reformers Luther and Calvin wanted to return to this biblical pattern, which would seem to rule out any kind of an at least "autonomous" merit apart from the prior mercy, love, and grace of God. "Be merciful, just as your Father is merciful" (Luke 6:36). Thus, the Reformers manifest the unconditional view of this clause of the fifth petition, that is, no one can merit—autonomously, if you will—God's forgiveness, although our actions of forgiving are a manifestation and a result of our having been forgiven.[26]

That teaching of the Reformers is also echoed, to some extent, in the Roman tradition of theology. Thomas Aquinas, for example, wrote that "no sin could ever be forgiven without charity. Charity covers all faults (Luke 6:36)." Here somewhat ambiguously, Thomas seems to argue for a more conditional view of this fifth petition: Our being forgiven depends on our forgiving others (showing them mercy). And that is partly the case, but

---

25. Johnson, *The Gospel of Luke*, 128.

26. See Calvin, *Institutes of the Christian Religion* 3.20.45; for a good collection of the relevant texts in Martin Luther, go to "Martin Luther's Explanation of the Lord's Prayer."

note that Thomas is citing the text from Luke we just noted: "Be merciful, just as your Father is merciful" (Luke 6:36). Although it is a bit ambiguous, I have the sense from Aquinas that he means that because God is always a God of mercy, we manifest God's own charity in our forgiving of others and showing them mercy. If we do not do this, there is something unreal about our saying the Lord's Prayer. "If, therefore, you say the words with your lips [that is, "Forgive us as we forgive"], fulfill them in your heart."[27]

Aquinas is ambiguous in a way, but his real concern is for the reality in our lives of what the Lord's Prayer should accomplish. His was not the time of the Reformation with its concerns about autonomously "earning" God's grace. His larger theology is well aware that this is not possible. Nonetheless, Aquinas does not seem to be so different from Luther on this petition. "But there is here attached a necessary, yet consolatory addition: As we forgive," Luther writes. And Luther continues, in commenting further on this petition: ". . . He forgives everything through grace . . . not on account of your forgiving, for God forgives freely and without condition, out of pure grace, because He has so promised, as the Gospel teaches, but in order that He may set this up for our confirmation and assurance for a sign . . . ."[28]

But if Aquinas might be thought ambiguous, Teresa of Avila from the Roman Catholic side is not: "Like someone who has accomplished something, we shall think that the Lord pardons us because we have pardoned others. Help us understand, my God, that we do not know ourselves and that we come to You with empty hands; and pardon us through Your mercy."[29]

The sixth and final petition — not to be brought to the time of trial and to be delivered from evil/the evil one — may well be the most controversial of all the petitions in the history of the churches, turning on whether God actually wants to lead us into trials or "the trial," or whether God simply "permits" this in some way, or whether God would want us to be able to avoid all trials. To some extent we might glimpse here something of an echo of what kind of God Christians believe in, that is, the loving God of Jesus' *Abba*, or a more punitive notion of God. But even if one opts for the loving *Abba*, then how do we explain the many obvious trials which we undergo in our historical experience?

---

27. See Murray, *Praying with Confidence*, 75, citing Thomas Aquinas, *The Lectures on St. Matthew*, ed. Tugwell, 474–75, and *In Orationem Dominicam*, 1068, 232.

28. Luther, *The Large Catechism*, 93.

29. Teresa of Avila, *The Way of Perfection* 36.6, 180.

The "We" Petitions

The general view, East and West, is that God, who is sovereign over all, somehow "permits" testings and trials of various sorts. "We are shown in this clause that the adversary can do nothing against us unless God allows it beforehand," wrote Cyprian.[30] This is not to say that there are not some difficult cases, in which God seems to more directly bring about our trials. For example, we might think of the *Akedah*, the summons to Abraham to sacrifice his son Isaac (Gen 22:1-19). But the more common and direct causes of our trials are the world, the "flesh" (the traditional term for our human condition), and the devil, to use the three traditional terms.[31]

Our trials are there in bounteous form, and there is simply too much evidence for a believer to draw any other conclusion than that God somehow allows these trials to occur. Origen in many ways is the great expositor of the role of trials in developing our moral and spiritual character. "The utility of testing is something like this: through testing the things which our souls have admitted, unknown to anyone except God, unknown even to ourselves, are made manifest, so that we should no longer be unaware of what kind of people we are, but may recognize this and, should we so wish, perceive our own evil and give thanks for the good things which have been made manifest to us through the testing."[32]

At the same time, we noted Paul's teaching that God will not allow us to be tested beyond our strength (1 Cor 10:13), and even in the case of the *Akedah*, God did finally rescue Isaac from being sacrificed. Jesus was paradigmatically tested in all ways, like us, but without sin (Heb 4:15). Because of our adoption in him, we may draw the conclusion that through him we too will be rescued from the trials we face. That does not mean that we will not face suffering. Jesus, after all, was crucified. But it means that there is a final deliverance, namely, resurrection. All of these themes are noted throughout the tradition in relationship to this last petition.

Finally, we come upon an ongoing difference between East and West over the last part of our last petition. The West, following Augustine, tends

---

30. See Cyprian, *On the Lord's Prayer*, 25, 84, following Tertullian, *On Prayer* 8, 48, perhaps echoing God's permissive, not "direct," will: "Suffer us not to be led" (*ne patiaris induci*); *The Book of Common Prayer*, 364, among others, reflects this in its alternate version: "Save us from the time of trial." Augustine accepts this and "lead us not" as appropriate (Stevenson, *The Lord's Prayer*, 41, 79, 93).

31. See Aquinas, for example, on the world, the flesh, and the devil in his *In Orationem Dominicam*, No. 1095, No. 1098, No. 1096, 233; Murray, *Praying with Confidence*, 84-85; and Luther, *The Large Catechism* 101.

32. Origen, *On Prayer* 29.17, 203; all of 29 is focused on testing (193-204).

toward a more general and "impersonal" view of "evil." The East, on the other hand, leans toward the more "personal" view, namely that we are speaking of the "evil one," Satan. Martin Luther, Trent, and some others in the West, however, seem to hold for both.[33] The East also tended to view this entire petition as one, although made up of two parts. This is similar to the notion, which we followed above, that these two parts are a typical example of biblical parallelism. The West, again following Augustine, separated the two parts, thus ending up with seven rather than six petitions, as we noted earlier.

Contemporary Transitions

Just to refresh our memory: the *modern transition* is a turn to human experience in our manner of reappropriating our Christian beliefs; the *late modern*, a heightening of our consciousness with regard to the sociopolitical and pathological (often "unconscious") dimensions of our experience, striving to avoid a too privatistic and inward understanding of our experience; the *postmodern*, a heightened consciousness of the fragile, humbled, and historical nature of our existence. To some extent, what brought the late modern and postmodern sensitivities about were the outbreaks in our modern time, supposedly the most "rational" of times, of many forms of human irrationality and pathology, personal, "unconscious," and societal: the world wars, which show little sign of letting up; the gulags; the Holocaust, human trafficking, and more. The modern "ego" has been decentered and revealed in all its fragility, even if many refuse to recognize that. And finally we have pointed to the *global transition*, a time in which all peoples and cultures and religions are becoming profoundly aware of one another, with all the tensions and frictions and challenges coming from that. In what way, then, are these final petitions of the Prayer "relevant" to these transitions? Or perhaps better put, in what way can these petitions come into dialogue with these various transitions? What might be the potential surplus of meaning?

By way of a "preface" we might begin by paying attention to the fact that the Lord's Prayer is a series of various forms of "petitionary prayer." We earlier spoke of the Prayer as a form of the genre of prayer, and noted

---

33. See Stevenson, *The Lord's Prayer*, 169; Luther, *The Large Catechism* 113–14; also in Teresa of Avila, *The Way of Perfection* 38–39, 185–92.

The "We" Petitions

the dimensions of adoration/elevation and conversation/communion that typically make up all forms of praying. Sometimes the focus is on the elevation side—hallowing the divine Mystery—and sometimes it is on the more human, conversational side, where we focus upon our own more obvious concerns and "converse" with God about these. But if we step back, we can see how these two sides are always present in some way. If we hallow God's name, we are recognizing our need to do that. If we pray for the kingdom's coming, and the realization of the divine will, we are recognizing our need for these. The focus is upon the divine pole, but the tacit implications flow over onto us. In these concluding three petitions, the focus seems reversed. We "converse" about our needs, focusing upon what these may be, but we tacitly own that it is only as we see these needs in their true light—that is, in the light provided by our hallowing of God and his reign and his will—that we are in the movement of the Prayer itself, letting it pray us.

The modern turn to experience prods us to think about petitionary prayer in some further ways. Why do we humans pray in the first place? Why do we petition God at all, if God is the divine Ground in whose power all is held? As we noted above with respect to the sixth petition—not to be led into temptation, but to be delivered from it—the biblical and postbiblical traditions argue that all things are embraced within God's permissive will, so to speak. God is the "almighty" one, we might say. Is prayer something that helps us only? Can God get along without our prayer, if need be? These are the kinds of questions typical of the "modern" turn to human experience, and perhaps they are questions more common in the developed West than in other territories. But as globalization occurs, perhaps these so-called "modern" and Western questions begin to become everyone's questions.

We have spoken of the difference between primary and secondary experience many times. In the first, we intuitively know that God, humans, cultures, and the world/universe are experienced in a more compact, undistinguished way. On this level, our experiences and symbols are more holistic, less "dualistic," and somehow experience simply leads us to the realization that all of these "partners" in reality somehow work together in a kind of symphonic celebration. God does God's part; we do our part. It seems to work. But of course, there are crises: Tragedies occur, cultures, empires, even religions seem to fail. And so questions arise, pushing primary theology into various forms of secondary theology. The experiences of our modern period have caused this push in many and even massive ways.

But it is well to remember that our modern age is not the first to think about some of these questions. Origen (d. c. 254) actually prefaces his exposition of the Lord's Prayer with a long discussion of these so-called "modern" questions about the role of and need for petitionary prayer. In some ways, Origen was very "modern," for he was one of the church's first great intellectuals and systematic thinkers, well versed in the Greek philosophical tradition of his time. One of the things we may deeply appreciate in Origen is his stress upon the unsurpassable mystery of the Divine. He writes of Paul, for example, who was so well versed in the ways of prayer. He "sees, not only due to the moderation of his nature but also in his honesty, that after all this so much is lacking with regard to knowledge of the manner in which we ought to pray." He references Romans 8:26: ". . . for we do not know how to pray as we ought . . . ." For this we need the Spirit. It is as if Paul and Origen remain rooted in the deep soil of primary experience, and all their recommendations flow from that. When then Origen comes to an attempt at an explanation of our praying, he seems to make an appeal both to the example of Jesus and the saints, but also to our own free will. He seems to be saying that God chooses to work through our free will. ". . . it is impossible to assent to any statement of human affairs which leaves no place for our free will."[34]

Archbishop Rowan Williams offers us a good commentary on Origen's approach:

> Origen's little book on prayer is the first really systematic treatment of the subject by a Christian. And one of the questions he asks is one you probably have asked yourself from time to time: "If God knows what we are going to ask, why bother to pray?" Origen has as good an answer as anyone has given: God knows, of course, what we are going to say and do, but God has decided that he will work out his purposes through what we decide to say and do. So if it is God's will to bring something about, some act of healing or reconciliation, some change for the better in the world, he has chosen that your prayer is going to be part of a set of causes that makes it happen. So you'd better get on with it, as you and your prayer are part of God's overall purpose for the situation in which he is going to work. It is a pretty good answer—and it is one that certainly keeps us on our knees working hard, which is just as well.[35]

---

34. Origen, *On Prayer* 6.2, 125; 2.3, 114; see 1–17, 111–52.
35. Williams, "In the Place of Jesus."

The "We" Petitions

Theologian John Macquarrie is well within the tradition of Origen on this matter of prayer, and shares with Archbishop Williams a similar perspective. It is what he refers to as "unitive Being," that is, the Holy Spirit, which draws us into prayer. Our prayer is a response to Being's self-communication, "a communication that is possible because Being is immanent in every being." It is not simply a subjective attempt to "produce a right frame of mind" in the one who prays. Referring to the prayer for the coming of the kingdom, we might well think of this as a "strengthening of one's own commitment to Christ's kingdom . . . [but] may we not also believe that the sincere prayer of faith is a strengthening of the movement of Being itself in its threefold action of creation-reconciliation-consummation? For this . . . is not something that proceeds just automatically, but something that needs [our] free response and cooperation."[36]

Questions remain, but at least some attempt must be made not to dodge the questions felt about prayer from long ago, and emerging with new force in today's modern and postmodern world. The context needed to supply the soil out of which much of this may make sense is our primary experience of partnership in the community of being and reality: God, humans, societies, and universe. Beautifully the Lord's Prayer, as it prays us in the Spirit ("unitive Being"), lifts us toward a consciousness of our primary communion with the divine Ground in its first three petitions, aligning our aspirations with the divine Ground's aspirations, and from that perspective brings us to the final petitions looking toward our human needs.

Since I have referred frequently to primary experience within our "primary field," and its always happening movement from remaining tacit in consciousness to a more differentiated awareness and expression in symbols and more narrow concepts, hopefully the following illustration will help.

---

36. Macquarrie, *Principles of Christian Theology*, 494, 496.

> **FIGURE 1**
>
>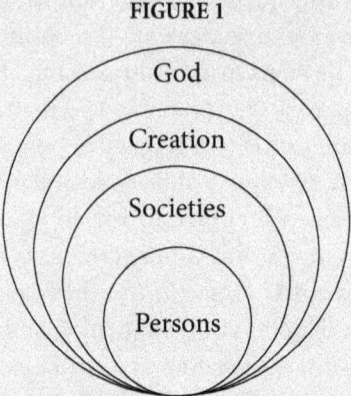
>
> **Our Primary Field of Existence: the Natural Soil of Prayer**
> Right brain
> Holistic/all within a flowing connectivity
> Uses imagination and images/symbols
> Tends to avoid either/or ("dualistic") thinking
> Appreciates depth and mystery
>
> **Secondary Field:**
> More left brain
> Analytic; separating for the sake of narrowing down and grasping; likes clear concepts
> Symbols too fuzzy . . . tends to want to reduce them to clear concepts/ideas ("Let me tell you what the picture means . . ." kind of person)
> Tends toward the either/or, dualistic (which has its place)
> Mystery is an irritant; thinks of reality as a series of "problems" that can be solved.
>
> **Ideally there should be a back and forth between these, all the while realizing we never really leave our primary field, but grow in our consciousness of it; secondary field work can help with this.**

The Lord's Prayer is in many ways an expression of these various and always interconnected dimensions of our primary field or experience in rich symbols: The invocation (epiclesis) and first three petitions look more to the divine Ground, and humans' attempts to align their lives with that, but as rooted in and drawn by the divine Ground. The final three petitions

The "We" Petitions

look more toward cosmos, societies, and history and human persons in various forms of relationships and the "needs" these generate. One of the key challenges for all forms of "secondary," more conceptual attempts to "explain" these matters is that these secondary attempts remain rooted in the larger, primary field, and return to that. As Origen noted about Paul, we pray in the Spirit, and all authentic prayer is flowing along with the Spirit, and ultimately surrendering to that Spirit. "Likewise the Spirit helps us in our weakness; for we do not know how to pray as we ought, but that very Spirit intercedes with sighs too deep for words. And God, who searches the heart, knows what is the mind of the Spirit, because the Spirit intercedes for the saints according to the will of God" (Rom 8:26-27).

This diagram might enable us to imagine the Lord's Prayer in as holistic a manner as possible. I use the word "imagine" deliberately, because our attempts to pin all this down and lock it up into clear conceptualizations need to be severely relativized. Not denied, but relativized. The secondary fields of conceptualization need to return us to the primary field. That, I believe, is one of the blessings of the Lord's Prayer. And our various transitions—modern, late modern, postmodern, and globalization—might well be imagined as various ways in which we are being drawn toward a more holistic consciousness and living out of the Lord's Prayer and its "depths."[37]

Let us work with the fourth petition, for bread. We have seen how biblical scholars and the later tradition come upon various layers of meaning: bread as basic material food and goods; bread as a spiritual nourishment of our souls, bread as the incarnate Word and as Scripture as well; bread as the sacramental, eucharistic food; and bread as the eschatological manna, which is the foretaste of the coming reign of God. These multiple meanings keep emerging throughout the later tradition, not always together, but more serially, almost. It is as if when one dimension is emphasized, another somehow makes its way into our consciousness in rather short order. The realism of our turn to experience pressures us, so to speak, to recover the holistic, Jewish, and biblical way of keeping body and spirit united as one. We do not need to choose one of these over another. In varying ways and

---

37. As mentioned earlier in chapter three, in the section on primary theology and secondary theology, I have been aided by these perspectives as developed in liturgical theology especially. But philosophically I have been especially helped by Voegelin's work on "cosmological order" and on "primary experience," in his *Israel and Revelation*, 51–150, and *The Ecumenic Age*, 118–28, respectively. Wilber, *The Integral Vision*, is doing analogous work, but largely from a social science perspective.

at various times in our pilgrimage each has its place, each is the "manna" of the reign toward which we are moving.

This petition for bread is very earthy and humble as well. It looks to our basic needs. It does not pretend to be lofty. It offers us a spirituality that is very incarnational, which is one of the major reasons it "speaks" to our modern turn to experience. It has all the features of human authenticity. We are not most spiritual when we are aloft in the clouds, but when we are humbly aware of our own and of others' various forms of hunger. Perhaps it will make us revisit our earlier comments about spirituality as the "way of imperfection" more than the "way of perfection"!

In this respect, the eucharistic bread, which nourishes us bodily as well as "spiritually," might be seen as the sacramental icon that brings together for us the multiple dimensions of being nourished. Inasmuch as we recognize that our bread is God's gift and not simply our own, our sense of control and ownership of the goods of the earth begins to be relativized. Although we might like to pretend that we are sitting down at our own table when we eat, we are really being invited to sit down at the Father's table. And that table is much more inclusive than our own. That is all tacitly noted in this fourth petition. And that is why the Eucharist is a thanksgiving experience, a giving of thanks to the provider of our food. And as the one loaf is made up of many grains, so the Father's family is made up of many. And although we do not like to think about it, the bread was broken, as Jesus was broken. This is the "sacrificial" dimension of our being nourished. This links up with the next petition regarding sin and forgiveness, for it is sin and the evil from which it comes that caused the breaking of Jesus. And yet there is something life-giving in this breaking, and this we believe has to do with this breaking as an expression of consummate love on the part of Jesus. Abbot Jeremy Driscoll beautifully gets to the heart of this:

> In our communion with his sacrifice, his perfect forgiveness of others is shared with us. We swallow his energy for love and forgiveness and are empowered to love as he did, far beyond what we could ever accomplish on our own. And thus our trespasses will be forgiven not to the measure of our own puny efforts at forgiving others, but to the measure of Christ himself.[38]

We can see some of the concerns of our other contemporary transitions in these remarks. The late modern awareness of our social formation and of the pathologies, personal and social, which can corrupt entire

---

38. Driscoll, *What Happens at Mass*, 116.

societies, might be seen in our awareness that this fourth petition needs to be widened in a correspondingly social way. And nowadays in a more cosmocentric way. The Father's table is a cosmically wide table, meant for all. "Given for the many," as the eucharistic prayers express it. It is the bread of the kin-dom, the alternative community of inclusive love. Our food is on loan. If people, and animates as a whole, are not receiving their daily bread—material, intellectual, "spiritual"—then this raises questions about ownership. The Lord's Prayer relativizes our absolute ownership. In a global world this will likely become a challenge more and more addressed to each of us. A wholesome "softly" postmodern critique of the ever present tendency of modern, "developed" societies to absolutize themselves at the expense of others, reducing others to mere instruments of themselves, is being sensed here.

This fourth petition manifests a fascinating combination of intimacy and sharing. What is more intimate than eating food? It literally enters into and becomes our very own fabric. And this is likewise true for intellectual and other spiritual forms of nourishment. Body and soul are one, intimately one, and so then are our material and spiritual nourishment. And yet we pray here for *our* bread: We are petitioning for the nourishment of our fellow human beings, but also for all creatures, if we are to move into that neocosmocentrism spoken of earlier. Here the image of the heavenly wedding banquet to which Jesus invites us seems very relevant (Matt 22:1–14; Luke 14:7–24). The "heavens" include us all.

That sense of the "our" perhaps helps us see something of the danger of eating degenerating into boring and lonely narcissistic self-feeding or almost a soul-forgetting materialism when we find ourselves continually unable to share our meals and our table with others. That kind of sharing seems to try to bring out the best in the intimacy of eating, for then this intimacy turns into something social, into love and caring, at least in hope and often in practice. The word *companion* derives from the Latin *cum pane*, "with bread."[39] True companions are those with whom we share bread, "bread" in all the senses of this fourth petition.

In "real" life, of course, food and scarcity are interlocked. That is the way it is in primary experience. Perhaps if we all knew better, it might not be so. But in practical experience, it is so. Some are well nourished; others are malnourished and worse. And so the Lord's Prayer immediately turns to the fifth petition regarding sin and forgiveness. This may well be

---

39. See Ayo, *The Lord's Prayer*, 69.

an example of biblical parallelism too, as I am inclined to think. For if we are truly being given our bread (the fourth petition), then this would imply that we are aware of our hoarding tendencies and are moving beyond them through facing them, seeking forgiveness, and manifesting the fruits of that forgiveness among others (the fifth petition).

As we have noted, Matthew uses the word *debt* and Luke uses the word *sin*, at least in the first clause of our fifth petition. So there is some discussion about whether "debt" is simply a metaphor for "sin," or whether "debt" might not also be a somewhat wider notion. Certain kinds of debts would be considered sinful, of course. Psalm 37:21 provides us with a classical example: "The wicked borrow and do not pay back." Are we to think of all forms of sin as examples of this kind of debt, namely, a debt qualified by something immoral attaching to it? It would not be the debt so much, but the immorality of not repaying that is in focus. And from the other side, we have the debts that people owe, and yet the one who gives the loan forgives the debtors who are unable to repay (Luke 7:42). This last example is more of a refinement on Psalm 37:21, for it indicates that not all refusal to pay back is necessarily immoral. Sometimes debtors simply cannot repay. And when they cannot, does this mean that the one who refuses to forgive the debt is sinful?

And the matter becomes very thick when we consider our relationship with God. For who is not in some kind of debt to God? Is there necessarily something sinful about this fact? Or would certain kinds of attitudes which those of us who are indebted to God might manifest be the sinful matter? For example, we might be resentful of our debts to God, just as we might be resentful of our debts to others. And people can develop a sense of entitlement and prestige when they are in the position of placing people in debt. It is hard to accept that God would act that way, however, although perhaps people have projected that sentiment onto God. And what about our debts to nature and animals? Can we develop attitudes of indifference and callousness toward them? Sometimes it is hard to learn to be dependent.

The language of "debts" does surface the interpersonal and more social dimensions of human existence, and that is helpful. In a way, this fifth petition is one of the most "late modern" petitions in its way of imagining, because it gets us beyond thinking in purely individualist ways of imagining evil and sin. And even more, we may now be led to think through the relationship between the forgiveness of debts and Jesus' master symbol of the reign of God. That reign is a social reality, and debt-talk, as noted,

The "We" Petitions

pushes us in a more social direction. The forgiveness of debts and the being forgiven them might be a rather strong way of thinking of the nature of the reign of God. Perhaps here is a good place to mention the connection some made in the tradition of this petition with the sacrament of penance (or now more commonly of reconciliation). The sacrament expresses both the "Godward" and the "social-ecclesial" dimensions of our sin.

Can we push this further and imagine a form of society in which there are no debts, in which debts and, most radically, even debt-thinking would not exist? This would be a way of imagining that is in more conformity with mutuality and love rather than with a kind of exchange approach to existence, where as one gives, the other returns in kind. Is the parable of the prodigal son (Luke 15:11–32), for example, illustrative of an exchange, debt-laden "economy," or of an entirely different "economy" altogether? Is this what is behind the celebrated Jubilee Year (Deut 15:1–2), with its remission of debts, even if those Jubilees never fully happened concretely? Is that a foretaste of the radicality of Jesus' new reign of God? Does Jesus' God, for example, want us to think of ourselves as in debt, or does that God want us to move beyond that? If so, this would then be a warrant for thinking of this fifth petition as radical indeed, for it would then mean seeking a form of existence of no sin, no sinful debts, and even of no debt. That is clearly utopian apart from grace, but if we remember that the Lord's Prayer in Matthew comes within the Sermon on the Mount, and that it follows the beatitudes, and that it is the prayer of the in-between eschatological times, perhaps this is not so utopian? "Owe no one anything, except to love one another," said Paul (Rom 13:8). The utterly decentered self, so celebrated in some forms of postmodern discourse, which has broken through the pretended absolutisms of the autonomous ego, or the autonomous society, peeks out at us here in some way.

As we noted, in the postbiblical tradition discussion typically turned to whether God's forgiveness was conditioned upon our forgiveness of others: "as we also have forgiven our debtors" (Matt 6:12). This again moves us back into the kind of thinking typical of an exchange economy, if we come to accept this conditional interpretation. It gets us quickly into the kind of merit-thinking against which the Reformers revolted. In exchange for our doing such and such, God will respond in kind. Both Luther and Calvin, and Teresa of Avila after them, were very clear that the "as" clause did not indicate the cause of God's forgiveness, but rather manifested it, which is also the biblical teaching as well. "I forgave you all that debt . . . should you not have had mercy . . . as I had mercy on you?" (Matt 18:32–33). As spiritual writer and Franciscan Richard Rohr expresses it: "There are two utterly different forms of religion: one believes that God will love me if I change; the other believes that God loves me so that I can change!"[40]

Trials, evil, and the evil one (Satan) are not far from our imaginations, as we ponder debts, sins, and the mystery of forgiveness. In the primary field of our experience, they are interlocking phenomena. Being forgiven our debts and sins would certainly be another way of speaking of being delivered from evil. Again, here we have another form of our crescendo, ever-growing biblical parallelism in the Lord's Prayer. As we spiral along one intuition, going a bit deeper, we stumble upon another; in this case, the mystery of evil. Of course, we believe that the crescendo effect is not the evil, but the liberation from it. If this truly be the climax of these ever-crescendoing petitions, then we are back where we began. Our own hallowing of God's hallowed name manifests itself in God's own liberation of the divine family from the anti-hallower. The ending is the beginning. But it is a new beginning of the beginning.

We saw earlier that an irritating question for some of the postbiblical tradition was how it was that Jesus and his followers could even offer the petition not to be led into temptation. Did this not necessarily "project" onto God a responsibility for temptation, thus embroiling the Divine in the mystery of evil and sin? Perhaps, looking back, some of the irritation caused by this persisting question can be alleviated by the recovery of the genre of biblical parallelism, and its presence here in the various petitions of the Lord's Prayer. For, following this genre's lead, if we think of the second clause of Matthew's version as the "parallel" to the first, then we might appropriately interpret the first clause by way of the second. It would be the second that offers us the "new" insight into the first clause, the "new twist," so to speak. That would indicate that being rescued from the evil one is the or at least another meaning unlocking the potential meaning of the first clause. God is not a tempter; God is rather a deliverer from temptations. It is not that God sometimes leads us into temptations, and sometimes does not, perhaps when we pray this petition. That would land us back into that exchange kind of thinking that Jesus seems to be seeking to move us beyond. Jesus' God is always a deliverer from evil, not a lurer toward it.

---

40. Rohr, *What the Mystics Know*, 104. Rohr, in his daily meditations online, frequently talks about the exchange approach to life, and how different the mystical approach is.

The "We" Petitions

But the problem of trials and temptations in the sense of contests with evil or the evil one, still remains. Biblical parallelism might ease the problem; it does not erase it. The tradition from very early on knew that God is supreme and almighty, and if so, at a minimum God must be said to somehow "permit" the existence of evil and sin. Is not this mere "permission" itself a kind of delivering us into temptation? We might respond that if God truly be the deliverer, then God is there with us always in the trial. We are never alone. Somewhat like a parent ready to help his or her child, although knowing that as the child grows one must step back and restrain one's presence as much as possible. The presence can be there as a kind of safeguard, and perhaps at times it may more actively intervene. But for the most part, it restrains itself. Why? So that the child can become an adult. Along the lines of Origen's view that in the testing virtue is developed.

This line of questioning, long present in the tradition and showing no signs of letting up, might be a sign of maturity, as long as it is not used as one of those "arguments" disproving God's existence, which has been a line of thinking long present in the tradition as well. We are growing up in some ways with respect to how we imagine God. But perhaps if we are truly to hallow the divine name, truly to reverence the Mystery and strive to avoid any form of manipulation of the Divine, we must at some point surrender to a surplus of irrationality that explodes our comprehension. For though there may be many fine examples of great virtue coming through the fires of testing, there are far too many examples of iniquity that would seem to offer very little if any virtuous consolation in the history of creation. This is the stubborn and painful reality of the mystery of iniquity in its fuller amplitude: the suffering of the innocent, the magnitude of pain unleashed, the mystery of the suffering of our animate companions too throughout history. God delivers us from evil? Perhaps so. But if so, it would seem that much of this could only occur in another "dimension" of reality, what is sometimes called the "afterlife" or "end time" (eschatological) realm of existence.

The reader will notice that we have strayed rather far from our "primary field of experience and symbolization" in these last thoughts. We are in the thicket of conceptual, secondary theology and philosophy, and we have only been able to get so far. In many ways, thoughts like these have emerged with an ever greater intensity because of the modern and late modern and even postmodern transitions. We may think of them as signs of our growing up, in a way. Some would argue that "God has to grow up."

But from within the perspective of this great Prayer, we might rather argue that "we should grow up." That is a good lesson for us. When some people say that "God must grow up," they might be thinking rather of our own infantile projections onto God. The primary field is just too dense, too deep, for us to ever expect more than a very limited clarity. We are brought back to a consciousness of our inadequacy, of our non-control. That is why these thoughts are arising within the context of petitionary prayer. Maybe the mystery of iniquity can lead us into a deeper experience of what petitioning really means.

Petitioning, not as an exchange form of bartering, but as a form of hallowing the divine name, a form of knowing we cannot manipulate by making any "deals," is a gesture of hope. It would seem to imply that evil is a contrast reality, something known only by contrast with its negation. That is, a sense of the good, of the possible triumph of love, may well be what fills us with a consciousness of the utter irrationality of evil. And so we keep petitioning, which is hoping.

The trial is a contest with evil. Or with the evil one. As we noted, the postbiblical tradition wavered on this, and the Greek in Matthew's version might mean either. As we may recall, the translation of the Greek *ponēros* as "the evil one" evokes the figure of Satan and seems to go along with Matthew's more eschatological perspective. For Satan is the endtime figure with whom Jesus is doing battle: "But if it is by the Spirit of God that I cast out demons, then the kingdom of God has come to you" (Matt 12:28). Satan is the Beelzebub who leads the kingdom of devils (Matt 12:26–27), and so as Jesus enters the contest with the demons, he enters it with Satan.

What might be gained for us in deeper understanding if we remain with "Satan" language? This need not necessarily be a replacement of "evil" language, as the tradition and even Scripture indicate. The realities of evil —whether personal or social or even cosmic—and the reality of demons and Satan seem to overlap. That is why Satan is so formidable. But does the language of "Satan" add something helpful for us? Since the modern turn to experience, the tendency has been to replace Satan-talk with evil-talk. The tendency has been to "demythologize" Scripture, to remove the layer of "myth," and to find clear replacements for what the mythical talk of Satan might mean in terms of our human and social and even cosmic experience. But the postmodern transition has grown uneasy with the notion that myth is outdated, that we can live without the myth. Thinking that we can is one of those hubristic pretensions of modernity.

The "We" Petitions

Is this another way of suggesting that the primary field of our existence is simply too thick and profound to be reduced to neatly delineated concepts? There is a mysterious depth to it which only the language of symbol can suggest. For example, the symbol of the "kingdom of Satan" found in Matthew 12:26 suggests a profound interconnection between all forms of evil. As a kingdom it is a sort of structure, a kind of situational organization, that has the ability to transmit and even outlast the actions of the people who first constitute it, thus placing more and more people and creatures in positions of "trial" or temptation. Is this connected with that "sin of the world" found in John 1:29? In other words, the primary "field" of which we have spoken is also a "field" under siege. The figures of demons and Satan suggest something of the "personal" and "concrete" nature of this siege. That is, our contest is not so much with "abstract principles" having to do with what constitutes evil and sin, but with "living sources" of a "malevolent" kind, which "take on an objective metaphysical reality," as theologian Leonardo Boff suggested.[41] That is, we encounter evil in persons, in the way in which they and we have internalized the temptations toward evil which surround us. There is a very "personal" dimension to it all. Theologians Karl Rahner, SJ, and Herbert Vorgrimler had suggested that "the personal nature of the devils" might mean that "every essential disorder in the world is personally realized." And in an interesting twist on this, theologian Hans Urs von Balthasar suggested that the demonic is a form of "un-person," that is, a person in the state of disintegration.[42] The symbolic language of our primary field of experience goes no further than this, nor can it. We do not enjoy a vantage point beyond this field from which we can take a look and pin down our adversary, so to speak. But that adversary seems vast indeed.

The Lord's Prayer is alluring here in a special way, because this final petition is the final one; that is, it is preceded by a veritable mountain range of positive, highly salvific aspirations and prayers. Is this a way of suggesting again that our consciousness of the mystery of iniquity is a contrast consciousness? That is, because the Holy Mystery has made known the divine name, and its kingdom, and its will, in our experiences of being nourished by the "bread," and of forgiveness, therefore by way of contrast with these very real experiences we can somehow name iniquity and trust in its overcoming? The truly final reality is one of deliverance, of hope, and

---

41. Boff, *The Lord's Prayer*, 110–12, 115.

42. Rahner and Vorgrimler, *Theological Dictionary*, 127; Balthasar, *Dare We Hope*, 145.

not of iniquity. Here our biblical parallelism leads us to a kind of massive interpretation of the "evil one" by way of the more massive earlier, five petitions of this great prayer. This should help us emphasize the word *deliver* in this final, sixth petition. The crescendo of the Lord's Prayer is not the evil one, but deliverance. Or better, a journey of *being* delivered, for we are in the in-between, the period of anticipatory vibrations of the fruits of the resurrection victory of Christ.

Before moving on, a pictorial expression of the Lord's Prayer as a triptych, and then as a spiraling, ever luring, series of crescendo parallelisms, may be helpful.

Figure 2

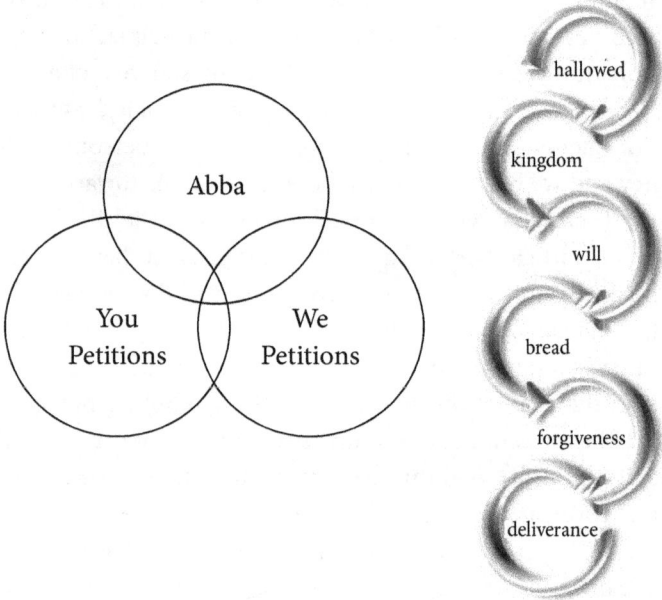

A Redemptive Pattern in History and Cosmos?

The reader will recall that at the end of our consideration of the first three petitions, we offered some suggestions about a possibly tacit anticipation of the trinitarian and incarnational structure of the Christian faith, along with a gesture toward interreligious hospitality. Divine name (Father), kingdom (incarnate Son and his mediation of the reign of God), and the realization of the divine will (Holy Spirit and our sanctification or divinization through the Spirit), find their roughly equivalent experiences and symbolizations

The "We" Petitions

arising from the primary field of experience in which all creatures, persons, and religions find themselves.

Now, as we softly hinted earlier, and as we gaze back upon these final three petitions, I will hazard another tacit pattern coming into focus. We can express it as the redemptive pattern moving from (1) creation (the petition for bread, symbolizing God as the giver of life), to (2) creation's struggle with the trial of sin and evil (the petition for forgiveness), and on to (3) the gift of salvation and deliverance from evil, through deification and transformation (the final petition for deliverance). The pattern is partly linear, in the sense that it is moving toward a final deliverance. This is certainly suggested by the resurrection event of Jesus. But for us, this "side" of that final deliverance, it is also a kind of an ongoing dialectic, that well known cross and resurrection interplay which seems to characterize our existence. I have expressed this in Christian language, but some form of this pattern would seem to characterize not only the Abrahamic traditions of Judaism, Christianity, and Islam, but also most or all of the other religious traditions of the world. And if this Prayer be truly ecumenical in the sense of moving toward the universal, it must somehow suggest these same patterns for all persons and creatures, but each in their own analogous ways. We are all in the primary field of experience, which is this great Prayer's soil. Somehow we are all companions, despite what our "secondary" conceptualizations may sometimes cause us to think.

seven

The Lord's Prayer and Spirituality: Liturgical and Personal, Cathedral and Monastic

By now the reader may have developed an interest in looking more closely at the use of the Lord's Prayer in the official liturgies of the churches, since we have mentioned its appearance especially at baptisms and at Eucharists. We began with Pope Francis' leading people in this prayer while visiting the Anglican martyrs' shrine in Uganda. While this may not have been strictly "liturgical," it was something of a public, quasi-official use of the prayer. At the same time many readers will be used to falling back on the Prayer in their personal devotions and experiences. Margaret Atwood's example in her novel *The Handmaid's Tale* exemplifies this "personal" use in a very dramatic way. A close friend of many years told me that she prayed the Our Father during her cancer treatments. "It's what I recited silently every time I had radiation. That's about how long it took for the huge machine to do its thing."[1] Another friend mentioned that he finds the "personal tone of the Lord's Prayer striking and novel . . . for someone who never knew [his] biological father—I barely knew mine who left when I was six—there is an extraordinary melting of my heart occurring praying with the Lord's Prayer."[2] Hemingway's more controversial form of the prayer moves us into a possibly non-believer's form of "praying," or at least a doubter's. In that way it is of special interest in our modern, "nonreligious" context. A

---

1. Thank you, Bonnie Hilbert, email of 12/16/14.
2. Thank you, Norm Weinstein, email of 12/21/14. Norm also noted how his Jewish background caused him to find the Prayer's "personal tone" something "striking and novel," and alerted me to Dante's citation of the Prayer in his *Purgatorio*.

further consideration might be to think about the relationship between these forms. We can imagine a wide spectrum, from congeniality to friction, and lots between, not the least of which might be ample confusion about the matter.

The reader will note that we are using the word *spirituality* as our overarching notion. Some may think that this is a trendy thing to do, since the word seems to be a popular one, sometimes as a way of referring to those who want to maintain some religious practices yet without any church or institutional allegiance. Even within the churches it can be a default term for some, as a way of expressing a critical distinction between church practices and teachings, on the one hand, and a "personal" relationship with God, which is not always congenial with the former. In other words, it is a way of "protesting" against ecclesial domination, or worse, ecclesial idolatry. In terms we have used before, it is a way of seeking to avoid being colonized.

While we may well recognize the dangers of lapsing into a narcissistic individualism that may lurk in the darker corners of the "turn to spirituality," nonetheless, I think that many of us still value and even cherish the term. It keeps us connected with our sisters and brothers who hang rather loosely, and maybe not at all, with church institutions. Why do we think we have nothing to learn from them? And I suspect that some of their concerns are our own. The word *spirituality* also has a long pedigree in Christian theology, and in the end it links up with Paul's theology of the Christian life as one that is rooted in the Spirit. "[Y]ou are in the Spirit, since the Spirit of God dwells in you . . . he who raised Jesus from the dead will give life to your mortal bodies also through his spirit that dwells in you" (Rom 8:9, 11). Paul uses the term *pneumatikos* ("spiritual") to describe people who have received the Spirit's gifts and have a gift for discernment (1 Cor 2:15).

If we think of spirituality in that way, as the Spirit's work within us, then I think we ought to think of spirituality as a dynamic process at work wherever the Spirit is at work. And where would this not be? Certainly not just when we are alone, supposedly removed from our fellow humans or even God's good creation. The Spirit is the life-giving energy for all of creation, the "wind" sweeping over the face of the waters (Gen 1:2), the one who drives us to search out always the common good (1 Cor 12:7), and the one in whom we, "though many, are one body" (1 Cor 12:12). Yes, the Spirit enables us to be "individually members" of Christ's body; our personalities and personal talents are not demolished (1 Cor 12:27). Indeed, our bodies, too, are temples of the Holy Spirit (1 Cor 6:19), illustrating how our entire being, and not just some immaterial aspect of us, is Spirit-energized. But that same Spirit is the life-giving source for the body of Christ, and indeed for all of creation as well. The implication of all of this is that spirituality embraces our totality as creatures: humans in their personal, social, and indeed cosmic network of relationships.

Insofar as liturgy is "the people's work" (this is the meaning of the term in Greek), it, too, is a form of spirituality. And perhaps thinking of the liturgical, larger ecclesial matrix of spirituality as a first way to imagine spirituality brings some advantages with it. In terms of our "primary field" of experience, it alerts us to the fact that we as persons dwell within a larger social-cosmic field. It also alerts us to the fact that liturgy and other public rites are meant to be Spirit-energized; without that Spirit they degenerate into empty "shells." And this indicates to us that the ecclesial-liturgical and the personal are already, on a deep-down level, united. We do not need to make artificial bridges between them. If we get into bridge-thinking, it is already too late. Yes, our consciousness of the dimensions of our primary field may heighten, and it can, because we are already participating within the larger field.

Anglican liturgist Paul Bradshaw has suggested the distinction between "monastic" and "cathedral" prayer as a way of getting beyond some of the problems noted above. It is a helpful distinction, and it does seem to make sense of much of the actual history of the liturgical and prayer practices of the Christian churches, at least. "Cathedral" prayer looked to the more public, social, and ecclesial needs of the churches, while monastic prayer looked more to the personal development of one's Christian discipleship. Yet elements of each overlapped, even in the earliest beginnings of the church, and this again would seem to go back to the Spirit-led dynamic between cosmos, social groups, and persons. Of course, at times the history has manifested signs of crisis: Sometimes the "monastic" and more personal has dominated, to the detriment of the cathedral, more liturgical strain. But this may have been in reaction to various forms of liturgical corruption: highly clericalistic liturgies, greatly removed from people's concerns, or rituals that had degenerated into highly elaborate, rococo-like encrustations. In a way, each form goes back to St. Paul's teaching to "pray without ceasing" (1 Thess 5:17). Each is a way of attempting to do just that.[3]

---

3. Bradshaw, *Two Ways of Praying*, 40–42.

The Lord's Prayer and Spirituality

The Lord's Prayer: An Expression of the Union between the Cosmic, the Liturgical, and the Personal

From a Christian point of view, what gives expression to these dimensions of the Lord's Prayer—cosmic, liturgical, and personal—is the very movement and energy of the prayer itself. It is the *Lord's* Prayer, and under his guidance, it expresses our adoptive sonship and daughtership in his mystical body. But two more thoughts are needed: We are incorporated in that body as persons, indwelt by the Spirit of Christ who knows our deepest aspirations more profoundly than we do ourselves. "Likewise the Spirit helps us in our weakness; for we do not know how to pray as we ought, but that very Spirit intercedes with sighs too deep for words" (Rom 8: 26). And the second thought: That Spirit is the Spirit of the cosmos itself. Our incorporation is into a cosmic body of Christ, a "creation [that] waits with eager longing for the revealing of the children of God." And Paul continues, "We know that the whole creation has been groaning in labor pains until now; and not only the creation, but we ourselves, who have the first fruits of the Spirit, groan inwardly while we wait for adoption, the redemption of our bodies" (Rom 8:19, 22–23). Paul is a wonderful theologian of the primary field of reality. He is holistic, moving easily and fluidly between body and spirit, creation, churches, social groups, and persons. His language is the richly symbolic language that gestures and evokes, rather than pins down and seeks to define: Spirit, redemption, adoption, groaning, interceding, language too deep for words, body, and more. This primary field is that of the Lord's Prayer, too, as we have frequently suggested. (At this point, the reader may want to revisit our discussion in chapter two of how Paul's writings express the various parts of the Lord's Prayer.) If we allow ourselves to be guided by the symbol of "Father," or *Abba*, it is difficult not to sense a certain evocation of personal intimacy, and we have noted many instances in the preaching of Jesus that point to this personal dimension in our relationships. The shepherd "calls his own sheep by name" (John 10:3). And yet, too, the Lord's Prayer invokes "our Father," and uses the plural in its We petitions, evoking the ecclesial and social dimensions. And we have likewise suggested that the phrases that allude to "heaven" and to "heaven and earth" evoke the universal and cosmic sweep and movement of the Lord's Prayer. It is a prayer embracing the cosmos and all its creatures; all peoples; and disciples, who express their discipleship in liturgy and in other forms of prayer, public, and personal.

Thus it is really not too surprising to find the Our Father appearing throughout the churches' traditions in social, liturgical actions, as well as in more personal devotions and expressions of prayer. Both are noted frequently. The Prayer's very energy moves in both of those directions, and as the Prayer prays us, it moves us likewise into those dimensions.

In Liturgy

We mentioned earlier that the addition of the doxology to the Lord's Prayer would have been a common thing to do in a Jewish context of public (liturgical) prayer. We noted the text in 1 Chronicles 29, in the context (1 Chron 28) of David gathering the officials and peoples together to celebrate God's choosing his son Solomon to be the one to build the temple, and to celebrate what had already been pledged in this regard. "Then David blessed the Lord in the presence of all the assembly; David said: 'Blessed are you, O Lord, the God of our ancestor Israel, forever and ever. Yours, O Lord, are the greatness, the power, the glory, the victory, and the majesty; for all that is in the heavens and on the earth is yours; yours is the kingdom, O Lord, and you are exalted as head above all'" (1 Chr 29:10–11).

It is not hard to believe that a similarly public note of solemn liturgy enabled the Lord's Prayer to find attached to it early on a similarly doxological thrust. That also nicely coheres with the biblical parallelism of the Prayer, the glory of the hallowed name, especially in heaven, and the power of the kingdom, finding their parallel echo in this final doxology. The Prayer's final petition does not end with the evil one, but with *deliverance* from the evil one. This is also another way of proclaiming the "power" and "victory" of God, which is more expressly noted in the doxology. This is the kind of victory expressed in the doxology we find in 1 Peter: "To him belong the glory and the power forever and ever" (4:11). So it seems, from the perspective of biblical parallelism, that the doxology is well within the flow of the entire Prayer. In a similar move, Bradshaw noted that the addition of the *gloria patri* ("Glory be to the Father, and to the Son, and to the Holy Spirit, as it was in the beginning, is now, and will be forever") to the psalms that were antiphonally chanted was also a doxological way to conclude these psalms in the context of the cathedral liturgies, as the monastic praying of the psalms found its way into cathedral prayer.[4]

4. Ibid., 50. See Ayo, *Gloria Patri*. At 42, he suggests that the second part of the "Glory be . . ." functions like the parallelisms of the psalms, reading it on both the level of

The Lord's Prayer and Spirituality

The two liturgical acts that early on assimilated the Lord's Prayer were baptism and Eucharist. The *Didache* (c. 100), which as we noted was perhaps the first text to have a doxology added to the Lord's Prayer, placed its brief discussion of and version of this prayer between baptism (number 7) and Eucharist (number 9), suggesting its liturgical or at least public, communal nature as a prayer of the body of Christ.[5] Of course the Prayer's origins in the preaching and ministry of Jesus, along with its heavy communal language, which is even more emphatic in Matthew's invocation, lend the Prayer a certain liturgical appropriateness. And many of its themes do as well. When one is being baptized, it is into the same family as other Christians that one is being baptized, with one Father. A baptism is a sign of the coming of the kingdom. So, too, is the Eucharist. Baptism celebrates forgiveness and victory over the evil one; so does the Prayer. When we receive communion, we are eating the manna of the new covenant, the bread we need for our daily living, and we are expressing our union in the body of Christ, gesturing forth in anticipatory manner the coming of the kingdom. The Prayer just may be "the oldest prayer of consecration" of the eucharistic elements, as theologian Robert Hughes suggested.[6] And in a kind of summary way, all liturgy—baptismal, eucharistic, and otherwise—is a hallowing or a glorifying of the glory of God's name.

Let us look at a few representative examples in the tradition. It is difficult not to sense both a baptismal and a eucharistic reference in Tertullian's commentary (200–206) on the Lord's Prayer. In commenting on the petition to hallow the name, he notes that while we do this, "should we prove worthy, [we are putting] on angelic vesture . . . already learning that heavenly song to God and that task of future glory." The vesture indicates the putting on of the white clothing that was a part of the baptismal ritual in Tertullian's Africa. And what was the "task of future glory" to which he is referring? Perhaps the angels' unceasingly proclaiming "holy, holy, holy" before the throne of God (see Isa 6:3) mentioned in this same passage of his treatise. That is why the baptismal robe is angelic. Likewise, when commenting on the petition for daily bread, he makes reference to the

---

eternity and time simultaneously, the "as it was in the beginning" paralleling the Father most emphatically; the "is now" paralleling the Son more emphatically; the "and will be forever" more focally paralleling the Spirit (63–111).

5. See Roberts and Donaldson, eds., *Didache*.

6. Thank you, Robert Davis Hughes, email of 12/30/14. It is an intriguing suggestion.

eucharistic bread at the Last Supper, where "his body is accounted bread: 'This is my body' (Matt 26.26; 1 Cor 11:24)."

Cyprian, the bishop of Carthage, and like Tertullian, representing the North African tradition, in his treatise (252) continues Tertullian's trend, which largely set the tone for the West in later centuries. As he introduces his commentary on the Prayer, he seems to have the Eucharist in mind when he says: "And when, together with our brothers, we gather to celebrate the divine sacrifices with the priest of God, we should be mindful of reverence and order, not forever tossing ill-judged phrases into the air, nor seeking to commend our requests by bombarding God with a tumultuous verbosity, because God is a hearer not of the voice but of the heart . . . ." Later, in commenting on the petition for daily bread, he becomes even more explicit: "We ask that this bread should be given to us daily lest we who are in Christ, and receive his eucharist daily as the food of salvation . . . should be separated from the body of Christ . . . ." Likewise, in commenting on the hallowing of the name, he links this petition with our need to maintain our being made holy in baptism: "We ask and beseech that we who are made holy in baptism should have the ability to persist in the way we have begun."[7] Cyprian's treatise on the Lord's Prayer is also echoed in the early Gregorian Sacramentary, going back to Pope Gregory the Great, with its language of praying as Jesus has taught us. That sacramentary also has the traditional introduction of our daring to say the Lord's Prayer.[8]

The evidence we have from the Eastern Christian tradition reflects trends similar to those in the West, although the early evidence also seems to manifest the importance of the Lord's Prayer in the early monastic offices of the church, Matins and Vespers especially. Maximus the Confessor, for example, in his eucharistic treatise, the *Mystagogia* (c. 628–30), describes the Lord's Prayer as "the symbol of adoption," which seems to reflect, according to Bishop Stevenson, "strong baptismal undercurrents." The phrase, "adoption by grace," in one way or another is frequently found in his treatise on the Lord's Prayer as well. The *Apostolic Constitutions*, from the fourth century, is perhaps our earliest evidence for the recitation of the Lord's Prayer by the newly baptized and anointed, and it also gives us the entire text of the Prayer, with the doxology included. Cyril of Jerusalem's

---

7. For Tertullian, *On Prayer* 3, 44; 6, 46; for Cyprian, *On the Lord's Prayer* 4, 67; 18, 78; 12, 73. See Stevenson, *The Lord's Prayer*, 28–35.

8. Cyprian, *On the Lord's Prayer* 2, 65 ("Among his other saving guidance and divine instructions"); 3, 66 ("Therefore . . . let us pray . . . as God the Master has taught us"); Stevenson, *The Lord's Prayer*, 101.

The Lord's Prayer and Spirituality

Mystagogical Catecheses (possibly fourth century or later) illustrates how the Lord's Prayer was recited between the end of the eucharistic prayer and the distribution of communion.[9]

There was some variance as to when the Lord's Prayer was to be prayed during the Eucharist. The general pattern seems to have been to do this between the eucharistic prayer and the distribution of communion, however. Whether the Prayer was thought to belong more properly to the eucharistic prayer, or more properly to the communion, was perhaps a variable, and may still be. The Byzantine Rites in the East, and Pope Gregory the Great (c. 540–604) in the West, placed the Prayer before the fraction of the bread, and this is a very common practice today in perhaps most of the rites of East and West. Would this indicate that it forms a part of the eucharistic prayer, as Pope Gregory argued in one of his letters? However, if the tradition is to place the Prayer after the fraction, as it is in the East and West Syrian rites, would that indicate that it introduces the communion portion of the eucharist?[10] This variance, should it have any special meaning, perhaps reflects the two-sided nature of the Lord's Prayer itself; that is, whether one puts the stress upon the first three petitions, focusing upon praise and hallowing of the Father; or whether the stress falls upon the second set of three petitions (the fourth through the sixth, on our counting), where our nourishing with our daily bread comes into focus, as well as our need for forgiveness and reconciliation, which is something we should seek before receiving communion. As we are taught in Matthew 5:23–24: "So when you are offering your gift at the altar, if you remember that your brother or sister has something against you, leave your gift there before the altar and go; first be reconciled to your brother or sister, and then come and offer your gift."

These appearances of the Lord's Prayer in liturgy, then, manifest how that prayer is the family prayer of the church, the body of Christ. As we become members of that ecclesial body in a formal way, at baptism, and as we seek our daily nourishment so that we might persevere in that membership, at Eucharist, we pray this Prayer, and the Prayer prays us. At the same

---

9. Stevenson, *The Lord's Prayer*, 61, 64, 244–45; Maximus the Confessor, "On the Lord's Prayer," 287, 291, 295; Roberts et al., eds., *Apostolic Constitutions* 7.24–26; St. Cyril of Jerusalem, *Lectures on the Christian Sacraments* 5.11–22.

10. See Bradshaw and Johnson, *The Eucharistic Liturgies*, 177, 335; the Reformation liturgies varied (233–92). See Stevenson, *The Lord's Prayer*, 99–100, for relevant evidence and some of the unresolved historical issues involved here. Apparently before Pope Gregory the Great (c. 540–604), the Roman practice was to recite the Lord's Prayer after the fraction.

time, the prayer is a prayer for each of us, not apart from the community, but as unique persons within that community and for that community. The shepherd "calls his own sheep by name" (John 10:3).

As we now turn to the Our Father in personal devotion, let us begin with a fascinating text from the *Rule of Saint Benedict* (mid-sixth century):

> The morning and evening Offices should never be allowed to pass without the Superior saying the Lord's Prayer in its place at the end so that all may hear it, on account of the thorns of scandal which are apt to spring up. Thus those who hear it, being warned by the covenant which they make in that prayer when they say, "Forgive us as we forgive," may cleanse themselves of faults against that covenant. But at other Offices let the last part only of that prayer be said aloud, so that all may answer, "But deliver us from evil."[11]

The monastic "Offices" are a fascinating combination of the personal and the public, illustrating those two sides of the Lord's Prayer. If liturgical theologian Paul Bradshaw is correct, the monastic cycle of prayers began as essentially personal forms of prayer, but they took on more of the public, "cathedral" forms of praying especially as the monks gathered into monastic communities and as those monasteries became public centers of prayer. Here in this text from Benedict's *Rule* we can notice how the Prayer reflects a kind of public, official perspective within the community, represented by the Superior's reciting of it at the morning and evening offices, and by the Superior's recitation of only the last part at the other offices. At the same time, the Prayer enables each monk to reflect personally on the "thorns of scandal" present within the community and afflicting each personally, and also implying that each is to assess one's own responsibility for them. At the same time, the role of the Prayer within the community offices also expresses rather forcefully the fact that, although we may pray in a quiet, more contemplative and personal manner (as each monk is being asked to do here in this text), at the same time we are never really alone in our prayer. As Bradshaw puts it, "There is, strictly speaking, no such thing as private prayer for a Christian. Whenever we pray, we do so as a member of the body of Christ and united by the Spirit with the whole company of earth and heaven. We pray as the church and with the church."[12] It is probably also good for us to comment here that our "cathedral," more public liturgical prayer also always needs its personal and "interiorizing" dimension, if

---

11. Benedict, *Rule of St. Benedict* 13.
12. Bradshaw, *Two Ways of Praying*, 41.

it is not to turn into an empty ritual. The feedback—public and personal—works both ways.

In Personal Prayer

An interesting example of how the cathedral, public styles of praying influenced and maybe even "tutored" personal forms of praying is represented by Paternoster Row, in London, England. Apparently this had been the site where rosary ropes, with knots at every tenth bead, were made for those who wanted to pray frequently, like the monks, imitating their daily offices, but who were unable to afford the books that would be needed, even very abbreviated books, or who may not have been able to read them in any case, and found themselves also unable to memorize appropriate psalms. But they could learn the Lord's Prayer, and use the ropes for that, and in time, perhaps from the twelfth century on, Marian devotions led to the use of the *Ave Maria* as well, along with the *Pater noster*.[13]

Turning to the Lord's Prayer as a guide for personal prayer was and is a very appropriate thing to do. It is a guide for liturgical, cathedral-style prayer, helping it to maintain its rooting in the gospel and its call to live out the great commands of love of God and love of neighbor. It is likewise a way to keep personal prayer rooted in that same gospel. It helps keep personal prayer from lapsing into so-called "private" prayer, which would probably end up becoming a subtle form of narcissism. But beyond that, there would seem to be no fixed "rule," just perhaps more or less wise advice from people who seriously work at prayer.

Some will be drawn to recite the Lord's Prayer at some point in their daily expressions of prayer. Others will more or less think of the Lord's Prayer as a guide or an example of how to pray, not being too tied into one express form of prayer. As we have seen, this dialectic is a tension which goes back to Matthew's version itself, where verse 6:9 begins the Prayer with the Lord's words, "Pray then in this way." The word being translated "in this way" might also be translated "like this." It is the Greek adverb *houtōs*. One might take that adverb to mean that the Prayer is a guide, rather than something to be slavishly followed. As such, it seems to suggest that not only are translations and paraphrases into contemporary forms warranted, but also very different forms of praying are as well.

---

13. Ibid., 16–17.

The reader may find it interesting that Thomas Aquinas, from the Roman side, and John Calvin, from the Reformed side, both knew of that *houtōs* and took it quite seriously. Aquinas wrote, for example: "Notice that the Lord does not say, 'You shall pray this,' but 'You shall pray *like* this.' He does not rule out the possibility of our praying in other words." The Lord's Prayer, he wrote, is given us so that we might have its thoughts "in view, no matter how we express them or think of them." Similarly, John Calvin counseled that "We would not have it understood that we are so bound by this form of prayer that we are not allowed to change it in either word or syllable." In other words, when we pray, "though the words [we use] may be utterly different, yet the sense ought not to vary." For the Lord's Prayer is a "summary" of what to pray for.[14] Ranging even further, interestingly we find a similar perspective, it seems, among the members of the Church of Latter-Day Saints (Mormons), which recognizes the New Testament's versions of the Prayer as a pattern for prayer, and also offers a slightly different version in its *The Book of Mormon* (3 Nephi 13.9–13).[15]

The *Ave Maria*, for example, is a popular prayer in Roman Catholicism, Anglo-Catholicism, Lutheranism, and among Eastern Orthodox Christians. The reader may recall that Hemingway referred to it when giving his Our Father version. It might be said to reflect the "freer" view of the Lord's Prayer as a guide to all forms of prayer. This might seem surprising, since we think of the "Hail Mary" as a prayer to Mary, and not to the Father. But if we pause for a moment, we can see how the Lord's Prayer forms the "deep grammar" of the *Ave Maria*.

But first a historical note. Roman and Anglo-Catholics will think of the *Ave Maria* as made up of two parts. The First part is: "Hail Mary, full of grace, the Lord is with you. Blessed are you among women, and blessed is the fruit of your womb, Jesus." The second part, which may have been added in the fifteenth century—its exact origins are debated—and found its way into the Roman Breviary of 1568, is: "Holy Mary, mother of God, pray for us sinners, now and at the hour of our death. Amen." Romans and

---

14. Aquinas, *The Lectures on St. Matthew*, ed. Tugwell, 454; *Summa theologica* 2-2.83.14.3, 1549; see Murray, *Praying with Confidence*, 14; Calvin, *Institutes of the Christian Religion* 3.49, 917. Stevenson, *The Lord's Prayer*, 172–83, describes the struggle within early Anglicanism between the Puritan/Reformed wing, which followed Calvin in a quite radical way on this "freer" use of the Prayer, and the more Catholic wing, seeking to adhere to the traditional version.

15. Riess, "Why Don't Mormons Recite the Lord's Prayer?" and Anonymous, "Why is the Lord's Prayer Different in 3 Nephi?"

The Lord's Prayer and Spirituality

Anglo-Catholics use both parts; Lutherans and Eastern Orthodox, typically only the first part.

Notice how the first part reflects the first part of the Lord's Prayer. Mary is blessed because she is gifted with grace, and her womb will give birth to Jesus, the son of the Father. Mary's being blessed reflects the hallowed Father's grace, whose will is done and kingdom is accomplished by the birth of Jesus. This part of the prayer is thoroughly biblical, reflecting the angel Gabriel's and Elizabeth's greetings to Mary (Luke 1:28, 30–31, 42). The second part of the prayer reflects the second part of the Lord's Prayer. It turns, like the Lord's Prayer, to our human concerns and needs, seeking forgiveness and deliverance. Praying *to* Mary is of course the hurdle for some, but what Mary is asked to do is to pray for us. She herself prays to God; she does not replace God. She, like us, belongs to the family of the Father, the fellowship of the saints, the body of Christ. Here perhaps the deep grammar that the Lord's Prayer is in the *Ave* is deep, but if we are one family, then it would seem that interceding for one another in that fellowship reflects the energy of the Lord's Prayer. In a way, we might say that we are asking Mary to pray the second part of the Lord's Prayer on our behalf. "Forgive *us* our sins . . . deliver *us* from evil": As we pray this, are we not praying *for* one another?[16]

Perhaps the deepest reason we turn to prayer, and the deepest reason that we find the Lord's Prayer an attractive guide, has to do with the "primary field of experience," to which we have made appeal so often. This is the air we breathe, the soil on which we live. We may try to cut ourselves away from it, we may get ourselves in various ways alienated from dimensions of it, but come what may, we are within it. Because it is our home, we are drawn to it, and to the various relationships with which it makes appeal to us. And because God, our Holy Mystery, is the divine Ground of our primary field, in the end we can wager that it is the Spirit who draws us into prayer. That is partly what we mean when we say that the Prayer prays us. It simply reflects the pattern or flow of our existence.

16. See Geert's Ave Maria Pages, "The Ave Maria Prayer"; Wikipedia, "Hail Mary." Also illuminating is Ayo, *The Hail Mary*, 70–71, who indicates that the ending of the prayer's first part with the name "Jesus" is biblical, reflecting Gabriel's instruction to Mary to name her child "Jesus" (Luke 1:31; see Matt 1:21), although it was not used "in much of the Middle Ages," and although it is not found in Elizabeth's greetings. Thus, Aquinas's commentary on the *Ave Maria* does not refer to it. The name "Mary," while biblical (Luke 1:27), is not technically in Gabriel's salutation; Aquinas notes this in his "Sermon Conferences on the Ave Maria" (Ayo, 141, *The Hail Mary*, who offers the text, 141–49, from *The Catechetical Instructions of St. Thomas Aquinas*, 173–80).

I sometimes wonder if Paul is not expressing something of the connection between prayer and our primary field of experience when he tells us to "pray without ceasing" (1 Thess 5:17). Just how is it that we can do such a thing unless it is our very being to do such? Whenever we are, like the first part of the Lord's Prayer, breathing in the divine Ground of our primary field, reflecting the Holy Mystery's holiness; or whenever we are living into our relationships within the primary field, with the cosmos (the heavens and the earth), or with our family, near and "extended," by praying for forgiveness and seeking deliverance from evil for all, like the second part of the Lord's Prayer—is this one way of understanding praying without ceasing? For we would have to cease to breathe, were we to somehow completely cut ourselves from our primary field. Paul, in the same context (1 Thess 5:18), says to "give thanks in all circumstances." Is "all circumstances" another way of saying "primary field of experience"?

We can do that praying more or less well. That is why it is helpful to have guides, like the Our Father and the Hail Mary, and like the liturgy of the churches, especially the Eucharist, which remind us of, and immerse us in, the larger family and cosmic context of our prayer as the body of Christ. And in the primary field, all dimensions are always co-present, but not always in conscious focus. Some or one may be in focus, while the other or others are more or less tacitly on the borders of awareness. When the divine Ground is in focus, we might say that our thanksgiving (to God) is in consciousness focally. This is like saying that the first parts of the Our Father or the Hail Mary are in focal awareness. The other dimensions of the primary field (cosmos, social groups, persons) do not disappear; they remain tacitly present, and can come into focus easily at any time. The second parts of the Our Father and Hail Mary correspondingly do not disappear as we pray their first parts. Likewise, as we concentrate upon our other relationships within the primary field, bringing them into focus, our deepest relationship to the divine Ground does not disappear. It is our co-present tacit partner, always able to emerge into focus from the border regions of consciousness.

Thomas Aquinas a number of times describes prayer as that which "interprets our desires" or as "the interpreter of our desires."[17] In a way, prayer teaches us how to recognize our deepest desires, that which we truly need. And what do we need more than the nurturing of our primary relationships within our primary field of experience, or perhaps also the

---

17. Aquinas, *Summa theologica* 2–2.83.9, 1538–39; see Murray, *Praying with Confidence*, 36–37.

correction of those desires that have somehow swerved away from their healthiest direction?

Again, by linking up our prayer once again with our primary field of experience, we may potentially heighten our consciousness of the partners with whom and for whom we are praying. For it may well be, and I believe it is, that there is a vast network of prayer at work throughout the cosmos. Did not Paul say, "For the creation waits with eager longing for the revealing of the children of God; . . . it is groaning in labor pains . . . [along with us], who have the first fruits of the Spirit . . ." (Rom 8:19, 23)? As the Lord's Prayer speaks of a Father of heaven and earth, so Paul speaks of a Spirit that is cosmic in breadth and depth. Does the Lord's Prayer belong to the world, as Matthew's version suggests, or to Jesus' explicit disciples, as Luke's version implies, when the disciples ask for an explicit form of prayer? Bishop Stevenson thinks this tension between all and Christians is there from the beginnings of the New Testament.[18] Likewise, our viewing the Lord's Prayer along with all prayer within the context of our primary field would seem to manifest a similar tension, between the ecumenical-moving-toward-the-universal, and the personal, whether Christian or otherwise.

Could it be that the Lord's Prayer, and all Christian prayer modeled on it, like the Hail Mary, urge us consciously to link up with the prayers of all creatures? And if we do not, maybe we are somehow shrinking the family of the Holy Mystery, and thereby attempting to shrink the Mystery. In place of hallowing the divine name, we might be, albeit unknowingly, inadequately and at times falsely hallowing. Let us think a bit more about that.

A promising example of ecumenical prayer, perhaps for the first time bringing leaders from many of the world's religions together to pray for peace, took place under the leadership of Pope (and now St.) John Paul II in Assisi under the patronage of Saints Francis and Clare on October 27, 1986. "The Pope chose Assisi as the gathering place, because the spirit of Brother Francis has transformed it into the city of universal brotherhood and sisterhood," wrote Antonio Rosales, OFM, in his report on the gathering.[19] "There were costumes," Rosales writes, "but they were of a different kind, costumes associated with religion, with people of prayer: the Pope's white; the Christian ecclesiastics' red, purple, black, and brown; the Hindus' saffron yellow and many shades of it; the Buddhists' white with designs; the American Indians' colorful costumes and feathered headdresses; the Af-

---

18. Stevenson, *The Lord's Prayer*, 228.
19. Rosales, "The Day Assisi Became the 'Peace Capital' of the World."

ricans' robes; and so on." Of course, the goal was deeper than costumes, Rosales comments, for the Pope had arranged for and invited the leaders to this gathering so that they might not just "talk about peace but pray for it," thus illustrating the Pope's belief "that peace is the desire of every man and woman of whatever faith," a divine gift coming through our prayerful response to that gift.

What is hopeful about this gathering is that there was a healthy balance between each of the religions' participants praying in their own unique manners in their own special locations, in the morning, and then gathering to pray together as a united assembly in the afternoon, "giving witness to the more universal thirst for peace shared by all humanity," writes Rosales. And he notes that "the Holy Father rounded up all the supplications with the prayer Jesus taught us: the Our Father." Again, there is something about the intrinsic movement of that prayer which gives it such a universal role.

John Paul II, in his address to the event, actually quite remarkably spoke about the "common ground," as well as "the dimension of prayer, which in the very real diversity of religions tries to express communication with a Power above all human forces." As a Christian, of course, he said that that Power is "what we call God . . . [who] has revealed himself in Christ." And although "the forms of our prayers are very different, as we have seen, and there can be no question of reducing them to a kind of common denominator," still "there is something which binds us together." These are sentiments similar to those to which we have arrived throughout this meditation on the Our Father. Somehow the Pope is being decolonized by this prayer, and leading his Roman Communion toward a similar decolonization. He said in fact that the Assisi assembly was also "an act of penance" for all the times that Roman Catholics have not been peacemakers: "We have not been always 'peacemakers.'"[20]

John Paul II was insultingly described as someone who "mocks publicly the first article of the Creed and the first Commandment of the Decalogue" by dissident Archbishop Lefebvre.[21] Decolonization is not an easy task. Apparently at the commemoration of the Assisi meeting twenty years later, there was no common prayer together among the representatives of the world's religions, although there was a moment of silence, which at least somewhat allows the crack through which common prayer might arise, I

20. Pope John Paul II, "Address."

21. Lefebvre, "Assisi 1 (October 27, 1986)." Lefebvre founded a breakaway movement from the Roman Catholic Church after the Second Vatican Council.

believe. But the tone toward the meeting seemed rather defensive. Pope Benedixt XVI, then the pope in office, did not even attend, and his address, which came in the form of a letter to the bishop of Assisi, expressed concerns about syncretism and relativism, although it did acknowledge "that prayer does not divide but unites," and that "the recognition of God's existence," which can be derived from "the experience of creation (cf. Rom 1:20), must dispose believers to view other human beings as brothers and sisters." So perhaps, despite Archbishop Lefebvre, another small step forward, despite two backwards, occurred.[22]

Syncretism and relativism are worth pondering, by way of cautionary alertness. The first ignores, or perhaps better, insufficiently appreciates not only the differences between the religions, but also the rich diversity of gifts that the religions may bring. The miracle of Pentecost in Acts 2 is a rather fine example of this rich diversity of gifts. There is nothing monochrome about the Spirit. Relativism, in its extreme form of denying any kind of ultimate truth, thus leaving a vacuum which allows any kind of cultural norm to fill it—a "might makes right" ideology not the least of these possibilities—deserves attention, to be sure. But the other side of the condemnation of alleged relativism is the shutting down of voices that have a hard time being heard, or even represented at the table of those more powerful. Prayers like the Lord's Prayer are, for Christians at least, one way to work against premature invocations of syncretism and relativism. And that prayer asks us to forgive one another when we do engage in such premature invocations. I think Pope John Paul II rather courageously was hinting at this in his comment that the First Assisi Congress was an "act of penance."

Episcopal priest Eric Law offers a fascinating and relevant interpretation of the miracle of Pentecost in his work on multicultural ministry. He describes it as the miracle of not only the tongues, but the ears. That is, it was those without the authoritative power (the Galileans [Acts 2:7]) who were gifted with the ability to speak in various languages (the gift of tongues); those with the authoritative power (the "devout Jews" [Acts 2:5]), on the other hand, were given the ability to hear those languages (the gift of ears). Speaking in tongues can seem like so much disorderly babble to those who approve of only a particular way of speaking (and thinking). They perhaps need to listen—and hearken to—what is being said. This may well be another way of praying "hallowed be your name."[23] That is, one way

---

22. Pope Benedict XVI, "Italy."
23. Law, *The Wolf Shall Dwell with the Lamb*, chapter 5, 45–51. I was inspired toward

in which we avoid the great temptation to manipulate God, unknowingly or not, is to listen to what God may be saying. As Francis of Assisi prayed in his paraphrase of the Our Father:

> Hallowed be your name. May our knowledge of you become ever clearer, that we may know the breadth of your blessings, the length of your promises, the height of your majesty, and the depth of your judgments.[24]

Earlier we mentioned Hemingway's version or "antiversion" (?) of the Our Father. This prompts me to think in our context here about the Lord's Prayer and the prayer of non-believers in any "Power" of a transcendent nature. The Our Father, I believe, belongs to all, and so it belongs to those whose faith does not extend to the divine Ground. That is why, here and there within the movement of this book's meditation on this prayer, we have been led to think more on this question.

As we sat with Hemingway's "anti-prayer" (?)—the "Our nada who art in nada"—we were led to suggest something of an overlap with the Spanish mystical tradition of Juan de la Cruz's *nada*, the emptiness that marks the transition from self-absorption to invitation of others and the Other. The empty space provides room for others. Partly this was suggested by the plea, "Give us this nada our daily nada and nada us not into nada." It is as if there is a two-sided dimension in Hemingway's plea. On the one hand we seek the nada; on the other, we ask to be delivered from it. From what are we asking to be delivered? Perhaps the nada that locks us in our own self-absorption? And what, then, is the nada that we ask to be given? Perhaps the open space within which communion can occur?

We can certainly pray *for* such as Hemingway and/or those represented by the character in his short story, "A Clean, Well-lighted Place," who pray or "speak" the "Nada." The energy of the Prayer calls us to that, for the *Abba* is every person's *Abba*. And praying is a form of speaking, if only silently, but it is also a form of asking. Perhaps that asking is the crack within which the flower may grow, and the depths of the Mystery may be sounded. And so somehow our prayer may reach them. Is Buckminster Fuller, for example, giving expression to a crack or not in his "revision" of the Lord's Prayer? "God [partly refers to all the] scientifically explainable answers [that] may and probably will eventually be given to all questions as engendered in all

---

my views regarding relativism originally by a comment from my friend and theologian-colleague Pamela Kirk.

24. Francis of Assisi, "Inspired by the Lord's Prayer."

human thoughts by the sum total of all human experiences."[25] It sounds as if he thinks the crack is temporary. But only "probably." So perhaps there is a crack in the temporary crack. But even if there is no crack, which I doubt, our prayer may reach God, for we are one in *Abba*.

But perhaps we might also consider praying the Our Father *with* those who pray the "Nada." Perhaps we need to listen, or listen harder, to them, and to their prayer, and practice the Pentecostal miracle of the ears. What is it that they may be teaching us? From a Christian perspective it may be that some dimension of the crucifixion and even the descent into hell is being communicated to us through the Nada. That is, the depths of the Mystery's outreach, and the costliness of it? St. Thérèse of Lisieux wrote in her autobiography that at a certain point God "permitted my soul to be invaded by the thickest darkness, and that the thought of heaven, up until then so sweet to me, be no longer anything but the cause of struggle and torment."[26] Is this kind of solidarity with those in a land of torment what we learn when we pray the "Hemingway Nada" along with our version of the Prayer? Or perhaps we learn just not to be so smug in our faith, so "in control" and really still in a very subtle land of self-absorption?

One final thought: As we pray the Lord's Prayer, or let it pray us, we have been seeking to uncover its ecumenical and universal-leaning thrust and energy. Our examples here are just that, examples: our partners with other religions, and our brothers and sisters whose faith is not, at least explicitly, in the holy Mystery. And earlier we had mentioned many others who have been victims of one form of colonization and iniquity or another: all those who are victims of suffering and exclusion, which the Lord's Prayer's final petition particularly evokes. But I would like to end this chapter by returning to our theme of a neocosmocentrism, and the Prayer's summoning us toward a recovery of our communion with all of nature's creatures. And this would include the border areas, those whose consciousness is not so transparently obvious, whether at human life's "beginnings" or its "ending." *Abba* of heaven and earth, of the galaxies and the vast cosmos, of all that has been and will be, somehow your Prayer calls us to hallow your name as it manifests itself on a cosmic scale.

---

25. See Fuller, "Ever Rethinking the Lord's Prayer." Wikipedia, "Buckminster Fuller," describes him as a Unitarian. The sentiments in his "revision" would likely be largely shared by non-believers.

26. Thérèse of Lisieux, *Story of a Soul*, 211.

The Prayer belongs to all. So we are called to pray for all. And also to pray with all. *"Our* Father . . . give *us* . . . *our* daily bread . . . forgive *us* . . . *our* debts . . . deliver *us* . . . from the evil one." The Prayer calls us to realize the ecumenical and universal extent of the "us." The creatures of the cosmos have their own analogous ways of praying, of beseeching, of asking, of imploring. We know this tacitly and sometimes more focally within our primary field of experiences. As our dogs bring us their leash, or ask us to feed them; as our livestock communicate their needs to us; as we place the bird feeders in our backyards because we sense a bond with birds, and on the examples can go, these are so many precious ways in which we can find with a "second naivete" our communion with all of creation. It may be that one of the great callings of us humans is to become the more articulate, conscious voice of the creatures of the cosmos. Somehow creaturely evolution achieves articulate consciousness in us. But we need to honor the other side of it: Our consciousness cannot be adequately conscious without our heeding the analogous voices of the cosmos. And this needs to include seeking forgiveness for the many ways in which we have failed to do this. "Your will be done *on earth* as it is in *heaven*." As the seventeenth century mystic Jean-Jacques Olier prayed in his meditation "On Seeing the Sun":

> My God, I adore you in this beautiful star, where you dwell as in your tabernacle. He made the sun to be his tabernacle (Ps 19:5). In it I adore and conceive some small idea of what you are in yourself . . . my God, you give life to a countless multitude of creatures, all distinct and different, which subsist and have life through you . . . . Have you not expressed this wonder [of the sun]? . . . If it traverses the whole world, is it not to proclaim this truth: that you are the Father of every creature and the source of life in all that subsists?[27]

---

27. Olier, "On Seeing the Sun," 277. Olier suggests that the Our Father offers so many ways in which through the Spirit we participate with the Son in the glory of the Father, in his *Explication du Pater Noster*.

conclusion

A Prayer of Immense Hospitality

How ecumenical have we been? The reader will recall that we set out to offer an ecumenical interpretation of, and guide to, the Lord's Prayer. Why did this author choose to do that? It was not the way I started on this journey. Originally I had simply wanted to offer a series of study sessions on something that might be pastorally useful to people in the cathedral parish I attend and at which I sometimes assist. I was prompted to think that something that practicing Christian believers perhaps daily, likely frequently, do, is to recite and hopefully really pray the Our Father. Would it not be very pastoral to offer some reflections on that prayer, and thereby aid typical Christian parishioners to deepen their Christian discipleship?

I was including myself within that group of people who might be helped. I have been praying the Our Father probably since I learned to speak, and rarely had I really reflected upon it at any length. But still I have kept on praying it, perhaps letting myself be carried along with the conviction that the church knows what it is doing in fostering this prayer, and also maybe with the conviction that somehow this prayer reaches back to Jesus himself. That was good enough for me. And likely that is good enough for most practicing Christians. But I probably was also comforted by the fact that oftentimes I prayed this prayer with others: with my immediate family; with my *Amuma* (Basque for "grandmother") very frequently as a young child; with my school classmates and fellow seminarians, theologians, and clergy; with my spouse and our children; and with my fellow Christian believers, especially at the Eucharist. It just seemed natural that we prayed this prayer together. Just why we did so was something that I did not ponder very much, if at all.

So already in a way the Prayer was widening me, almost without my knowing it: into ever wider circles, from family to fellow students to practicing Christians within the family of the church, all perhaps through the grace of and with our brother Jesus, and on toward our Father. The movement into those widening circles is a flow, a field of energy, or in our symbolic language, an event in the Spirit. The prayer had been a kind of ecumenical, ever-widening energy in my life. Perhaps it has been similar for others, it now occurs to me to ask.

My first conscious memory of really engaging in serious study of the Prayer was in reading an essay titled "The Pater Noster as an Eschatological Prayer," by the famed and untimely deceased biblical scholar Raymond E. Brown, PSS.[1] I think I was originally attracted toward that essay—although almost anything by Father Brown was immediately something that attracted my attention—by my interest in Christology, and by the desire to study what the New Testament had to say about Jesus and his message and work. Of course, the essay carried me into the world of eschatology in, before, and after Jesus' time, and in so doing began something of a more studied ecumenical widening in my thinking. I was slowly discovering something of the Hebrew and Jewish horizon of Jesus and the New Testament. And perhaps the readers of this book so far will have noticed how that very early beginning in Jewish sensitivity has borne greater fruit here. For part of the ecumenical energy of the Our Father is its ability to lead us into the rich world of Jewish spirituality and prayer.

But I really had no idea of just how ecumenically I would find myself challenged as I began to consider the Lord's Prayer more carefully, in preparing my little study sessions, something I have since done again at another local parish nearby. At some point it occurred to me that perhaps there might be a book somewhere among all the research I was doing. And naturally it dawned on me, as a clergy friend said to me recently, "Can anything new really be said about the Lord's Prayer?" We do not need another book repeating, likely at a less attractive level, what has already been said by others. In any case, I began to study other writings on the Prayer, and found that, when one waded beyond the wonderful work of careful biblical exegesis, the commentaries became rather narrow, typically expressing the approved line in a particular denomination. This is not necessarily wrong, but somehow, perhaps because of my own ecumenical experiences and attractions, I began to sense that a more self-consciously ecumenical

---

1. Brown, *New Testament Essays*, 217–53.

A Prayer of Immense Hospitality

approach to the Prayer might find its own appropriate niche among the vast literature of books on the Our Father.

This "ecumenical" attraction is really something that has grown within me since the Second Vatican Council. The period of the Council was one of great ecumenical optimism, and I shared in that, and still do in many ways. But not too long after that Council a kind of ecumenical thinning out seems to have occurred. The official representatives of the various churches keep up their ecumenical duties, but all too commonly, with some few exceptions, I have the sense of being in a period of ecumenical retrenchment. This is similar to what some have called the "postmodern" tendency. If modernity might be characterized as the era of the "universal narratives," that is a time in which many believed, at least in the West, that humanity might be understood in grandly universal theories, then the late modern and postmodern periods might be characterized as eras in which that universal optimism grew more difficult to sustain. We are more and more within our tribal confines, and at best we have our tribal stories or narratives, nothing more. This has probably been necessary in many ways, so that if we are to move toward anything approaching a universal narrative, or at least broken narratives with sufficient cracks and openings within which to invite all who might wish to participate, then we do need to take a second look at our particular heritages and preserve as much as we can.

But we are moving into a more global period, and have been for some time. The ever present phenomenon of colonialism, in one way or another, almost always characterizing the human march, might be considered an incipient form of globalization. Empire building, particularly that of the multicivilizational empires, such as Greece and Rome, continued this trend, as our own many "debts" to those heritages illustrate, within the Christian churches and beyond those churches. If someone is in doubt of this, just ask yourself what style of architecture most state capitols, or church buildings, exhibit. The world wars are a symptom of how dreadfully difficult it is to enter into a global culture. And now today's global communications networks, the worldwide digital explosion, the outreach of the world's various economic systems, the near-universalization of "imperial" languages like French (at one time), and now English (and Spanish to some extent)—all of these are so many examples of the global march. And as this happens, the various religions come into ever more frequent contact with one another.[2]

---

2. Helpful is Wilson, *The Evolution of International Society*.

And thus it is almost inevitable that we have asked about the global implications of the Lord's Prayer. In a way we are challenged with an increasingly growing awareness of what it means when we speak of "heaven and earth." And of a Father of these, and of the "us" for whom we pray in this Prayer. A colonial reading of the Prayer imposes one culture's reading onto the text. Will globalization help us decolonize, or will it tempt us into various forms of neocolonialism? Will we seek to domesticate this Prayer, or will the Prayer subvert our colonizing tendencies? Those were some of the sensitivities we were led to bring to our interpretation. And to some extent we were aided in this by the emergence of the "sciences" of social and cultural and psychological pathology that emerged in the "late modern" period, as we noted. But we were helped, perhaps even more, by the inclusive love of the movement of Jesus, and its precedents within the Jewish tradition, and by a growing sensitivity to the religions of the world. And I continue to think that the mystic tradition—we have appealed to John of the Cross and Teresa of Avila especially—is perhaps the great "carrier" of an ever-widening movement of love. And so the reader will have noted here and there our "mystical lens" in our reading of the Prayer. And happily we Christians share this mystical tradition with many of the world's religions, and beyond them even with many "nature mystics," who help us attend to the cosmos and to our widening neocosmocentric perspective.[3]

I do not mean to downplay the role of the Christian church in our reading and praying of the Our Father. It has always been thought of as the church's prayer in a special way, all throughout the tradition. We recall Bishop Stevenson's answer to his own question, "But to whom does this Prayer belong?"[4] He averred that, if we follow Matthew's Gospel, we would tend toward a more universal answer: The Prayer belongs to all, even those without Christian belief. If we were to follow Luke's Gospel, we would incline to the narrower view: The prayer belongs to the believing disciples of the church, who asked Jesus for this prayer. There is a "tension" between these within the tradition, and that is as it should be. For how else might we move toward the universal, if not through the particular? I would only caution that we are involved in a movement *toward* the universal, or toward the

---

3. Some helpful works: Sorokin, *The Ways and Power of Love*, which is largely unknown, but it is one of those breakthrough works; Chardin, *On Love*; and Johnston, *Christian Mysticism Today*.

4. Stevenson, *The Lord's Prayer*, 228.

catholic in the fullest sense of the word. The tension here might be thought of as "eschatological," with all the ambiguities evoked by that term.

Perhaps for now our most appropriate option is to pray the Prayer within this particularity-ecumenical-toward-universality tension. We are not really imposing this option upon the Prayer, if we remember that the soil from which the Prayer springs is that of our primary field of reality, namely, God/cosmos/cultures-religions/persons, within all of which we dwell. Is it inappropriate to think that the Prayer wants to guide us into our primary relationships ever more fully? It is not the only guide, but it is a "summary of the gospel," a summary of the movement toward universality, or better, toward universal love.

How more concretely might we pray the Prayer within that tension? Actually the record indicates that we have been doing this, in ever widening ways, down through the ages. We are referring here to the history of the reception of the Lord's Prayer, in translations, in textual variations, in paraphrases, in commentaries, in baptismal, eucharistic, and other liturgical forms, in musical compositions, in artistic renderings, in plays, in ecumenical gatherings of various kinds, especially the Assisi gathering of world religions, in children's renditions, and more. We return, in each of these, to our precious biblical texts of Matthew and Luke, and yet as we do so, somehow our participation leads us on toward multiple meanings. And no ending of this is in sight. Nor could such an ending be really contemplated, if indeed the Prayer's soil is that of our primary field of reality.

The primary field of existence—the field within which we live and always have—has echoes, we might metaphorically say. As we Christians and others pray the Our Father, we are transmitting this echo. And as others pray their prayers, likewise they are transmitting their echoes. As we grow ever more conscious of these, perhaps we are able to overhear one another's echoes and enrich our own. For Christians, the "Our" in the Our Father seems to become richer, and the "Father" in the Our Father is more adequately hallowed. We may hope that something equivalent happens in the prayers of our fellow persons and creatures through the cosmos.

> Do not let your hearts be troubled. Believe in God, believe also in me. In my Father's house there are many dwelling places. If it were not so, would I have told you that I go to prepare a place for you? And if I go and prepare a place for you, I will come again and will take you to myself, so that where I am, there you may be also (John 14:1–3).

Your Kin-dom Come

Prayer Fragments as Echoes

Our Father—the "thousand names"—"the ninety-nine names"

Note: Hinduism speaks of the "litanies of a thousand names" regarding its major deities, and these litanies are recited by the devotees of those deities. The technical term for this is the *sahasra-nāma*. By one counting there are over 330 million gods in Hinduism, ranging from the thirty-three gods of the early Vedas (of earth, heavens, and the middle space), to the ultimate power of Brahman, of which all others are manifestations, in the later more philosophical Upanishads.[5]

Islam speaks of the "ninety-nine" or "beautiful names" (the *al-⊠asmâ⊠ al-ḥusnâ*) of Allah. The precise number is fascinating, and suggests the impossibility of ever adequately naming Allah (*Allâh*); we always fall short of perfection (100) in our attempts to achieve it.[6] Hinduism's 1,000 names, from the positive side, suggests the perfection of the divine as well. Thus, in some sense we are speaking of a kind of "equivalence" *in this respect* of perfection of the Divine between Hinduism, Islam, and Christianity. These are what I am calling "echoes." I believe the fact that we have names, some of a more or less personal kind, also suggests further echoes. These echoes help us or at least challenge us to widen our own personal name for the divinely perfect. May the challenge be mutual. In Chapter Four, "Addressing the Holy Mystery," we offered one approach by way of mystical non-clinging to names, accompanied by the simultaneous presence of symbols/names, as one way to work with these echoes.

In heaven—"The Master said . . . 'If you offend heaven, prayer is useless.'" (Confucius).—"The Dao of heaven is to provide benefit without doing harm." (Lao-tzu[Laozi])

The association of heaven with the Dao (Tao) evokes a transcendental dimension in Taoism. Likewise, there seems to be a strain of the transcendental and mystical in Confucius' language of "heaven." At the same time, as we suggested with the image of "heaven" or the "sky" in Hebrew and Christian

---

5. Klostermaier, *A Concise Encyclopedia of Hinduism*, 74–75.
6. Newby, *A Concise Encyclopedia of Islam*, 34–35, 26–27.

A Prayer of Immense Hospitality

Scriptures, there is another sediment of the cosmic dimension, which is also evoked in Confucius and Laozi.[7]

Hallowed be your name.—"Thou art holy and thy name is awesome"
(Amidah, 3)

We have seen reason to believe that as Jesus prayed his Prayer, he heard the echo of petitions or refrains like this one from the *Amidah*, the Eighteen Benedictions of Israel, not to mention other echoes recognizing God's holiness. In Jewish tradition it was common not to say the name YHWH, but to find substitutes. *Ha-Shem* (the name) was one of these. Was Jesus' address of *Abba* another substitute for the tetragrammaton of YHWH?[8]

Your kingdom come.—"Ruling a large state is like cooking a small fish."
(Laozi)—"The Master said: 'Lead them by political maneuvers, restrain them with punishments: the people will become cunning and shameless. Lead them by virtue, restrain them with ritual: they will develop a sense of shame and a sense of participation.'" (Confucius)

We have seen that Jesus' "kingdom," although having some historical precedents in Israelite history (the kingdoms of David and Solomon, for instance), was one of truly radical and unprecedented inclusivity, even to the point of love of the enemy. That is why we suggested referring to it as an "alternative community," for it truly is an alternative to the kinds of kingdoms known in human history. But all is not gloom, and as Dr. Martin Luther King Jr. reminded us, the arc of history does seem to bend toward justice.

Because of the radically different nature of Jesus' reign of God, we do not hear echoes in the normal course of our experiences, but we may just barely pick up echoes from very far away places, in this case, once again from Laozi and Confucius. There is something Taoist in Jesus' alternative community: supreme gentleness (not overcooking the fish). But there is also something that reminds me of Confucius' largely wonderful virtue

---

7. Confucius, *The Analects* 2.3, 6; Laotzu, *The Classic of the Way*, section 81,191. See especially the note on 5.13 in Confucius, *The Analects*, 141–42.

8. Harrington, *Amidah*, 98; Cohn-Sherbok, *A Concise Encyclopedia of Judaism* 82, 94–95.

ethic. Jesus was not a "political" quietist. He did lead, quite actively, and encourage active participation, and by virtue as well, although his virtues were more along the lines of inclusive love than of being "humane" in the Confucian sense, which included finding ways to implement education for virtue in rituals and actions. Passive (Taoist) and active (Confucian) qualities might help us Christians hear some equivalent echoes of this petition of the Prayer of Jesus.[9]

> *Your will be done, on earth as it is in heaven.* —"[B]e ye lamps unto yourselves.... Be steadfast in Resolve! Keep watch o'er your own hearts!" (Farewell Address of Gautama Buddha)

Something characteristic of Jesus' teaching is a healthy criticism of empty formulas and dogmatic declarations. This was likely one of the reasons he preferred to speak in parables, striving to challenge people who think they see and know to have to dig deeper and see and think again. Basing himself on Isaiah 6:6–13, he is reported by Matthew as saying, "The reason I speak to them in parables is that 'seeing they do not perceive, and hearing they do not listen, nor do they understand'" (Matt 13:13).

Perhaps this echo from the Gautama Buddha's final address will help us appropriate this petition from the Lord's Prayer with new eyes and ears. Like Jesus, Gautama was preaching in a context of many competing dogmatisms (the many sects of Hinduism), and he wanted his followers to resist turning his "reformation" into yet another empty shell. Neither Jesus nor Gautama were "individualists"; Jesus was forming his disciples, who would come to make up the "church," and Gautama had his monastic community (the Sangha) and his followers. But each wanted their followers to dig as deeply as possible, to the heart, so to speak.[10]

---

9. Laotzu, *Classic of the Way and Virtue*, section 60, 164; Confucius, *Analects* 2.3, 6; the quote from Dr. King is "The arc of the moral universe is long but it bends toward justice." King is perhaps quoting someone else, and there are a number of different ways in which he expressed this powerful saying. See Quote Investigator, "Arc of Universe."

10. Burtt, ed., "Buddha's Farewell Address," 23–26, at 25 and 26. See the Buddha's "Questions Not Tending to Edification," 8–12, for his struggle with sectarian dogmatisms. Cf. Thompson[-Uberuaga], *Jesus and the Gospel Movement*, 48–49.

A Prayer of Immense Hospitality

Give us this day our daily bread.—7,665,000 people starve to death each year; 1,250,000 children starve to death each year; 21,000 will starve to death today (World Hunger Statistics/the "religion" of the starving)—"I have enough daily bread, so I won't waste time on that. It isn't the main problem. The problem is getting it down without choking on it." (Offred, in Margaret Atwood's The Handmaid's Tale*)*

Can those who are starving transmit echoes? Are they strong enough physically to do this? But thank God we have those who seek out their voices, in effect becoming echoes for them. Is this an example of what we Christians mean by "the body of Christ," a body uniting us all? Perhaps this massive echo from the religion of the starving will challenge us to pray this petition with greater earnestness? How often have we prayed this without even a passing thought to the starving? What might this indicate with respect to the prior petition, of doing the Father's will? Do we have some serious "will work" to do? "Not everyone who says to me, 'Lord, Lord,' will enter the kingdom of heaven, but only the one who does the will of my Father in heaven" (Matt 7:21). Are we being called to be the "manna" for these sisters and brothers of ours who are starving? And what of animate soul friends? We use them for our food all too easily. What about our responsibilities toward them?

Margaret Atwood's Offred surfaces a necessary supplemental challenge, namely, that bread (or food or nourishment) is also a spiritual reality. Our souls need to be fed as well. Like the biblical "handmaids," who provide children for the infertile, thus being valued for their bodily fertility—Bilhah, Zilpah, Hagar (Gen 30:1–13; 16:1–6)—Offred also has a soul which is seeking nourishment. And if our souls are starving, then somehow this poisons even our physical nourishment. Is something of this insight what is at work in the tradition's noting that the prayer for bread is both a physical and a spiritual petition. And perhaps for Christians this two-sided reality is expressed in the eucharistic bread and wine?[11] Offred is like another handmaid, Mary, Jesus' mother, who told the "tale" of a God who "filled the hungry with good things" (Luke 1:53).

---

11. Statistic Brain Research Institute, "World Hunger Statistics"; Atwood, *The Handmaid's Tale*, 194. See also Wikipedia, "The Handmaid's Tale."

And forgive us our debts, as we also have forgiven our debtors.—"Every seventh year you shall grant a remission of debts." (Deut 15:1)—*If your debtor be in straits, grant him a delay until he can discharge his debt; but if you waive the sum as alms it will be better for you, if you but knew it."*
(Koran 2:280)

It is challenging to think of this petition as one of moving us beyond an "exchange economy," a *do ut des* way of thinking: I give this, so that you give that. I in effect am in debt to you, if you do fulfill the condition. Jesus does seem to suggest that his reign of God, his kin-dom, is one which moves to what Richard Rohr frequently calls an "economy of grace." Grace is completely free. No debt. The free gift of love makes us loving. If we are in sin, love loves us out of it. "I forgave you all that debt . . . should you not have had mercy . . . as I had mercy on you? (Matt 18:32–33). Some people do characterize the Jubilee Year freeing from debt noted in Deuteronomy as utopian, or at least not really required in Jewish society, or at least a practice about which we know very little. But with the reality of grace, and the incarnation, what seems utopian becomes a real possibility in history.

Is the text from the Koran also moving in the direction of an economy beyond debt, beyond merit and exchange? In some ways, it is an old kind of economy, reflecting a time when "ownership" was perhaps hardly yet thought of. Or perhaps we should speak of a family kind of economy, the one family of our primary field of experience, which indigenous cultures varyingly represent, even today, in some way. Here again we might want to think of reclaiming this old economy with a second naivete. In any case, a place to begin for thinking and *praying* along these lines might be the website of "Jubilee Economics."[12]

And do not bring us to the time of trial. But rescue us from the evil one—
"We don't teach meditation to the young monks. They are not ready for it until they stop slamming doors." (Thich Nhat Hanh to Thomas Merton in 1966)

As we have seen reason to believe, if we treat this last petition from the Our Father as yet another form of biblical parallelism, in this case an antithetic parallelism, then the Prayer can be said to be ending on a very

12. See Rogerson, "Deuteronomy," 160–62, on the Jubilee; Dawood, trans, *The Koran*, 41; and Ali, ed., *The Qur'an*, 113; Rohr, "Desmond Tutu"; Ham, "Jubilee's Roots."

A Prayer of Immense Hospitality

positive, affirmative note. The prayer to be rescued from the evil one repeats *and even deepens* the meaning of what is stated in a negative manner in the preceding part of the petition, namely, *not* to be brought to the time of trial. The paradoxical finding of the positive in the negative! This is possibly another way of stating the conviction, which I share with many throughout the traditions of mysticism, that evil is basically a contrast notion. It is known only by way of implied contrast with the positive, that is, the goodness of reality. That is why we can call the positive formulation of this final petition a *deepening*, and not simply an exact repetition, of the preceding part, for it brings out the implied positive foundation of the prayer, namely, the overwhelming goodness of reality. The final petition is really a petition for deliverance and redemption, and an affirmation of an overwhelmingly redemptive power at work in the universe.

I cannot resist citing a favorite saying from one of my very best professors in theology from my seminary days, namely, Father Peter Chirico, PSS, a Sulpician priest and quite brilliant thinker. I am remembering, for as far as I know, it was never published, so I may not be giving the exact formulation. Using the doughnut as a metaphor for the contrast nature of evil, he said: "You can have the dough without the hole; but you cannot have the hole without the dough!" The dough—the "bread" in the Prayer's sense, the life, the overflowing nourishing of reality—that is the grounding reality. The hole—the lack of life's flourishing, or even the chipping away at it—that must feed on the dough and even depend on it.

The citation from Thich Nhat Hanh, the South Vietnamese reformist Buddhist monk who met Thomas Merton briefly in 1966, during the miseries of the Vietnam War, is something of an Eastern form of mystical wisdom.[13] It is also something of a form of mystical, poetic antithetic parallelism. In this case, the positive side is expressed in the image of "meditation," which is by implication being evocatively suggested to be an "opening of doors." Its negative parallel is that of "stop slamming doors." This suggests to us that our ecumenical reading and praying of the Prayer is one of learning to open doors. To return to our primary field once again, as the Prayer prays us, whatever doors we have closed to our possible relationships—with our fellow humans and creatures; our societies and cultures

---

13. Rohr, Thich Nhat Hanh's citation to Thomas Merton in 1966, *What the Mystics Know*, 35. For a fine biography of Thich Nhat Hanh, see Laity, "If You Want Peace." "Thich" is a title given to Buddhist monks and nuns in the Vietnamese tradition, a transliteration of "Sakya," the Gautama Buddha's clan. "Nhat Hanh" is the monastic name given at ordination, meaning "One Action."

and religions; our cosmic home; and our divine Ground of reality—those doors are opening once again. The more deeply the Prayer prays us, the more we find that there really are no doors.

Opening doors: May this be something of what we mean when we pray: "For yours is the kin(g)dom, and the power, and the glory, forever and ever. Amen."

May the reader agree that "opening doors" and the Prayer's doxology are yet another form of poetic and echoing parallelism. But perhaps we might call this a form of equivalent and echoing parallelism.

Bibliography

Ali, Abdullah Yusuf, ed. *The Qur'an*. Elmhurst, NY: Tahrike Tarsile Qur'an, 2001.
Alighieri, Dante. *The Divine Comedy*, vol. 2, *Purgatory*. Translated by Mark Musa. Harmondsworth: Penguin, 1985.
Andreopoulos, Andreas. *The Sign of the Cross: The Gesture, the Mystery, the History*. Brewster, MA: Paraclete, 2006.
Anglican Communion News Service. acnslist@anglicancommunion.org.
Anonymous. "Why Is the Lord's Prayer Different in 3 Nephi?" https://nothingwavering.org/2016/10/07/60885-why-is-the-lords-prayer-different-in-3-nephi.html.
Aquinas, Thomas. *Catena Aurea. The Gospel of Matthew*. Translated by John Henry Parker. London: Rivington, 1842. http://dhspriory.org/thomas//CAMatthew.htm.
———. *The Gospel of Luke*. Translated by John Henry Newman. London: Parker, 1841. http://dhspriory.org/thomas/CALuke.htm.
———. *Compendium theologiae*. Translated as *Aquinas' Shorter Summa*, by Cyril Vollert. Manchester, NH: Sophia Institute, 2002; originally 1947. http://dhspriory.org/thomas/Compendium.htm.
———. *In Orationem Dominicam videlicet 'Pater Noster' expositio*. In *Opuscula theologica*, vol. 2, *De re spirituali*, edited by Raymundus Spiazzi, 221–35. Rome: Marietti, 1954.
———. *The Lectures on St. Matthew*. In *Albert and Thomas: Selected Writings*, Classics of Western Spirituality, edited by Simon Tugwell, 445–75. New York: Paulist, 1988.
———. "Sermon Conferences on the Ave Maria." In *The Catechetical Instructions of St. Thomas Aquinas*, translated by Joseph B. Collins, 173–80. New York: Joseph F. Wagner, 1939.
———. *Summa theologica*. 3 vols. Translated by the Fathers of the English Dominican Province. Boston: Benziger Brothers, 1947–48.
Ashton, John. "Abba." In *Anchor Bible Dictionary*, volume 1, edited by David Noel Freedman, et al., 7. New York: Doubleday, 1992.
Atwood, Margaret. *The Handmaid's Tale*. New York: Anchor, 1986.
Augustine. *Commentary on the Lord's Sermon on the Mount*. Translated by D. J. Kavanagh. Washington, DC: CUA Press, 1951.
———. *On Christian Doctrine*. Translated by D. W. Robertson Jr. Mineola, NY: Dover, 2009.
———. *Sermo 341*. In *The Later Christian Fathers*, edited by Henry Bettenson, 240. Oxford: Oxford University Press, 1970.
———. "Sermon on the Mount." In *The Nicene and Post-Nicene Fathers*, First Series, vol. 6, 38–47. Edinburgh: T & T Clark, 1996.
Ayo, Nicholas. *Gloria Patri: The History and Theology of the Lesser Doxology*. Notre Dame, IN: University of Notre Dame Press, 2007.

BIBLIOGRAPHY

———. *The Hail Mary: A Verbal Icon of Mary.* Notre Dame, IN: University of Notre Dame Press, 1994.

———. *The Lord's Prayer: A Survey Theological and Literary.* Notre Dame, IN: University of Notre Dame Press, 1992.

Balch, David L. "Luke." In *Eerdmans Commentary on the Bible*, edited by James D. G. Dunn et al., 1104–60. Grand Rapids: Eerdmans, 2003.

Balthasar, Hans Urs von. *Dare We Hope "That All Men Shall Be Saved"?: With a Short Discourse on Hell.* Translated by David Kipp and Lothar Krauth. San Francisco: Ignatius, 1988.

Bass, Diana Butler. *Grounded: Finding God in the World: A Spiritual Revolution.* New York: HarperCollins, 2015.

Bauckham, Richard. *Jesus: A Very Short Introduction.* New York: Oxford University Press, 2011.

———. *Jesus and the Eyewitnesses: The Gospels as Eyewitness Testimony.* 2nd edition. Grand Rapids: Eerdmans, 2017.

Baugh, S. M. *A New Testament Greek Primer.* 3rd ed. Phillipsburg, NJ: P & R, 2012.

Benedict. *Rule of St. Benedict.* Translated by Leonard Doyle. http://osb.org/rb/text/rbefjo.2.html#13.

Benedict XVI. "Italy: interreligious congress 'For a world of peace' in Assisi." http://www.dici.org/en/news/Italy-interreligious-congress-for-a-world-of-peace-in-assisi/.

Blackman, E. C. "Amen." In *A Theological Word Book of the Bible*, edited by Alan Richardson, 18. New York: Macmillan, 1950

———. "Truth." In *A Theological Word Book of the Bible*, edited by Alan Richardson, 269–70. New York: Macmillan, 1950.

Boff, Leonardo. *The Lord's Prayer: The Prayer of Integral Liberation.* Translated by Theodore Marrow. Maryknoll, NY: Orbis, 1983.

The Book of Common Prayer. New York: Oxford University Press, 2007.

Bradshaw, Paul F. *Two Ways of Praying: Introducing Liturgical Spirituality.* Maryville, TN: OSL, 2008.

Bradshaw, Paul F., and Maxwell E. Johnson. *The Eucharistic Liturgies: Their Evolution and Interpretation.* London: SPCK, 2012.

Brockington, L. H. "Height, Highest, Hosanna, Heaven(s), Firmament, Throne." In *A Theological Word Book of the Bible*, edited by Alan Richardson, 105–6. New York: Macmillan, 1950.

Brown, Raymond E. *The Gospel according to John.* 2 vols. Anchor Bible 29 and 29A. New York: Doubleday, 1966, 1970.

———. *New Testament Essays.* New York: Doubleday, 1982.

Burtt, E. A., ed. "Buddha's Farewell Address." In *The Teachings of the Compassionate Buddha: Early Discourses, the Dhammapada and Later Basic Writings*, 23–26. New York: New American Library, 1982.

———. "Questions Not Tending to Edification." In *The Teachings of the Compassionate Buddha: Early Discourses, the Dhammapada and Later Basic Writings*, 8–12. New York: New American Library, 1982.

Calvin, John. *Commentary on a Harmony of the Evangelists, Matthew, Mark, and Luke.* Volume 1. Translated by William Pringle. Grand Rapids: Christian Classics Ethereal Library, 1845. http://www.ccel.org/ccel/calvin/calcom31.ix.liv.htm?highlight=harmony,of,the,gospels#highlight.

Bibliography

———. *Institutes of the Christian Religion.* 2 vols. Edited by John T. McNeill, translated by Ford Lewis Battles. Louisville: Westminster John Knox, 1960/2006.

Caruso, Steve. "Tag Archives: abba." http://aramaicnt.org/tag/abba/.

Catholic Apologetics. "The Lord's Prayer." In *The Catechism of the Council of Trent.* http://catholicapologetics.info/thechurch/catechism/trentc.htm.

Catholic Prayers. "A Prayer before Reading the Bible." http://www.catholic.org/prayers/Prayer.php?=p=3134.

Catholic Resources. "Embolism." Latest English translation of the Mass. http://catholic-resources.org/ChurchDocs/Mass-RMS.htm.

Chandler, Michael. *An Introduction to the Oxford Movement.* New York: Church Publishing, 2003.

Chardin, Teilhard de. *On Love and Happiness.* London: William Collins Sons, 1973.

Chrysostom, John. "Homily 19 on Matthew 6." Translated by George Prevost (1851), revised American translation by Matthew B. Riddle (1888). http://www.orthodoxprayer.org/Lords_Prayer.html.

Church of England. "The Lord's Prayer." YouTube, 11/22/2015.

Cohn-Sherbok, Dan. *A Concise Encyclopedia of Judaism.* Oxford: Oneworld, 1998.

Confucius. *The Analects of Confucius.* Translated by Simon Leys. New York: W. W. Norton, 1997.

Congar, Yves. *Tradition and Traditions: An Historical and a Theological Essay.* 2 vols. Translated by Michael Naseby and Thomas Rainborough. New York: Macmillan,

Countryman, L. William. *The Mystical Way in the Fourth Gospel: Crossing over into God.* Philadelphia: Fortress, 1987.

Cox, Harvey. *Many Mansions: A Christian's Encounter with Other Faiths.* Boston: Beacon, 1988.

Cranfield, C. E. B. "Bread." In *A Theological Word Book of the Bible,* edited by Alan Richardson, 37–38. New York: Macmillan, 1950.

Crossan, John Dominic. *The Greatest Prayer: Rediscovering the Revolutionary Message of the Lord's Prayer.* New York: HarperOne, 2010.

Cyprian. *On the Lord's Prayer.* In *Tertullian Cyprian Origen, On the Lord's Prayer,* Popular Patristics Series, 29, edited and translated by Alistair Stewart-Sykes, 65–93. Crestwood, NY: St. Vladimir's Seminary Press, 2004.

Cyril of Jerusalem. *Lectures on the Christian Sacraments: The Procatechesis and the Five Mystagogical Catecheses.* Popular Patristics Series, 2. Edited by F. L. Cross. Crestwood, NY: St. Vladimir's Seminary Press, 1977.

D'Angelo, Mary Rose. "Abba and 'Father': Imperial Theology and the Jesus Tradition." *Journal of Biblical Literature* 111 (1992) 611–30.

Dawood, N.J., trans. and notes. *The Koran.* Rev. ed. New York: Penguin, 1997.

Delio, Ilia. *Making All Things New: Catholicity, Cosmology, Consciousness.* Maryknoll, NY: Orbis, 2015.

Didache 8.2. Text in Kenneth W. Stevenson, *The Lord's Prayer: A Text in Tradition,* 19–21. Minneapolis: Fortress, 2004.

DLTK. "Bible Stories for Children." www.dltk-bible.com/cv/lords_prayer.htm.

Douglas-Klotz, Neil, comm. and trans. *Prayers of the Cosmos: Reflections on the Original Meaning of Jesus' Words.* Foreword by Matthew Fox. New York: HarperOne, 1990, 2009.

Driscoll, Jeremy. *What Happens at Mass.* Rev. ed. Chicago: Liturgy Training, 2011.

Bibliography

Dulling, Dennis C. "Kingdom of God, Kingdom of Heaven." In *The Anchor Bible Dictionary*, vol. 4, edited by David Noel Freedman et al., 49–69. New York: Doubleday, 1992.

Errico, Rocco A. *Setting a Trap for God: The Aramaic Prayer of Jesus*. Rev. exp. ed. Unity Village, MO: Unity, 1997.

Francis of Assisi. "Inspired by the Lord's Prayer: St. Francis of Assisi (1182–1226)." http://1stholistic.com/Spl_prayers/prayer_lords-prayer-assisi.htm.

Francis. "Uganda Martyrs." www.anglicannews.org/news/2015/11/pope-francis-uganda-martyrs-continue-to-proclaim-jesus-christ-and-the-power-of-his-cross.

Fuller, Buckminster. "Ever Rethinking the Lord's Prayer: Buckminster Fuller Revises Scripture with Science." https://www.brainpickings.org/2013/07/12/buckminster-fuller-ever-rethinking-the-lords-prayer.

Gadamer, Hans-Georg. *Truth and Method*. 2nd rev. ed. Translated by Joel Weinsheimer and Donald G. Marshall. New York: Continuum, 2004.

Geert's Ave Maria Pages. "The Ave Maria Prayer." http://www.avemariasongs.org/ave/ave/aveMaria.htm.

Gerhardsson, Birger. *The Shema in the New Testament: Deuteronomy 6:4–5 in Significant Passages*. Lund: Nova, 1996.

Gregory of Nyssa. "Fifth Homily on the Lord's Prayer." Translated by Theodore G. Stylianopoulos, 2003. http://www.orthodoxprayer.org/Articles_files/GregoryNyssa-Homily5%20Lords%20Prayer.html.

Hahn, Roger. "Matthew 5:1–48." http://www.crivoice.org/biblestudy/bbmatt4.html.

Ham, Lee Van. "Jubilee's Roots: Indigenous Peoples Living Jubilee Opened My Eyes." http://www.jubilee-economics.org/indigenous-economics/.

Harrington, Daniel J. *Amidah*. In *The Gospel of Matthew*, 98–99. Sacra Pagina Series. Collegeville, MN: Liturgical, 1991.

———. *The Gospel of Matthew*. Sacra Pagina Series. Collegeville, MN: Liturgical, 1991.

Heath, Elaine A., and Larry Duggins. *Missional, Monastic, Mainline: A Guide to Starting Missional Micro-Communities in Historically Mainline Traditions*. Eugene, OR: Cascade, 2014.

Heidegger, Martin. *Being and Time*. Translated by John Macquarrie and Edward Robinson. New York: Harper and Row, 1962.

Hemingway, Ernest. "A Clean, Well-Lighted Place." In *The Short Stories of Ernest Hemingway*, 343–52. The Hemingway Library Edition. New York: Scribner, 2017.

Hogan, Linda. *Dwellings: A Spiritual History of the Living World*. New York: Touchstone, 1995.

Hopkins, Gerard Manley. *Gerard Manley Hopkins: A Critical Edition of the Major Works*. Edited by Catherine Phillips. Oxford Authors. Oxford: Oxford University Press, 1986.

Howard-Brook, Wes. *"Come Out, My People!": God's Call out of Empire in the Bible and Beyond*. Maryknoll, NY: Orbis, 2010.

Hügel, Friedrich von. *The Mystical Element of Religion as Studied in Saint Catherine of Genoa and Her Friends*. 2 vols. London: J. M. Dent and Sons, 1961.

"Icon of Christ and His Friend." https://frjamescoles.wordpress.com/2009/06/22/icon-of-christ-and-his-friend/.

Jerome. *Commentary on Matthew*. In *The Gospel of the Nazarenes*, in *The Apocryphal Gospels: Texts and Translations*, edited and translated by Bart D. Ehrman and Zlatko Pleše, 204–9. Oxford: Oxford University Press, 2011.

Bibliography

John of Damascus. *On the Divine Images: Three Apologies against Those Who Attack the Divine Images*. Translated by David Anderson. Crestwood, NY: St. Vladimir's Seminary Press, 1980.

John of the Cross. *The Ascent of Mount Carmel*. In *The Collected Works of St. John of the Cross*, translated by Kieran Kavanaugh and Otilio Rodriguez, 100–349. Washington, DC: ICS, 1991.

John Paul II. "Address of John Paul II to the Representatives of the Christian Churches and Ecclesial Communities and of the World Religions." http://w2.vatican.va/content/john-paul-ii/en/speeches/1986/october/documents/hf_jp_spe_.

———. *Ut Unum Sint*. http://w2.vatican.va/content/john-paul-ii/en/encyclicals/documents/hf-jp-ii_enc_25051995_ut-unum-sint.

Johnson, Luke Timothy. *The Gospel of Luke*. Sacra Pagina Series. Collegeville, MN: Liturgical, 1991.

Johnston, William. *Christian Mysticism Today*. New York: HarperCollins, 1984.

Käsemann, Ernst. "The Problem of the Historical Jesus." In *Essays on New Testament Themes*, translated by W. J. Montague, 15–47. London: SCM, 1964.

Kavanagh, Aidan. *On Liturgical Theology*. Collegeville, MN: Pueblo/Liturgical, 1984, 1992.

Keble, John. "Preface," October 21, 1847. In *Sermons, Academical and Occasional*, ixx–ixxiii. Oxford: Parker, 1847. https//archive.org/stream/sermonsacademicaookebirich/sermons Academicaookebirich_djvu.t.

Kelly, James J. *Baron Friedrich von Hügel's Philosophy of Religion*. Bibliotheca Ephemeridum Theologicarum Lovaniensium, 62. Leuven: Leuven University Press, 1983.

Klostermaier, Klaus R. *A Concise Encyclopedia of Hinduism*. Oxford: Oneworld, 1998.

Knowles, Brian. "Which Language Did Jesus Speak—Aramaic or Hebrew?" http://www.godward.org/hebrew%20roots/did%20jesus%20speak%20hebrew.htm.

Labriola, Albert C., and John W. Smeltz, eds. *The Bible of the Poor (Biblia Pauperum)*. Pittsburgh: Duquesne University Press, 1990.

Laity, Annabel. "If You Want Peace, You Can Have Peace." http://www.buddhist-canon.com/PUBLIC/MASTERS/TNYNIOG.htm.

Laotzu. *The Classic of the Way and Virtue: A New Translation of the Tao-te-ching of Laotzi as interpreted by Wang Bi*. Translated by John Richard Lynn. New York: Columbia University Press, 1999.

Law, Eric H. F. *A The Wolf Shall Dwell with the Lamb: A Spirituality for Leadership in a Multicultural Community*. St. Louis, MO: Chalice, 1993.

Lefebvre, Marcel. "Assisi 1 (October 27, 1986): Letter of Archbishop Lefebvre to Eight Cardinals (August 27, 1986)." http://www.dici.org/en/documents/assisi-i-october-27-1986-letter-of-archbishop-lefebvre-to-eight-cardinals.

Levine, Amy-Jill. "Bearing False Witness: Common Errors Made about Early Judaism." In *The Jewish Annotated New Testament*, edited by Amy-Jill Levine and Marc Zvi Brettler, 501–4. Oxford: Oxford University Press, 2011.

———. *Short Stories by Jesus: The Enigmatic Parables of a Controversial Rabbi*. New York: HarperOne, 2014.

Levine, Amy-Jill, and Marc Zvi Brettler, eds. *The Jewish Annotated New Testament*. Oxford: Oxford University Press, 2011.

Louth, Andrew. *Modern Orthodox Thinkers: From the Philokalia to the Present*. Downers Grove, IL: IVP Academic, 2015.

BIBLIOGRAPHY

Luther, Martin. *The Large Catechism.* In *Triglot Concordia,* translated by W. H. T. Dau and F. Bente, no. 22. St. Louis: Concordia, 1921. http://bookofconcord.org//c-5-ourfather.php.

———. "The Liberty of a Christian." http://www.theologynetwork.org/unquenchable-flame/luther/-the-freedom-of-the-christian.htm.

———. "The Lord's Prayer." In *The Large Catechism.* In *Triglot Concordia,* translated by W. H. T. Dau and F. Bente, no. 22. St. Louis: Concordia, 1921. http://bookofconcord.org//c-5-ourfather.php.

———. *The Small Catechism.* In *Triglot Concordia,* translated by W. H. T. Dau and F. Bente. St. Louis: Concordia, 1921. http://bookofconcord.org/smallcatechism.phpsetFont=Times.

Macquarrie, John. *Principles of Christian Theology.* 2nd ed. New York: Charles Scribner's Sons, 1966, 1977.

Maloney, George A. *The Cosmic Christ: From Paul to Teilhard.* New York: Sheed and Ward, 1968.

Martin, James. *Jesus: A Pilgrimage.* New York: HarperOne, 2014.

"Martin Luther's Explanation of the Lord's Prayer." https://downloadily.com/docs/martin-luther-s-explanation-of-the-lords-prayer.html.

Mary Magdalene Apostle Catholic Community. "May your kin-dom come." http://storage.cloversites.com/marymagdaleneapostlecatholiccommunity/Documents/WorshipA.

Maximus the Confessor. "On the Lord's Prayer." In *The Philokalia,* volume 2, translated and edited by G. E. H. Palmer et al., 285–305. London: Faber and Faber, 1981.

McCall, Richard D. "Versions of the Lord's Prayer." http://re-worship.blogspot.com/2012/02/inclusive-lords-prayer.html.

Mersch, Emile. *The Whole Christ: The Historical Development of the Doctrine of the Mystical Body in Scripture and Tradition.* Translated by John R. Kelly. London: Dennis Dobson, 1938.

Metz, Johann Baptist. *A Passion for God: The Mystical-Political Dimension of Christianity.* Translated by J. Matthew Ashley. New York: Paulist, 1998.

———. *Theology of the World.* Translated by William Glen-Doepel. New York: Herder and Herder, 1969.

Moore, Stephen D. *Empire and Apocalypse: Postcolonialism and the New Testament.* The Bible in the Modern World, vol. 12. Sheffield, TN: Sheffield Phoenix, 2006.

Murray, Paul. *Praying with Confidence: Aquinas on the Lord's Prayer.* New York: Continuum, 2010.

A New Zealand Prayer Book. New York: HarperOne, 1997.

Newby, Gordon D. *A Concise Encyclopedia of Islam.* Oxford: Oneworld, 2002.

Nielsen, Cynthia R. "St. Augustine: The Principle of Charity, the Gift of Multiple Meanings, and *Scriptura ex Scriptura explicanda est.*" http://percaritatem.com/200802/02/St-Augustine-the-principle-of-charity-the-gift-of-multiple-meanings-and-Scriptura-ex-Scriptura-explicanda-est.

O'Collins, Gerald. *Christology: A Biblical, Historical, and Systematic Study of Jesus.* Oxford: Oxford University Press, 1995.

———. *The Lord's Prayer.* New York: Paulist, 2007.

Olier, Jean-Jacques. *Explication du Pater Noster.* In *Tentations diaboliques et possession divine: Édition critique, d'après les manuscrits suivie d'une étude sur la spiritualité d'Olier: Les "petits mots" d'un aventurier mystique,* by Mariel Mazzocco, 45–87. Mystica. Paris: Honoré Champion, 2012.

Bibliography

———. "On Seeing the Sun." In *The Christian Day*, in *Bérulle and the French School: Selected Writings*, Classics of Western Spirituality, edited by William M. Thompson[-Uberuaga], translated by Lowell M. Glendon, 277–90. New York: Paulist, 1989.
Origen. *On Prayer*. In *Tertullian Cyprian Origen: On the Lord's Prayer*, Popular Patristics Series 29, translated and edited by Alistair Stewart-Sykes, 95–214. Crestwood, NY: St. Vladimir's Seminary Press, 2004.
Orthodox Page. Divine Liturgy of Saint John Chrysostom. www.ocf.org/OrthodoxPage/liturgy/liturgy.html.
Orthodox Prayer. "The Lord's Prayer." www.orthodoxprayer.org/Lords_Prayer.html.
Palamas, Gregory. *The Triads*. Classics of Western Spirituality. Edited by John Meyendorff, translated by Nicholas Gendle. New York: Paulist, 1983.
Quote Investigator. "Arc of Universe." http://quoteinvestigator.com/2012/11/15/arc-of-universe.
Rahner, Karl. "The Concept of Mystery in Catholic Theology." In *Theological Investigations*, vol. 4, translated by Kevin Smyth, 36–73. Baltimore: Helicon, 1966.
Rahner, Karl, and Herbert Vorgrimler. *Theological Dictionary*. Edited by Cornelius Ernst, translated by Richard Strachan. New York: Herder and Herder, 1965.
Ricoeur, Paul. "Biblical Hermeneutics." *Semeia* 4 (1975) 29–48.
———. *Interpretation Theory: Discourse and the Surplus of Meaning*. Fort Worth: Texas Christian University, 1976.
———. *The Symbolism of Evil*. Translated by Emerson Buchanan. Boston: Beacon, 1967.
Riess, Jana. "Why Don't Mormons Recite the Lord's Prayer?" http://religionnews.com/2013/10/14/don't-mormons-recite-lords-prayer/.
Roberts, Alexander, and James Donaldson, eds. *Didache*. http://www.earlychristianwritings.com/text/didache-roberts.html.
Roberts, Alexander, et al., eds. *Apostolic Constitutions*. In *Ante-Nicene Fathers*, vol. 7, edited Alexander Roberts et al., revised by Kevin Knight, 24–26. Grand Rapids: Eerdmans, 1886.
Robertson, Ronald. *The Eastern Churches: A Brief Survey*. 6th ed. Rome: Orientalia Christiana, 1999.
Rogerson, John W. "Deuteronomy." In *Eerdmans Commentary on the Bible*, edited by J. D. G. Dunn and John W. Rogerson, 153–73. Grand Rapids: Eerdmans, 2003.
Rohr, Richard. "Daily Meditation for December 3, 2015." https://cac.org/step-11-the-contemplative-mind-2015-12-03/.
———. "Desmond Tutu: Economy of Grace." Daily Meditation for Friday, October 30, 2015. http://myemail.constantcontact.com/Richard-Rohr-s-meditation-Desmond-Tutu-economy-Grace-html?soid=1103098668616&aid=bjC.
———. *What the Mystics Know: Seven Pathways to Your Deeper Self*. New York: Crossroad, 2015.
Rosales, Antonio M. "The Day Assisi Became the 'Peace Capital' of the World." http://www.americancatholic.org/Features/Assisi/PeaceCapital.asp.
Saldarini, Anthony J. "Matthew." In *Eerdman's Commentary on the Bible*, edited by James D. G. Dunn and John W. Rogerson, 1000–63. Grand Rapids: Eerdmans, 2003.
Schofield, J. N. "Adversary (Satan, Enemy, Foe, Devil, Demon, Beelzebub." In *A Theological Word Book of the Bible*, edited by Alan Richardson, 17–18. New York: Macmillan, 1950.
Simon, Ethelyn, et al. *The First Hebrew Primer: The Adult Beginner's Path to Biblical Hebrew*. 3rd rev. ed. Oakland, CA: EKS, 2005.

Bibliography

Sorokin, Pitrim A. *The Ways and Power of Love: Types, Factors, and Techniques of Moral Transformation*. Introduced by Stephen G. Post. Philadelphia: Templeton, 1982, 2002.

Statistic Brain Research Institute. "World Hunger Statistics." http://www.statisticbrain.com/world-hunger-statistics/.

Stevenson, Kenneth W. *The Lord's Prayer: A Text in Tradition*. Minneapolis: Fortress, 2004.

Taylor, Jeremy. *The Great Exemplar of Sanctity and Holy Life according to the Christian Institution, Described in the History of the Life and Death of the Ever-Blessed Jesus Christ, the Saviour of the World*. London: Longmans and Green, 1876. http://babel.hathitrust.org/cgi/pt?id=yale.39002013112611;view=1up;seq=468,471.

Teresa of Avila. *The Interior Castle*. In *The Collected Works of St. Teresa of Avila*, vol. 2, translated by Otilio Rodriguez and Kieran Kavanaugh, 263–452. Washington, DC: ICS, 1980.

———. *The Way of Perfection*. In *The Collected Works of St. Teresa of Avila*, vol. 2, translated by Otilio Rodriguez and Kieran Kavanaugh, 15–204. Washington, DC: ICS, 1980.

Tertullian. *On Prayer*. In *Tertullian, Cyprian, Origen, On the Lord's Prayer*, Popular Patristics Series 29, edited and translated by Alistair Stewart-Sykes, 41–64. Crestwood, NY: St. Vladimir's Seminary Press, 2004.

Thérèse of Lisieux. *Story of a Soul: the Autobiography of St. Thérèse of Lisieux*. Translated by John Clarke. Washington, DC: ICS, 1976.

Thompson, Colin. *St. John of the Cross: Songs in the Night*. Washington, DC: CUA Press, 2003.

Thompson, Patricia Kobielus. *From Dark Night to Gentle Surrender: On the Ethics and Spirituality of Hospice Care*. Scranton, PA: University of Scranton Press, 2010.

Thompson-Uberuaga, William. *Jesus and the Gospel Movement: Not Afraid To Be Partners*. Eric Voegelin Institute Series in Political Philosophy: Studies in Religion and Politics. Columbia, MO: University of Missouri Press, 2006

———. *The Struggle for Theology's Soul: Contesting Scripture in Christology*. New York: Crossroad, 1996.

———. "Thomas Merton's Transcultural Christ." In *Jesus, Lord and Savior: A Theopathic Christology and Soteriology*, 250–76. New York: Paulist, 1980.

Underhill, Evelyn. *Abba: Meditations Based on the Lord's Prayer*. London: Aeterna, 2015.

Vatican. *Catechism of the Catholic Church*. Second Vatican Council. http://www.vatican.va/Archive/ENG0015/_P9V.HTM.

Voegelin, Eric. *The Ecumenic Age. Order and History*, vol. 4. Collected Works vol. 17. Edited by Michael Franz. Columbia, MO: University of Missouri Press, 2000.

———. "Equivalences of Experience and Symbolization in History." In *Published Essays 1966—1985*, edited by Ellis Sandoz, Collected Works vol. 12, 115–33. Baton Rouge: Louisiana State University Press/Columbia, MO: University of Missouri Press, 1990.

———. *Israel and Revelation. Order and History*, vol. 1. Collected Works vol. 14. Edited by Maurice P. Hogan. Columbia, MO: University of Missouri Press, 2001.

Wainwright, Geoffrey. *Doxology: The Praise of God in Worship, Doctrine and Life: A Systematic Theology*. Oxford: Oxford University Press, 1984.

———. "Theology of Worship." In *The New Westminster Dictionary of Liturgy and Worship*, edited by J. G. Davies, 506. Philadelphia: Westminster, 1986.

Wesley, John. *Journal*. http://www.ccel.org/ccel/wesley/journal.vi.ii.xvi.html.

Wikipedia. "Buckminster Fuller." https://en.wikipedia.org/wiki/Buckminster_Fuller.

———. "Hail Mary." https://en.wikipedia.org/wiki/Hail_Mary.

Bibliography

———. "The Handmaid's Tale." https://en.wikipedia.org/wiki/The_Handmaid%27s_Tale.

Wilber, Ken. *The Integral Vision: A Very Short Introduction to the Revolutionary Integral Approach to Life, God, the Universe, and Everything*. Boston: Shambhala, 2007.

Williams, Rowan. "In the Place of Jesus: Insights from Origen on Prayer." *The Christian Century*, July 23, 2014. http://www.christiancentury.org/article/2014-07/place-jesus?print.

———. *Teresa of Avila*. London: Continuum, 1991.

Williams, Rowan, and Wendy Beckett. *Living the Lord's Prayer*. Edited by Su Box. Oxford: Lion Hudson, 2005.

Wilson, Adam. *The Evolution of International Society: A Comparative Historical Analysis*. London: Routledge, 1992.

World Council of Churches. *The Church: Towards a Common Vision*. Faith and Order 214. Geneva: World Council of Churches, 2013.

YouTube. "The Lord's Prayer for Children." 6/17/2013.

Index

Abba, 7, 12, 16, 26, 41, 43–44, 48, 50–51, 53, 55, 56, 56n10, 57n12, 71–72, 73n36, 74, 79–80, 80n5, 81, 94, 96, 99, 116, 137, 149–50, 159
Abhinu Malkenu ("Our Father, Our King," Jewish festal prayer), 22
Abrahamic religions, see Semitic religions
Adoration, 44–47, 119, see Prayer
Agnostic, atheists, 75
Akedah, the, 116–17
Alighieri, Dante, 5, 30, 31, 31n37, 42, 44, 134n2
Allegory, postmodern openness to, 31, 64
"Amen" (part of a doxology), 19, 19n18
Amidah (Jewish Benedictions), 21, 22, 106, 159
Anamnesis, global vs global amnesia, 98
Ananias, 85
Andreopoulos, Andreas, 47n15
Angels, 87, 90, 138
Anglican Church, Anglicans, 3, 18, 18n16, 24, 29, 31, 37, 59, 69, 88n18, 112, 133, 143n14
Anglo-Catholic(s), 69, 97, 144–45, 144n14
Anthropocentrism, see Cosmocentrism
Anonymous, 144n15
Aorist tense, 14, 83, 85, 106
Apostolic Constitutions, 140

Aquinas, Thomas, St., 64, 64n23, 64n26, 86–87, 87nn14–15, 89, 89n21, 94, 101, 112–13, 114n22, 115, 116, 116n27, 144, 144n14, 145n16, 146, 146n17
Aramaic, and Jesus, 16nn9 and 11, 20n21, 21, 38n6, 41, 50, 50n1, 56–57, 57n12, 104–5, 105n6
Arrobamiento, vs. *Abobamiento*, see Ecstasy
Ashton, John, 55, 55n8
Atwood, Margaret, 33–34, 34n42, 36, 42, 44, 59, 134, 161, 161n11
Augustine, St., 48, 48n17, 63–64, 64nn23 and 27, 77, 77n1, 87n15, 89, 89n20, 91, 96, 101, 112–13, 113n21, 117, 117n30
Ave Maria ("Hail, Mary") Prayer, 6, 144–45, 145n16, 146–47
Ayo, Nicholas, CSC, 25n30, 26, 91, 91n24, 95, 95nn29–30, 138–39n4, 145n16

Balch, David L., 15n6, 56, 56n10, 80n6, 105–6, 106n8, 111n16
Balthasar, Hans Urs von, 131, 131n42
Baptism, see Spirituality and Lord's Prayer
Bass, Diana Buttler, 40n8
Bauckham, Richard, 16n11, 23n27, 25, 25n31
Baugh, S. M., 14n5
Beckett, Wendy, 92n25
Benedict, XVI, Pope, 149, 149n22

Index

Bibles of the Poor (*Biblia Pauperum*), 29, 29n35
Biblical Interpretation, 35–37
Bilhah, 161
Blackman, E. C., 42n10
Boff, Leonardo, 131, 131n41
The Book of Common Prayer, 18, 18n16, 24–25, 28, 31, 117n30
Bradshaw, Paul F., 136, 136n3, 141n10, 142, 142n12
Brahman, see Hinduism
Brettler, Marc Zvi, 20n22, 50n1
Brockington, L. H., 59
Brown, Raymond E., PSS, 19, 19n18, 26, 26n33, 51, 154, 154n1
Buddha, Gautama, 160, 160n10, 163n13
Buddhism, 6
Byzantine Rites, 141, see Eastern Christians and Churches

Calvin, John, 24, 47, 47n16, 64–65, 65n28, 87, 87n16, 88, 88n17, 101, 101n1, 113, 115, 115n26, 127, 144, 144n14
Caruso, Steve, 57n12
Cassian, John, 63
Cathedral vs. Monastic, see Prayer
Catholic, see Ecumenical
Catechism of the Catholic Church, 18, 18n14, 78n3
Catholic, see Ecumenical
Chalcedon, Council of, 102
Chandler, Michael, 98n34
Chardin, Teilhard de, SJ, 90, 156n3
Chirico, Peter, PSS, 162
Chrysostom, John, St., 62, 62n21, 87n15, 113
Christology, 9, 96, 153
Church(es), 82, 88–89, 94, 135–36, 138, 153–55, 160
Clare, St., 147
Cohn-Sherbok, Dan, 159n8
Colonize, see Decolonize
Comedy/Joking, in the mystics, 75
Communion, of Saints, 63

Community, of Being and Reality, 121
Companion, etymology of, 125, 125n39
Confucius, 158–59, 159n7
Congar, Yves, OP, 8n10
Contemplation, 4, 60, 61
Context, historical, see Lord's Prayer
Contrition, as form of prayer, 45–47, see Prayer
Conversation, as form of prayer, 44–47, 103–4, see Prayer
Cosmic Christ, 98–99, 99n36, 160
Cosmocentrism, vs. Anthropocentrism, 57–60, 63, 70, 81, 84, 86, 90, 96, 98, 101, 103, 125, 130, 136–37, 146, 151–52, 156–59
Countryman, L. William, 26n32
Coverdale, Miles, 23
Cox, Harvey, 37n3
Cranfield, C. E. B., 107n10
Cross, Sign of, 46–47, 47n15
Crossan, John Dominic, 38–40, 40n7, 58, 85, 108, 110n14, 112, 112n18
Crucifixion, 151
Cultural Conditioning, vs. Cultural Determinism, 71–72
Cyprian, St., 10, 10n1, 62, 62n20, 78, 78n3, 87n15, 117, 117n30, 140, 140nn7–8
Cyril, of Jerusalem, St., 61, 61n18, 140–41, 141n9

D'Angelo, Mary, 56, 56n10
Dante, see Alighieri, Dante
Dao, the, see Tao
David, 137, 159
Dead Sea Scrolls, 54, 56
Debt(s), 107–10, 125–28, 161, see Lord's Prayer and Sin
Decolonize, vs. Colonize, 5, 32, 42, 57–58, 66, 70, 72, 75–76, 83, 135, 148, 151, 155–56
Deification, 61, 83, 96, 101–4, 133

Index

Delio, Ilia, OSF, 4nn5–6, 32n40, 83–84, 84n9, 90
Demarest, Richard, xi
Demons, Devil, 102, 111, 118, 128–31, 131nn41–42
Deprivatize, 32, 42, 47, 93, 109, 118
Detachment, as Non-clinging, 72–76
Didache, 18–19, 19n17, 21n23, 44, 139, 139n5
Discipline, of the Secret, 61n18
Divine Ground, the, see Father and Mystery
Divine Liturgy, the, see Eucharist and Lord's Prayer
The Divine Liturgy, of St. John Chrysostom, 18n15
Donaldson, James, 21n23
Douglas-Klotz, Neil, 16n9
Doxology, the, 17–19, 78, 112, 138, 164; see *Gloria Patri* and Lord's Prayer
Driscoll, Jeremy, OSB, 96, 96n31, 124, 124n38
Dualistic Thinking, 96, 103, 106, 119, 122 (Figure 1)
Duggins, Larry, 40n8
Dulling, Dennis C., 80n7
Durkheim, Emil, 70

East, and West, Churches of, 62–64, 101–4, 140–41
Eastern Catholic Churches, 3
Eastern Christian Churches, 18, 23–24, 47n15, 101–4, 112–13, 140, 144–45
Echoes, within the primary field, 157–64
Ecology/Ecological Awareness, 32, 42, see Cosmocentrism
Ecstasy, in prayer, 46
Ecumenical (Catholic, Universal), 4, 18, 33, 37, 61, 68, 70, 74, 76, 94–100, 112, 133, 147–52, 154–55
Edward, VI, King, 24, 25n29
Elizabeth, 145, 145n16
Enlightenment, the, 67

Episcopal Church, Episcopalians, 18, 24
"Epiclesis," 60, 122
Erasmus, Desiderius, 23
Errico, Rocco A., 16n9
Eschatology, 14, 82–83, 85, 104–7, 105n6, 114, 123, 154, 157
Eucharist, see Lord's Prayer and Eucharist
Eusebius, 19
Evangelical Churches, 3
Evil, 93, 103, 108, 125–32, 163, see Debt(s), Lord's Prayer and Sin
Exchange Economy, of Religion, vs Grace/Gift Economy, 127–28, 128n40, 162
Exegesis, vs Eisegesis and "Sausagesis," 60
Experience, 42–43, 67, 69, 71–72, 74, 89, 92, 98–99, 116, 118–19, 123, 131

Faith, 1, 17, 28, 40, 42–43, 47, 61, 64–66, 75, 87, 91, 96–98, 111, 121, 132, 148, 150–51
Family, of God, 72, 74–76, 85, 97, 109, 141, 146, 162, see Lord's Prayer
Farrer, Austin, 101
Father, God the, 2, 4, 7, 10–13, 16, 18n15, 20–24, 26–27, 30–32, 41, 44–45, 48, 50–76, 80–82, 86, 88–91, 95–96, 98, 110, 114, 124, 132, 139, 153–54, 161
Feminist Critique, 70
Francis, Pope, 1, 1n1, 37, 134
Francis, St., 147, 150, 150n24
Free Will, 120
Freud, Sigmund, 70
Fuller, Buckminster, 150–51, 151n25

Gabriel, 145, 145n16
Gadamer, Hans-Georg, 36n2
Geert, 144n16
Gender Justice, 5, 32
Geneva Bible, 24

Index

Gerhardsson, Birger, 21, 21n25
Globalization, Global, 3, 33, 118–19, 155–56, see Transitions, Contemporary
Gloria Patri ("Glory to the Father") Prayer ("Lesser Doxology"), 138, 138–39n4
God, see The Divine Ground, Father, Mystery, Trinity
Gospel of the Nazarenes, 104–5, 105n6
Grace, 72, 82, 87, 96, 103, 114, 115, 127, 140, 145, 154, 157, 162
Greek Philosophy, 104
Gregorian Sacramentary, 140
Gregory, of Nyssa, St., 85, 87n15, 94, 112, 114, 114n24
Gregory, the Great, Pope, 140–41, 141n10

Hagar, 160
Hahn, Roger, 79n4
"Hail, Mary" Prayer, see *Ave Maria*
Harrington, Daniel, SJ, 13, 14n4, 20, 20n21, 21, 21n24, 85n12, 106, 106n9, 159n8
Healings, and Exorcisms, of Jesus, 83
Hearing, and Hearkening, 44, 75, 149
Heart, the One, of the Church, 3, 9
Heath, Elaine A., 40n8
Heaven, see Cosmocentrism
Hebrew Passive, the reverent, 44, 78–79, 79n4, 87
Heidegger, Martin, 44
Hell, Descent into, 150
Hemingway, Ernest, 6, 6n9, 31, 33, 36, 42, 44, 59, 75, 134, 144, 150–51
Henry, VIII, King, 25n29
Herod Antipas, 16
Hezekiah, 43
Hilbert, Bonnie, 134n1
Hinduism, 158, 158n5
Hogan, Linda, 58, 58n13
Hopkins, Gerard Manley, SJ, 43, 43n11
Hoppock, Amy, 16n9
Hosea, 20

Hospitality, see Lord's Prayer
Hospitality, Interreligious, 98–100
Howard-Brook, Wes, 56n11
Hügel, Friedrich von, 69, 70n33, 108n11
Hugh, of St. Victor, 64
Hughes, Robert Davis, 2, 2n2, 139, 139n6
Humanocentrism, see Cosmocentrism

"I Am," as name of and address for God, 26, 51–53
Icon, of Friendship, Coptic, 103–4, 104n3
Icons, 102–4
Ignatius, of Loyola, St., 43
Ildefonsus, of Toledo, 94
Imperfection, Way of, vs Way of Perfection, 124
Incarnation, the, of Jesus Christ, 45–46, 94–101, 103, 114, 124, 132, 162
Indigenous Cultures, 162
Individual, vs Person/Self, 81
"Inscape" and "Instress," 43
Intercession, as form of prayer, 45–47, 145
Interreligious, see Ecumenical, Religions
Irenaeus, St., 19
Islam, 158, 158n6, 162, 162n12
Ivanov, Vyacheslav, 3n4

James (apostle), 74
James, I, King, 24
Jerome, St., 104–5, 105n6
Jesus, Christ, 4–8, 10–11, 11n2, 12, 14–15, 18nn13 and 15, 22, 25, 27–28, 35–36, 38, 47, 50, 53–59, 63, 65–66, 68–69, 71–74, 78, 81–82, 83, 85–86, 88–89, 89n20, 91, 95–96, 99, 102–3, 107, 109–12, 114, 117, 120, 127–28, 132, 137, 139–40, 142, 145, 145n16, 148, 154, 159–60

Index

Jewish Spirituality and Prayer, 12–13, 19–22, 154
John, Gospel of, 59, 69, 74, 86, 95n30, 103
John, the Baptist, 15
John, of Damascus, St., 102, 103n2
John, of the Cross, St., 6, 9n11, 72n35, 74–75, 75n39, 83, 92, 92n26, 150, 156
John Paul, II, Pope and St., 3n4, 147–49, 148n20
Johnson, Luke Timothy, 11n1, 15n6, 104–5, 105n7, 115, 115n25
Johnson, Maxwell E., 140n10
Johnston, William, SJ, 156n3
Josephus, 53
Jubilee Year, 127, 162, 162n12, see Deut 15:1–2
Jung, Carl Gustav, 70
Justification, by Faith through Grace, 87

Kaddish, 21–22
Käsemann, Ernst, 22n27
Kavanagh, Aidan, OSB, 40n8
Keble, John, 69, 70n33, 97, 97n33, 98n34
Kelly, James J., 108n11
King James Version of the Bible, 24
King, Martin Luther, Jr., 159, 160n9
Kin-dom, 32, 32n40, 48, 57, 81, 84, 108, 125, 162, 164, see Lord's Prayer, Symbols of
Kingdom, of God, the, 41, 48, 80–84, 118–20, 139
Kirk, Pamela, 150n23
Klostermaier, Klaus R., 158n5
Knowles, Brian, 50n1
The Koran, see Islam

Labriola, Albert C., 29n35
Laity, Annabel, 163n13
Lao-tzu (Laozi), 158–59, 159n7, 160n9
Late Modernity, see Transitions, Contemporary

Law, Eric H. F., 74n37, 149, 149–50n23
Law, Tablets of, 47, 77
LDS, see Mormons
Lefebvre, Marcel, 148–49, 148n21
Levine, Amy-Jill, 16n10, 20n20, 35, 35n1, 50, 50n1, 51, 51n2, 53, 53nn3–4, 56, 64
LGBTQ, 42, 70
Lincoln, Abraham, 41
Lord's Prayer, the
    allegorical interpretations, table of, 30
    and Aramaic language, see Aramaic and Jesus
    and baptism, 27, 61, 65, 138–42, 156
    and eschatology, see Eschatology
    and Eucharist, 37, 96, 96n31, 104–7, 106–7, 123–25, 124n38, 138–42, 153, 157, 161
    aorist, in Matthew's version, 83, 106; in Luke's version, 14
    as decolonizing, see Decolonize
    as diptych/triptych, 47–48, 132
    as globalizing, see Ecumenical and Globalization
    as guide for how to pray, 48, 143–44
    as hospitality, 152–63
    as personal and liturgical prayer, 9, 30n36, 43–47, 134–52
    as prayer before reading the Bible, 48–49
    as prayer for church union in John Keble, 97
    as prayer of a family, 36–37, 54, 57
    as prayer of agnostics, atheists, non-theists, 5
    as prayer of the imperfect, 5
    as primary theology, 40–43
    as restricted to Christian believers, in Luke's version, 146
    as summary of the Bible, 2, 8

Index

Lord's Prayer, the (*continued*)
   as summary of the Eucharist, 2, 8
   as summary of movement toward universal love, 156, 156n3
   as universal, in Matthew's version, 61–62, 62n19, 147
   at Church Offices (Divine Office), 27–28, 103
   Atwood's version, 33–34
   comparisons between Matthew's and Luke's versions, 12–13
   contemporary and artistic versions, 29–34
   context and language in Matthew's and Luke's versions, 12–17
   context, text, surplus of meaning in, 8, see Surplus of Meaning
   doxology in, 17–19, 19n17, 24, 45, 112, 138, 164
   ecclesial dimension, in Cyprian and John Chrysostom, 62
   ecumenical nature of, 1, see Ecumenical
   English versions commonly used, 23–25
   form/structure (medium) and message/content, relation between, 35–49
   global nature of, 3–4, see Ecumenical and Global
   handing over, in baptism, 27, 61, 61n18
   Hemingway's version, 6
   in liturgy, 30n36, 134–52
   invocatory address of, 7, 12, 50–76
   Jesus, as author of, 10–11, 15–17
   Jewish background of, 20–22
   Kingdom's coming, textual variations of
      Father's will as preceding petition for the kingdom's coming, in Tertullian, 85
      Holy Spirit as coming, rather than the kingdom, in Gregory of Nyssa and Maximus the Confessor, 85
   "Lead us not" vs "Let us not be led," 25n29
   literary genre of, 37–40, see Parallelism, Biblical
   Matthew's and Luke's versions, 12, 51, 55, 59, 104–7, 110, 156–57
   musical renditions of, 17–18, 60
   New Zealand Prayer Book version of, 31
   parallelism in, see Parallelism, Biblical
   pictorial versions of, 60
   present tense, in Luke, 14, 106
   royal road to Church's one heart, 3
   symbols of (*Abba*, bread, debts/sin, Evil One, hallowing, heaven and earth, temptation, reign of God), 41
   texts, translations, and versions, 10–34
   title as "Lord's Prayer," 10–11
   "We" petitions of, 8, 12–13, 20–21, 47–48, 51, 101–32, 161–64
      petition for bread, 13, 104–7, 112–14, 123–25, 161
      petition for deliverance, 111–12, 116–18, 128–32, 162–64
      petition for forgiveness, 13, 107–10, 114–16, 125–28, 162
   "You" petitions of, 8, 12–13, 20–21, 47–48, 77–100, 159–60
      petition for doing the Father's will, 85–86, 90–92, 160
      petition for hallowing the name, 77–80, 86–88, 159
      petition for the kingdom, 14, 80–85, 88–90, 159–60
Louth, Andrew, 3n4
Love, 53, 56, 77, 125, 127, 130, 143, 156, 156n3, 159–60, 162

Index

Lungs, the Two, of the Church, 2
Lure, Holy, the, see Mystery
Luther, Martin, 23, 30, 64–65, 65n28, 87, 87n16, 101, 113, 113n20, 115, 115n26, 116, 116n28, 117n31, 118, 118n33, 127
Lutherans/Lutheranism, 144–45

Macquarrie, John, 121, 121n36
Maloney, George A., SJ, 99n36
Malotte, Albert, 42, 60
Marian Devotions, 142
Martin, James, SJ, 16n9
Marx, Karl, 70
Mary, I, Tudor, Queen, 24
Mary, Magdalene, 73, 73n35
Mary Magdalene Apostolic Catholic Community, 32n40
Mary, Mother of Jesus, 6, 102, 144–45, 145n16, 160, see *Ave Maria*
Mass, see Lord's Prayer and Eucharist
Matthew, Gospel of, 7, 12–17, 19, 20n22, 35, 47n16, 85, 126
Maurice, F. D., 69–70, 70n33
Maximus (Maximos), the Confessor, St., 61, 64, 85, 94, 94n28, 96–97, 97n22, 140, 140n9
McCall, Richard D., 32n40
Mercy, 115–16, 162
Mersch, Emile, SJ, 89n20
Merton, Thomas, OCSO, 99n36, 162–64, 163n13
Metz, Johann Baptist, 42n9
"Middle Way," the, see *Via Media*
Modernity, see Transitions, Contemporary
Monastic Prayer, vs Cathedral Prayer, see Prayer
Moore, Stephen D., 32n41
Mormons (LDS), 144
Moses, bar Kepha, 64
Mother, God as, 31–32, 72
Multiple Meanings, 48n17, 105, 157, see Surplus of Meaning
Murray, Paul, OP, 5n8, 89n21, 114n22, 116n27, 144n14, 146n17

Music/Song, see Primary Theology
Mystery, Holy, the, 50, 54, 67–68, 71–73, 77, 82, 92–93, 93n27, 94, 111, 120, 129, 131, 145, 147, 150–51, 158
Mysticism/Mystics, 6, 26, 26n32, 45, 69, 70n33, 73, 75, 83, 88–89, 92, 96, 108n11, 128n40, 150, 152, 156, 156n3, 158, 163
Myth, postmodern openness to, 130

Narratives/Stories, see Primary Theology
Nephi, Book of (LDS/Book of Mormon), 144, 144n15
New Quest, the, for the Historical Jesus, 22, 22n27
New Zealand Prayer Book (Anglican), 31, 31n38, 32n39, 59–60
Newby, Gordon D., 158n6
Newman, John Henry, 69, 70n33
Nielsen, Cynthia R., 48n17
Non-clinging, see Detachment
Ntagali, Stanley, 1
Numbers, Book of, 19

O'Collins, Gerald, SJ, 54, 54n6, 73n36, 78–79, 80n5, 106, 107n10, 110, 110n15, 115, 119–20, 120n34
Office (Divine), Offices (Liturgical), 142
Old Quest, the, for the Historical Jesus, 22n27
Olier, Jean-Jacques, 152, 152n27
Oriental Orthodox Church, 3
Origen, 46, 46n13, 63, 63n22, 104, 104nn4–5, 105, 105n6, 109, 109n12, 117, 117n32, 120, 120n34, 123
Orthodox Church, 3
"Our Father" (prayer), see Lord's Prayer
Oxford Movement, the, 97, 98n34

Palamas, Gregory, St., 83, 83n8
Papias, 104

Index

Parables, 160
Parallelism, Biblical, 12–13, 38–40, 44, 59, 77, 85, 90, 108, 118, 126, 128–29, 132, 138, 138–39n4, 162–64
Participation, 36, 43–44, 59, 65, 72–73, 78, 84, 96, 98–99, 160
Pater Noster Guild, 29
Paternoster Row, 142
Paul, St., 6, 11n2, 12, 15, 25, 44, 56, 59, 68, 75, 82, 84–85, 95n30, 111, 117, 122, 135, 137, 146–47
Pelagians, 91
Penance (Reconciliation), Sacrament of, 127, see Reconciliation
Pentecost, 149
Peter, 111
Peter, First Letter of, 27
Petition, as form of Prayer, 45–47, 91–92, 118–21, 130, 145
Platonists, 63, 101
Polybius, 4n5
Postcolonial Critique, 70, see Decolonize
Postmodernity, see Transitions, Contemporary
Protestants/Protestant Churches, 3, 18, 24
Prayer, see Adoration, Contrition, Conversation, Intercession, Petition, Thanksgiving, Lord's Prayer
"Prayer before Reading the Bible, A" 48–49, 49n18
"Prayer interprets our desires"/"interpreter of our desires" (Thomas Aquinas), 146, 146n17
Prayer, liturgical, 134–52
Prayer, monastic vs cathedral, 134–52
"Prayer prays us, the," 36, 36n2, 43, 46, 48, 65, 92, 96, 98, 119, 120–21, 138, 141, 145, 151, 163–64
"Pray without ceasing," 146, see 1 Thessalonians 5:17

priest (presbyter), 18, 18n15, 26, 30, 59, 69, 140
Primary, vs Secondary Theology, 40–43, 52, 54–56, 72–74, 76, 80, 84–85, 90–91, 95, 98, 107–8, 111, 119–32, 123n37, 136–37, 145–47, 152, 157, 163–64
Primary Field, see Primary vs Secondary Theology
Psalms, 20, 143
Puritan, see Reformed

Rahner, Karl, SJ, 93n27, 131, 131n42
Reconciliation, Sacrament of, 127, see Penance
Redemptive Pattern, the threefold, 108, 132–33
Reformation, 64, 87–88, 91, 116, 141n10, 159
Reformed Christianity, 18, 144, 144n14
Reformed (Presbyterian), 24
Reformers, the, 31, 65–66, 89, 115, 127
Relativism, 148
Religions, of the World, 6, 68, 70, 76, 93, 98–100, 132, 147–48
Renaissance, 64
Revelation, 20, 67, 72, 94
Richard, of St. Victor, 64, 64n25
Ricoeur, Paul, 8n10, 15, 15nn7–8, 37, 38n5, 57
Riess, Jana, 144n15
Ritual, see Primary Theology
Roberts, Alexander, 21n23
Robertson, Ronald, CSP, 3n4
Rohr, Richard, OFM, 4–5, 5n7, 128, 128n40, 161n12, 162n12
Roman Catholic Church, 3, 18, 24, 116, 144, 148, 148n21
Romantic Movement, 68
Rosales, Antonio, OFM, 147, 147n19
Rosary, the, 143
Rule of St. Benedict, 142, 142n11

Saints, 102, 120
Saldarini, Anthony J., 110n13

Index

Satan, see Demons
"Sausagesis," 60, 67
Schofield, J. N., 112n17
Secondary theology, see Primary Theology and Primary Field
Secular Ideologies, 93
Semitic/Abrahamic Religions, 108, 133
Sermon on the Mount, 64n23, see Augustine, St., and Matthew, Gospel of
Shema, 21, 21n25
Sign of the Cross, Prayer of the, 47, 47n15
Silence, 44, 96, 142, 148, 150
Simon, Ethelyn, 79n4
Sin, 108, 125–28, see Debt(s) and Evil
Smeltz, John W., 29n35
Sociopolitical Analysis/Criticism, 32, 41–42, 70, 80, 93, 113, 118, 124–25
Solomon, 58, 138, 159
Son of God, the, see Jesus Christ
Song, Music, see Primary Theology
Sorokin, Pitrim A., 155n3
Spirit, Holy, the, 1, 7, 14, 18n15, 30, 30n36, 31, 47, 65, 87–88, 95–96, 99, 120, 123, 134–52
Starving, Religion of the, 161
Statistic Brain Research, 161n11
Stephen, 111
Stevenson, Kenneth W., 14n5, 19, 19n17, 19nn19–20, 20n22, 21, 21n25, 22n26, 23n28, 29n35, 30, 30nn36–37, 60n16, 61, 61nn17–18, 64nn24–25, 65n29, 70n33, 85n11, 88n19, 90n23, 94, 94n28, 101, 101n1, 114, 114nn23–24, 117n30, 118n33, 140, 140nn7–8, 141nn9–10, 144n14, 147n18
Suffering, of the Innocent, 129
"Supersubstantial," 104–7
Surplus of Meaning, 8, 8n10, 59–60, 86, 94–95, 105, 110, 112, 118, 157
Symbols, see Primary Theology

Syncretism, 149
Synoptic Gospels, 95n30, 103
Syrian Rites, the, 141

Tao (Dao)/Taoism, 158–59, 159n7
Taylor, Jeremy, 65, 65n29, 83, 88, 88n19, 90, 92–94, 113
Teresa, of Avila, St., 9, 9n11, 46, 46n14, 65–66, 66n30, 83, 88, 88n17, 89n22, 90, 99, 100n37, 116n29, 118n32, 127, 156, see *Arrobamiento vs Abobamiento*, Ecstasy
Tertullian, 2n2, 46, 46n13, 63, 77–78, 78n3, 85, 85n10, 86, 86n13, 87n15, 101, 117n30, 139–40, 140n7
Thanksgiving, as form of prayer, 45–47, see Prayer
Theater, see Primary Theology
Theocentric, 60
Thérèse, of Lisieux, St., 151, 151n26
Thich Nhat Hahn, 162–64, 163n13
Third Quest, the, for the Historical Jesus, 22–23n27
Thom, Brian, 74n37
Thomas Aquinas, St., see Aquinas, Thomas, St.
Thompson, Colin, 75n39
Thompson, Patricia Kobielus, 75n39
Thompson-Uberuaga, William, 17n12, 26n32, 37nn3–4, 38n6, 58n13, 70n34, 73n36, 99n36, 159n10
Titus, of Bostra, 60
Tradition(s), 8, 8n10
Transference, Symbolic, 79–80, 80n5
Transitions, Contemporary, 31, 65–71, 108, 118–32, 155–56
Trent, Council of, 66, 88, 88n17, 89, 114
The Catechism of the Council of Trent, 66, 66n31, 88n17
Trinity, the, 55n9, 94–100, 102, 132
Truth, 42–43, 42n10
Tugwell, Simon, OP, 116n27, 144n14
Tutu, Desmond, 162n12

Index

Tyndale, William, 23–24, 25n29

Uganda, Martyrs of, Anglican and Roman Catholic, 1, 37, 134
Underhill, Evelyn, 69, 70n33
Unitive Being, see Spirit, the Holy
Universal, see Ecumenical
Upanishads, the, see Hinduism

Vatican, 78n3
   Catechism of the Catholic Church, 78n3
Vedas, see Hinduism
Via Media (of Anglicanism), 18, see Oxford Movement
Vico, Giambattista, 70
Voegelin, Eric, 4n5, 43n10, 60, 60n15, 67, 99n35, 123n37
Vorgrimler, Herbert, 131, 131n42
Vulgate, the, 23

Wainwright, Geoffrey, 37n4, 40n8
Weber, Max, 70

Weinstein, Norm, 134n2
Welby, Justin, 29
Wesley, John, 30, 68–69, 68n32, 70n33
Western Christians, 47n15, 113
Wettstein, David, xi
Wilber, Ken, 74n38, 123n37
Williams, Rowan, 65–66, 66n30, 92, 92n25, 120, 120n35
Wilson, Adam, 155n2
Witherington, Ben, III, 35
Witnesses, Role of, in Jesus Traditions, 16, 16n11, 25, 25n31
World Council of Churches, 98, 98n34
World Hunger Statistics, 161, 161n11

York Mystery Plays, 29

Zigabenus, Euthymius, 94
Zilpah, 161

Scripture and Sacred Documents Index

OLD TESTAMENT

Genesis
1:2	135
16:1–6	160
22:1–19	20, 117
30:1–13	160

Exodus
3:1–16	79
16:8	105
16:15	20
20:1–17	47
32:32	20

Leviticus
11:44	86
17—26	79
19:2	79
20:7	78
20:26	79
22:32	87, 91

Numbers
5:22	19
11:6	20

Deuteronomy
5:1–12	109
5:6–21	47
6:4–5	21
8:3	20
10:1	47
15:1	162
15:1–2	127

Ruth
4:14	79

1 Kings
8:27, 30	58
21:7	80

2 Kings
20:3	43

1 Chronicles
28	137
29:10–11	19, 20, 138
29:11–12	112

Psalms
6:2	20
8:4	39
11:5	111
18:35	20
19:5	151
23:1	38–39
26:2	111
31:5	43

33:19	20
37:21	109, 126
42:7	74

Psalms (continued)

46:7	20
68:5	53
74:12	80
79:9	79
84:3	80
89:26	53
89:27	20
95:3	80
113:3	79
116:4	79
119:27, 30, 32, 37	20
121:5	20
130:2	21
150:1	57

Isaiah

6:1–3	58
6:3	139
6:6–7	57
6:6–13	3, 160
11:2–3	30
25:6–8	105
28:5	89, 94
44:6	52
45:5–6	80
46:9	20
55:10–11	84–85
63:16	20, 54
64:8	53, 54
66:13	32

Jeremiah

5:1	43
7:11	20
10:10	43
31:9	53, 54

Ezekiel

20:33	20
36:23	20, 80

Habakkuk

3:17	39–40

APOCRYPHA

Psalms of Solomon

17:3	80n7

NEW TESTAMENT

Matthew

1:21	145n16
3:16–17	59
4:1–11	111
4:12–17	80
5:1–48	79n9
5:22	109
5:23–24	141
5:44	86
5:44–45	53
6:1–18	13, 21
6:3	64n23
6:7	31, 38
6:9	20, 50, 77, 48, 143
6:9–13	12–17, 20n22, 47n16
6:10	20, 80, 82, 85
6:11	104
6:12	107, 127
6:13	111
6:32	56
7:21	91, 161
10:23	82
11:27	56
12:24	112
12:26–27	130

12:28	14, 81, 82, 95, 112, 130	5:20–21	110
13:13	73, 160	6:12	15
14:3	36, 51, 53	6:20	105
14:33	47	6:36	115
16:16	55	7:36–50	114
18:32–33	115, 127	7:41	110
22:1–14	124	7:42	126
22:3	82	7:41–43	115
22:34–40	47	9:51—19:27	15
22:37	90	10:15	81
24:33	82	10:21	15
25:6	83	10:27	90
25:13	82	10:25–28	47
25:31–46	82	10:29–37	81
26:18, 26–29	107	11:1	15
26:26	140	11:2	50, 77, 80, 82
26:39	111	11:3	104, 105
		11:4	107, 111
		11:1–4	47n16
		11:2–4	12–17, 20n22
		11:20	81
		12:22–28	107
		12:35–38, 39–40, 42–46	91
		14:7–24	124
		14:15–24	106
		15:11–32	127
		16:5, 7	110
		17:10	110
		17:20	82
		21:18	81
		22:15–20	107
		22:40, 46	111
		22:44	15

Mark

1:14–15	80
1:15	82
9:1	82
11:25	25
12:28–34	47
12:30	85
13:30	80
14:14, 22–25	107
14:35–36	111
14:36	12, 50, 57n12, 74
15:39	55
16:3	79

Luke

1:27	145n16
1:28, 30	145
1:28, 38	6
1:31	145, 145n16
1:53	161
1:77	110
3:3	110
3:21	15
4:1–13	111
4:14–15	80
4:18–19	109
5:16	15

John

1:1	104
1:12	56, 61
1:29	131
3:5	61
3:14	26
4:34	91
6:25–40	106–7
6:25–71	107
6:35, 51	26

SCRIPTURE AND SACRED DOCUMENTS INDEX

8:12, 24, 28, 58	26
9:5	26
10:3	137, 142
10:7, 9, 11, 14	26
11:25, 52	26

John (*continued*)

12:28	78n3
13:19	26
14:1–3	157
14:2	xii, 3, 7, 76, 99
14:6	26
15:1, 5	26
17	26–27
17:1	78
17:1, 4, 5, 6, 9, 11, 12, 15, 16, 20, 21, 24, 25, 26	27
20:17	73, 73n35

Acts

1:24	15
2	149
2:5, 7	149
6:6	15
7:52–54	111
9:4	84
9:11	15
9:16	85
11:2–3	111
11:5	15
13:3	15
14:23	15
16:25	15
20:36	15
21:4–22	111
21:5	15
22:17	15
22:21–22	111
28:8	15

Romans

4:7–8	26
8	65
8:9, 11	135
8:14–15	56
8:14–16	56
8:15	50, 51, 53, 57n12, 96
8:15–16	44
8:17	96
8:19, 22–23	137
8:19, 23	147
8:26	120
8:26–27	123
9:19	91
11:33	68
12:2	26
13:8	127

1 Corinthians

2:15	135
3:3	99
4:6	91
6:19	135
10:13	26, 117
10:17	26
11:24	140
12:7	135
12:12, 27	135
15:3	25
15:4	79
15:28	26

2 Corinthians

3:17	73n35

Galatians

2:20	45
4:5–7	56
4:6	12, 26, 50, 53, 57n12
6:8	95

Ephesians

6:12	86

Philippians

2:5–6	75

Scripture and Sacred Documents Index

2:7   6
2:9   26

Colossians
1:15, 17   99

1 Thessalonians
5:17   136, 146
5:18   146

Hebrews
4:15   117
5:2, 6   53

James
1:13   111

1 Peter
1:3, 17   27
1:15–16   28
2:2   28
2:9, 15   28
3:15   28
4:2, 8, 11, 12, 19   28
5:7   28
5:8–10   28
11:4   57

2 Peter
1:4   96, 102

1 John
3:1–2   56
10:5–2   56

BOOK OF MORMON

3 Nephi 13.9–13   144, 144n15

DEAD SEA SCROLLS

1QH9, 34–35   54
4Q 372, 1   56n10
4Q 460   56n10

www.ingramcontent.com/pod-product-compliance
Lightning Source LLC
Chambersburg PA
CBHW031431150426
43191CB00006B/467